T0386538

THROUGH HER EYES

THROUGH HER EYES

Australia's Women Correspondents from Hiroshima to Ukraine

EDITED BY MELISSA ROBERTS & TREVOR WATSON

Hardie Grant

BOOKS

Published in 2022 by Hardie Grant Books, an imprint of Hardie Grant Publishing

Hardie Grant Books (Melbourne)
Wurundjeri Country
Building 1, 658 Church Street
Richmond, Victoria 3121

Hardie Grant Books (London)
5th & 6th Floors
52–54 Southwark Street
London SE1 1UN

hardiegrantbooks.com

 A catalogue record for this book is available from the National Library of Australia

Through Her Eyes
ISBN 978 1 74379 889 8

10 9 8 7 6 5 4 3 2 1

Cover design by Josh Durham/Design by Committee
Cover image courtesy of Getty Images
Typeset in 11.5/14 pt Bembo by Cannon Typesetting

Printed in Australia by Griffin Press, an Accredited
ISO AS/NZS 14001 Environmental Management System printer.

 The paper this book is printed on is certified against the Forest Stewardship Council® Standards. Griffin Press holds chain of custody certification SGSHK-COC-005088. FSC® promotes environmentally responsible, socially beneficial and economically viable management of the world's forests.

Hardie Grant acknowledges the Traditional Owners of the country on which we work, the Wurundjeri people of the Kulin nation and the Gadigal people of the Eora nation, and recognises their continuing connection to the land, waters and culture. We pay our respects to their Elders past, present and emerging.

For those young Australians who
aspire to life as a foreign correspondent.

Contents

PART THREE: BEING A CORRESPONDENT

Timeline

1939	Germany's invasion of Poland triggers war in Europe
1945	US atomic bombs destroy Hiroshima and Nagasaki
1947	India and Pakistan partitioned
1948	Israel created, large numbers of Palestinians flee
1967	Israel occupies Palestinian territory known as the Gaza Strip
1972	Australia recognises People's Republic of China
1975	Cambodian capital, Phnom Penh, falls to Khmer Rouge
	Saigon falls to North Vietnamese forces
	Civil war erupts in Lebanon
1979	Soviet forces invade Afghanistan
1984	Indian Prime Minister Indira Gandhi assassinated
1985	Mikhail Gorbachev becomes General Secretary of the Soviet Communist Party
1986	Marcos regime in the Philippines collapses
1987	Global stock markets crash
1989	Chinese military crushes Tiananmen Square protests
	Fall of Berlin Wall
1990	Collapse of the Soviet Union marks the end of the Cold War
1994	Rwanda genocide claims 200,000 lives. More than 2 million flee

2001 — 9/11 terrorist attacks in the United States

— US forces invade Afghanistan

2003 — Coalition forces invade Iraq, overthrowing President Saddam Hussein

— United Nations security forces arrive in Liberia to maintain peace after more than a decade of civil war and dictatorial rule

2004 — Boxing Day Tsunami claims nearly a quarter of a million lives

2005 — Israeli forces withdraw from the Gaza Strip

2006 — Blockade of Gaza begins

2008 — Barack Obama elected President of the United States

— Global Financial Crisis

— Beijing hosts Summer Olympic Games

2010 — Arab Spring uprisings begin in Tunisia and spread across Arab World

2011 — Uprising against Syria's President Assad begins; Russia, Iran, the US, Hezbollah and ISIS join civil war

— Arab Winter descends as authoritarian governments fight back. Civil war and terrorism spread

— Osama bin Laden shot dead by US forces in Pakistan

2012 — Xi Jinping becomes paramount leader of China

2014 — Russia annexes Ukraine's Crimean Peninsula

— Fighting between government forces and pro-Russian separatists breaks out in Ukraine's Donbas region. Separatists declare Donetsk and Luhansk independent

— Malaysian Airlines MH17 shot down over Ukraine

2019 — Anti-Beijing protests erupt in Hong Kong

— ISIS defeated in Syria. Kurds take control of traditional territory

2020 — Chemical explosion at the Port of Beirut kills more than 200 people

2021 — US abandons Afghanistan after 20 years of war. Taliban victorious

2022 — Beijing hosts Winter Olympic Games

— Russian forces invade Ukraine

Acknowledgements

Through Her Eyes had two objectives. The first was to highlight the struggle by women to take their rightful place in the once male dominated media industry, ensuring that it now enjoys a high level of gender equality. Our second was to chronicle a number of history-making world events as witnessed and reported by some of Australia's most talented journalists.

We believe that we have achieved both, but we also acknowledge that we would not have been able to do so without those outstanding journalists who have contributed their stories to *Through Her Eyes*, and a number of people who assisted with ideas, contacts, memories and quotes.

They include former *Newsweek* correspondents Tony Clifton and Carl Robinson; former *Sydney Morning Herald* foreign editor Stephen Claypole; former *Sydney Morning Herald* photo editor, Mike Bowers; former CNN vice president (Asia) Ian Macintosh; former News Corp executive and columnist Piers Akerman and the ABC senior economics correspondent, Peter Ryan. Many of them also mentored and supported women correspondents.

Women in the hot zone

By Melissa Roberts and Trevor Watson

IN THE HIGHLY unlikely event of Russia's President Vladimir Putin ever facing a war crimes tribunal, charged over the many atrocities committed by his forces in Ukraine, he must be questioned about dead journalists.

Fourteen were killed in the first six weeks of the war. Were they merely collateral damage or were they deliberately targeted, murdered to prevent the outside world learning of Putin's brutal behaviour; the missile attacks on children, hospital patients and refugees; the rape and the execution of bound civilians? Ukrainian leader Volodymyr Zelensky believes the reporters were executed to guarantee their silence. He maintains that 'Putin is frightened of journalists because they tell the truth'.

At this moment, Australian correspondents are telling the truth as they personally witness it. Many of those who inform far away audiences of the war in Ukraine, the rise of China, a divided America, Europe's immigration crisis and trauma in Africa are women. They are filing now from Jakarta, New Delhi, Tokyo, London, Jerusalem, Port Moresby, Washington, Kyiv and many places in between. They report the facts, and they interpret those facts in a compelling and meaningful way for us and for our decision makers. These correspondents, male or female, often risk their own safety for the story.

The gender of a correspondent shouldn't matter. But the reality is that until very recently, gender determined all in journalism, particularly opportunity. While it is now common to see women closely questioning world leaders, interviewing disaster victims or lacing up combat boots, that hasn't long been the case and change hasn't come easily. Women have needed single-minded determination, courage and, in some cases, the wherewithal to fund the launch of an international career if they were to break through the gender-based barriers that held them back.

To paraphrase British rabbi Lionel Blue, journalists are just like everyone else, only more so, and newsrooms have traditionally been just like many other male-dominated workplaces, only more so. They have been blokey places of clattering typewriters, cigarette smoke, booze at the desk and large amounts of adrenaline. The conversation has been of political upheaval, personal tragedy, football scores and sexual exploits. The nature of the work attracted big egos, larger than life characters, adventurers and voyeurs. The few women who managed to join the news industry were exposed to highly sexualised humour, and occasionally to verbal abuse laced with threats of gender-specific punishment from editors quick to fury over some minor misdemeanour.

Until relatively recently, women were largely confined to the 'women's pages'. Decked out in hats and gloves, they covered fashion and society events or wrote advice columns, which earned them the sneered nickname 'sob sisters'. When they had the chance to cover real news, they were confined to the 'women's angle' – nurses tending to the wounded, the home front, refugees. Their male colleagues covered the action, the tectonic shifts of history, the deeds of great men.

When working alongside their male counterparts, women lived with a miasma of sexism. In 1981, the term 'microphone stands with tits' entered the patois of the Parliamentary Press Gallery in Canberra. It was coined as a reference to a group of young women, including a co-editor of this book, who covered national politics for Australia's commercial radio networks. The insult, published in *The Bulletin* news magazine, came, the women believed, from a supposed friend and a highly respected member of the Gallery. The women did not challenge him on it – that's not what one did; they were the ones embarrassed by his betrayal, not him. He has since died, and the chance to discuss it has passed. 'They were really sexist days, but that was a reflection of the society,' one news presenter told the Australian Broadcasting Corporation's (ABC) online service. It was a time when women on the Senate side of the Press Gallery had to cross the building to the only women's toilets, when all women were obliged to wear skirts, and young women had to quietly accept being ogled.

FOR A WOMAN to graduate from the domestic newsroom to a much sought–after overseas assignment or a posting to a foreign bureau before the mid-1980s was a herculean task. You will distract soldiers, aspiring women correspondents were told, a conflict zone is no place for a woman. They were refused assignments because there would be no women's toilets, or separate sleeping quarters. They were told that an assignment was too dangerous, that women were too emotional and, by their very nature, unreliable. Lorraine Stumm, an accredited war correspondent in World War II, was obliged by fellow journalists to leave a military briefing on the grounds that women could not keep secrets. Radio and television outlets including Australia's national broadcaster, the ABC, argued that women didn't carry the authority of male reporters, that listeners didn't want to hear their voices or be told what to think by a woman. Diane Willman was told that the ABC didn't send women to foreign postings because they might get married and have children. Willman paid her own way to Beirut and became a household name on the strength of her coverage of the civil war that gripped Lebanon in the 1970s. The ABC's Helene Chung was refused a traineeship, despite being among the best candidates, because the training would be wasted on 'a girl'. Chung eventually became the ABC's first woman foreign correspondent when she was posted to China in 1983.

Women like Willman and Chung, as well as Kate Webb, UPI bureau chief during the Vietnam War, and groundbreaking *Sydney Morning Herald* China correspondent Margaret Jones, were pathfinders and trailblazers. According to her obituary in the *Herald*, Jones was responsible for much of 'the correction of the gender imbalance in Australian journalism during the second half of the last century'. (Jones and Webb both paid their own way overseas.) Correspondents who today cross borders with rebels, embed on Special Forces ops or interview the inhabitants of the Afghan women's tent owe them a debt.

There are many more female journalists who must be acknowledged for their contribution to Australia's understanding of our international environment. They include outstanding reporters like *The Wall Street Journal*'s Geraldine Brooks, the ABC's Sally Sara and Zoe Daniel, *The Sydney Morning Herald*'s Louise Williams and *The Australian*'s Jacquelin Magnay. Other exceptional Australian women covered China, and contributed to our book *The Beijing Bureau*.

GENDER MAY NO longer be a barrier to international assignments and postings, but it continues to play a role in the lives – and work – of female reporters. Like male correspondents, they work around the clock and face the risk of death, injury and kidnap. Female reporters also risk sexual violence. They are often reluctant to bring danger to an editor's attention, as it might impact on their career, but correspondents move in areas where the rules don't apply. Western women may be viewed as fair game, online threats can spill into real life and Australian journalists with a diverse heritage can pay a personal price when they push back against cultural norms. Women correspondents with children also talk of their battle with guilt as they struggle to balance the priorities of family versus work. Some worry about time spent away from home – or the office – and are uneasy about moving the kids from post to post. Others fear the effects of too much adrenaline or a dose of tear gas on an unborn child.

Women correspondents are the equal of their male counterparts. They are among the bravest and most insightful journalists we have at a time when the hot zone is more dangerous than it has ever been. Once, journalists were ignored by combatants as bystanders or valued as neutral observers who would tell their stories to the world. Now, they are targets.

The carpeted halls of the management floor, and many newsrooms, remain the domain of the white, middle class and mostly male. But as we increasingly see the world through the eyes of women, something has changed. Those people-focused stories that once earned women derision are the stories that now tell us about the human truths behind the first draft of history. All journalists, male and female, now report the world very differently as they cover the chaos overwhelming the lives of ordinary people caught up in the winds of change. Being empathetic is a job requirement rather than a cause for ridicule. We now hear more about the people huddled in basements in Kyiv than the specifications of the munitions they are sheltering from, or the name of the general who ordered the bombardment. Soft stories are now the big stories.

Women, as Mao Zedong famously pointed out, without ever fully acting on his idea, hold up half the sky. Women correspondents are vital to covering the news. Without hearing about women, without hearing from them, we hear only half the story.

PART ONE
BREAKING NEWS

'A thousand tanks massed on Polish border. Ten divisions reported ready for swift stroke.'

– Clare Hollingworth, journalist

With those few words, the London *Telegraph* broke the story of the twentieth century – Hitler's preparations to invade Poland and trigger a catastrophic war in Europe. The correspondent was a woman.

Today, Australian women correspondents are filing headline stories from every corner of the globe. As we write, these are the stories that are ongoing or have gripped our recent past.

1
EXODUS FROM UKRAINE

Barbara Miller
Ukraine March 2022, Europe 2013–2016
ABC

On camera, Lviv, Ukraine 2022

THE DAY WAS already playing out like some journalistic comedy of errors. We'd arrived at the main station in Lviv, in western Ukraine, where we'd heard hundreds of escapees from Mariupol were expected to disembark a train coming from the south-eastern city of Zaporizhzhia. Getting information about which platform it was due on seemed unnecessarily difficult. Our Ukrainian fixer, Tymur Zakriiaiev, couldn't seem to read the arrivals board without his glasses, which for some reason he wasn't wearing, and every official he asked gave a different answer.

I had decided I'd do a piece to camera as the train arrived, so camera-man Fletcher Yeung and I bolted up the stairs to knock that off as we heard one pulling in. It was an okay performance from me, but it soon emerged that the people getting off weren't from Mariupol at all.

We didn't really take time to find out their stories. Mariupol was the hot button issue. A city on the Sea of Azov of strategic importance to the Russians, who had invaded Ukraine several weeks earlier, it was now reported to be under a crippling and deadly siege.

Ukrainian authorities said several hundred people were unaccounted for under the rubble of a bombed theatre where they had been sheltering. Many more, they said, were surviving with little food and no running water or electricity, and were under threat of death should they venture from their basement hiding places. In the words of one resident, Anna, whom we had met a couple of days previously, and who'd managed to escape with her son, 'There is no Mariupol anymore.'

Another woman Tymur had tracked down that same day, Katya, sobbed as she told us of days spent in hiding, unable to make even soup for her children, of the bodies she saw lying on the street as she emerged, of apartment blocks in flames. These were among the first first-hand accounts of the sheer brutality of the Russian invasion, which was to be laid bare in shocking and graphic images and testimony a couple of weeks later when the invading forces retreated from areas around the capital, Kyiv.

BACK AT LVIV train station, the search was still on for the correct platform for this train rumoured to be full of Mariupol escapees. I use the word escapees deliberately as they were not evacuees. Establishing safe humanitarian corridors for people trying to flee the hell they were enduring there was proving difficult. Those who did get out and make it to cities like Zaporizhzhia and then further west to Lviv were largely doing so under their own steam and at huge risk.

Our bumbling attempts to pin down where and when the train would come in were interrupted by a rush to shelter when an air siren sounded, a frequent disruption to life in Lviv and a reminder that although the missiles, then at least, were largely falling elsewhere, this was a country at war. Finally I found some other media on platform one. Soon there were six or seven cameras and a bunch of other journalists and NGO types. 'This must be it,' we thought, though it wouldn't have been the first time a media pack had formed on a rumour and a hope rather than any actual intelligence.

Adding to the confusion, some of the cameras were pointing towards the west, which seemed strange to me, since the train clearly had to be coming from the east, so when another train pulled up on platform three, Fletch and I sprinted across the train tracks for my precious piece to camera — just in case. It was another false alarm.

By the time the correct train pulled in, I'd really nailed this piece to camera. I talked about how there weren't safe corridors but how some people were still managing to flee. Fletch panned away just as I finished, to capture some of these brave people disembarking. Only there were none. The train so eagerly awaited and now being avidly filmed and photographed by a bunch of crews was completely empty. It soon emerged the passengers had all got off at the previous station, a twenty-minute drive away.

We bundled into our car and headed there, arriving just in time to see the last of them board buses. 'Mariupol? Mariupol?' I ventured urgently to a few stragglers, who shook their heads. By this time, it was well into the afternoon. I could already feel the evening deadlines looming for the morning bulletins in Australia. Whatever I gathered here would have to be translated and edited and woven into a package for the AM program, complete with some lines and audio from other key developments in the war. Then there were radio news voicers on the major newslines to file, in coordination with my colleagues in London and Washington, a live cross with breakfast TV news to prepare for, perhaps a blog post or two to write. Finding time for dinner would be the usual challenge, it'd be late before I got to bed, there'd more than likely be an air raid siren or two in the night, and I'd be up early to finish and voice a script for the evening television news. The familiar pressure was gnawing away.

Finally I came across Oksana, who was from Mariupol and was willing to talk — briefly at least, she indicated. Oksana spoke Russian as her first language, as do up to one-third of Ukrainians. Our Polish colleague Agnieszka Suszko translated.

Oksana had been working in a factory in Poland, a country where many Ukrainians fled as war began but where hundreds of thousands already worked, filling in the gaps in the labour market left by the Poles who in turn headed west to work in more affluent European Union countries. When war broke out, Oksana had returned to Ukraine to try and get her kids out of Mariupol, where they had been staying with her mother. Her brother had managed to get the girls to a safer part of the city, where they hid out in a basement with another family. After a particularly bad night of shelling, they decided they had to try and get out of the city. Against considerable odds Oksana's brother managed to get the girls, aged eight and thirteen, to Zaporizhzhia, where their mum was waiting.

If that sounds like a happy ending, it's not.

Oksana's mother was still trapped somewhere in Mariupol, unreachable despite her daughter's frantic attempts to get through to anyone who might be able to check in on her. Her brother was trying to return to the besieged city to look for her, a highly dangerous undertaking. She was torn when I asked if she thought Ukrainian forces should lay down their arms there. 'Mariupol is Ukrainian – yes, I understand that,' she said. 'But there are people there and they need to be rescued … Ukraine needs to get people out of there.'

Oksana and the girls boarded a bus for Poland, joining the vast human convoys once again snaking through Europe as a refugee crisis of historic proportions unfolds. Women and children trudge in freezing conditions across Ukraine's western borders, carrying only what they could hurriedly pack as Russian leader Vladimir Putin made good on a threat that has long cast a shadow over this former Soviet republic.

There are noticeably fewer men in these caravans than there were during Europe's migrant crisis of 2015 to 2016; Ukraine has ordered all men under the age of sixty to stay and fight for their homeland. The women who arrive at the Polish, Moldovan and Hungarian borders weep when asked about the fate of the men that stayed behind.

Frankly, it's not looking good, is it?

My colleague Ben Lewis, from Australia's SBS, reports that he witnessed one man make a run for it, leaping over the Ukrainian checkpoint and sprinting towards Poland. He managed a few hundred metres before guards from both countries tackled him to the ground. The account gives me goosebumps with its echoes of the Cold War we naively, it now seems, took to be over.

In Berlin, where I lived for several years, and where they know a thing or two about war displacement and about the drawing of arbitrary borders, people are turning up at the main train station with homemade signs offering accommodation to the Ukrainian refugees arriving there.

In the opposite direction, into Ukraine, there's a smaller but steady stream of traffic: Ukrainian men going back to take up arms, and foreigners lured by a cause. Some are unwilling combatants, some relish the chance to do battle.

A report by National Public Radio (NPR) correspondent Leila Fadel sheds a light on the motivations of some of these fighters, including the guy who says he wants to string Russians up on lampposts and will find killing them easier than killing animals, he claims with menacing bravado, because he likes animals. It's chilling listening, and beautifully crafted radio.

I AM NOW back in Washington, where the invasion of Ukraine is of course huge news too and my days are filled with Pentagon, State Department and White House briefings. Six months after a chaotic and bloody exit from Afghanistan, US President Joe Biden is keen to make good on his promise that 'America is back'.

Russia's invasion of Ukraine also gives weight to the Biden mantra that the prevailing challenge of these times is to unite democracies against autocracies. In these early days of war, NATO is certainly invigorated, and Washington, Brussels and London are coordinating unprecedented sanctions on Russia. The acrimony of the Trump years and bitterness over Brexit have been brushed to one side.

As with all major news events, it's both exhilarating and exhausting to be caught up in it. I feel the buzz of a big story, that heightened sense of being, yet every bone in my body longs to be back on the ground in Europe. I experience it as a deep physical yearning – in the first instance, because I'm a reporter. Our instinct is to head towards the action, to be in the thick of it. It's where we feel most in our element – most alive. Up to a point at least.

Ukraine soon gets under your skin – its expanse, its stoicism, its beauty. I'd like to experience more of it. And this refugee crisis is playing out in parts of Europe that are old stomping grounds from the years I spent living in Germany and Austria. My desire to be there also stems from the enduring impact covering Europe's last migrant crisis has had on me. I hold close the experiences of those reporting trips in 2015 and 2016 to Greece, Serbia, Hungary, Macedonia, Austria, Croatia, Germany.

Now when I see those shimmering masses of refugees, I feel a connection. As silly as this may sound, I feel somehow that I know them. 'Oh, there you all are,' I think.

IT'S THE SOUNDS that stay with you long after you've left. The same sounds that seem to mark the final moments of each desperate voyage across a deceptively calm ocean – destination Europe.

No matter how long and hard you scan the inky waters as you stand gathered in the dead of night on a beach on a Greek island, shivering despite the time of year, you don't see the boats until they have almost arrived. Even then, we need the help of the wizened locals our locally engaged cameraman, Giorgos Moutafis, has engaged. The men spend the night scouring the coast, looking for the flimsy boats with their human cargo: a cargo which has turned this tourist island into a migrant hub in a crisis destined to grow to staggering dimensions.

One of the spotters has seen something on the horizon and phoned it in. We scramble to our cars and head to another beach. At first there's nothing but disappointment, and then it all happens in a rush. Suddenly a tiny light flickers and then, floating through the darkness, come the panicked voices of those onboard as their boat bobs into shore. There is the sound of splashing as someone jumps out and starts pulling the dinghy the final metres up the beach, and soon everyone is scrambling to disembark, as if the sea were about to swallow them up again. Children who one day will surely understand the significance of this moment are handed to those whose wet feet are now planted in Europe.

It all happens at a frantic pace. The lifejackets of dubious provenance are yanked off and abandoned, and the migrants make their way in small, hushed groups into the darkness. The local spotters give the boat's motor the once over, and if it checks out, they haul that off into the night too.

It's June 2015 and I'm on Kos with producer Sashka Koloff and cameraman Cameron Bauer on assignment for ABC TV's *Foreign Correspondent*. Around 70,000 migrants have already arrived on the Greek islands this year, a record number, but this is only the beginning.

The steady stream is about to become a flood. Soon, spotting migrant boats won't require any patience or skill at all.

That September, shocking images of the body of a three-year-old Syrian boy, Alan Kurdi, washed up on a Turkish beach, lying on his tummy, his little dead face planted on the sand, will bring the escalating crisis into sharp global focus. The toddler's death will come just days after German Chancellor Angela Merkel essentially opens her country's borders to Syrians fleeing a war already four years old by declaring, 'Wir schaffen das', translated as 'We can do this!' or 'We can manage this!'

Now that I am becoming more familiar with American lingo, I feel 'We got this!' might better reflect the sentiment, even if that seems not at all like something the dour German leader would have said.

By the end of the year, an estimated 800,000 migrants will have arrived in Greece from Turkey, many of them hoping to strike out further north to Germany. I don't know that yet as I stand that morning on a beach on Kos, a little stunned at what I have just witnessed.

'YALLA, YALLA, YALLA!' the coastguard shouts as he tries to encourage several dozen migrants to abandon their overcrowded rubber boat and board his vessel. Yalla, he explains, means let's go or come on in Arabic. It's the only word he knows of the language and that summer he's using it almost every night.

It's the wee hours, and after days of badgering the central authorities in Athens, our fixer, Menelaos Tzafalias, has convinced them to allow us to go out on the coastguard's boat. We haven't been at sea for long before a suspected migrant boat is detected on the radar and we speed towards it.

We pull up alongside, but no one is keen to leave the dinghy until they are sure they are dealing with the Greek coastguard and not their Turkish counterparts. If Turkey picks these boats up, it will turn them back.

'Where are we going?' one man shouts.

'Over here … Greece,' the coastguard tells him.

'Greece, are you sure? You promise?'

Soon the passengers are convinced and the three or four guys on our boat start to pull them on board, a hectic undertaking during which it feels as if someone could easily slip silently into the water.

It's only when you're up this close that you truly appreciate the perilous nature of the journey. There's no captain, there are no nautical instruments in the laden-down dinghy you have paid a smuggler for a spot on, just a guy trying to work the motor and follow the instruction to head for the lights across the dark expanse of ocean.

During the day, gazing out from under the tourist umbrellas on the Greek side, Turkey appears tantalisingly close, almost as if you could easily swim across. The night gives lie to that illusion. Many of the people on these boats can't swim anyway. Alan Kurdi is one of an esti-mated 800 migrants who drown in the waters between Turkey and Greece that year. The death toll on the longer and more treacherous crossing between North Africa and southern Europe is astronomical. In 2015, almost 4000 migrants drown in the Mediterranean.

On a previous reporting trip to Sicily with the ABC's Mark Douglas, aka Floyd, to cover a boat sinking shocking enough in its scale to briefly prick the conscience of a world largely inured to the tragedies on the Mediterranean migrant route, I'd met listless young men who had made it to Europe only to languish on the island. They were unable to get the paperwork to leave for the mainland, or to work legally. They couldn't go back to the families who had hoped they would prosper and send money home, and they couldn't go forward either.

Rana is on this first boat in the Aegean we see being intercepted, a pediatrician from Aleppo travelling with her cousin. She's left her two boys behind and it'll be more than two years before she's reunited with them. She weeps when we interview her later at the port on Kos about where she hopes to settle.

'Any country, please,' she says. 'Any country ... we will be safe again, together again.'

In November 2017, she will send me a photo after her boys finally arrive in Denmark, where she has wound up. The older boy, who in the years his mother hasn't seen him has become almost a man, takes the selfie. All three are beaming. The image warms and breaks my heart. In June 2015, sitting on the ground at the harbour that morning as she and her fellow passengers are processed, Rana says she was shocked to see kids on her boat. She didn't think it would be safe to bring her boys.

Rana features in the half-hour documentary we put together, as do three young men who arrive on another boat. Mohamed is a sound engineer from Damascus. He's introspective, intelligent and has a wry sense of humour. We're filming with him as he takes one look at the abandoned Captain Elias Hotel, where many migrants wait on Kos for the paperwork to allow them, inshallah, to depart the island and get to the mainland.

'Oh, very nice place!' he quips as we tour derelict rooms full of miserable-looking migrants lying on the floor or huddling in small groups. Mohamed can afford a shared room in town for the duration.

He probably wouldn't have made it here without the help of his friend Yamen, a dentist. Yamen is the street-savvy one who dealt with the smugglers in Turkey and convinced Mohamed to leave with him, rather than stay in a country where the Syrians are often treated as second class citizens, condemned to a life on the fringes, overcharged and underpaid. Mohamed and Yamen end up in Germany, although in different cities. A third young man, a pharmacist called Azar, winds up in Sweden, becoming something of an activist for the rights of asylum seekers.

There was a time when I would think of these three young men several times a week. Like some distant and vaguely annoying aunt, I would worry and wonder about them and feel a strange sense of responsibility for their wellbeing in Europe. Perhaps they represented the hundreds of thousands who trudged through the continent that summer. I couldn't allow myself to be weighed down by all their stories but focusing on a few was manageable. Perhaps feeling as if I have a real connection to them assuages some of my guilt for crashing into their lives at a precarious moment, taking their story and offering nothing in return. Maybe what I am really doing is convincing myself that I am a good person who didn't just suck up their experience for my own journalistic gain and then leave.

Whatever the motivations, I keep in sporadic touch with all three, and with Rana, and I catch up with Azar on a visit to Sweden a year or so later. I fantasise about making a *Where Are They Now* program about them, but there's been so much coverage of the migrant crisis, so many similar stories, that it never gets off the ground.

Mohamed and Yamen buy fake passports to get them to Germany, via France. Azar takes the less expensive option and crosses the continent by land. He says it was pretty dicey at times, but I never do hear the full story. Initially, European countries set aside the regulation requiring those seeking asylum to apply in the first safe haven they land in, but it wasn't a sure bet and crossing borders could still be risky.

It was the year when everyone seemed to be Syrian. But there were also migrants from Iraq, Pakistan, Afghanistan, even the Balkans, hoping to use the prevailing winds to make it too. Some carried fake documents, some just chanced their luck. On Kos we met another Muhammad, a young electricity factory worker from Lahore in Pakistan. He'd acquired a new pair of pants and seemed to see them as a good omen.

'I will take these pants to Athens!' he declared triumphantly. 'Now I am free. Now I have chances, because in front of me is the whole of Europe. I have lots of opportunities and, inshallah, I will do something better for myself.'

His goal was to work in a restaurant in Paris. We never managed to track him down again to find out if he made it there, or if he even made it off the island. Sometimes I imagine him working in the kitchen of some cosy Parisian bistro, washing dishes or working as a sous chef, grinning from ear to ear.

Chances are that's not the case. Syrians fleeing war were given special treatment that summer, Pakistanis fleeing a crushing lack of opportunity were not. The likelihood of Muhammad making it to France without being turned back wasn't great, but by inadvertently getting caught up in what before the war in Ukraine was the greatest migration Europe had seen since World War II, his chances were probably as good as they were ever going to get.

WHEN YOU HEAR that a million people flooded into Europe within the space of a year, mainly from the Greek islands, you imagine the continent overrun with migrant convoys. In reality, the influx was confined to shifting hot spots and corridors.

A disused rail track led from the village of Horgoš in Serbia directly into Hungary, and therefore into the European Union. For weeks, the Syrian migrants who'd made it from Greece to the Serbian capital Belgrade would board buses to Horgoš or pay locals a couple of hundred euros to drive them north. Then they'd flood along the tracks and into Hungary.

The first time I walked the tracks, I was going against the tide. Cameraman David Sciasci and I arrived at a sprawling makeshift camp on the Hungarian side just in time to go live into the ABC's 7 pm news bulletin. With the morning rush into the evening news program over, time was on our side. As I ambled towards the rail track, streams of people began washing past me and I found myself welling up. Many of those passing greeted me joyfully; with Hungary in sight they appeared energised. Despite the length and difficulty of the journey behind them, they were going at an impressive speed, including a man with a wooden leg. I'd see this same haste a few years later when I watched images of migrant caravans making their way from Central America to the US–Mexico border, and I'd wish I were there too.

I know few details about the lives of the people we interviewed, about the specific circumstances behind the decision to leave their home and embark on a long and dangerous journey to a foreign country where grief and guilt would gnaw away. Did I think the reasons why they might want to up sticks were just so painfully obvious that, short on time, I too readily accepted the brevity of their responses?

Many people didn't want to give details, at least until they were sure on which side of Syria's brutal civil war their fellow travellers came down. Rebel and regime supporters warily rubbed shoulders on the migrant route, now uncomfortably united in a common goal to get out.

It's worth taking a moment to reflect on these lines from the 2015 Human Rights Watch World Report: 'In 2014, Syria's armed conflict grew increasingly bloody with government and pro-government militias intensifying their attacks on civilian areas and continuing use of indiscriminate weapons. Government forces also continued to arbitrarily arrest, disappear, and torture detainees, many of whom died in detention. Non-state armed groups opposing the government also carried out serious abuses including deliberate and indiscriminate attacks on civilians, use of child soldiers, kidnapping, and torture in detention. The extremist group Islamic State, also known as ISIS, and al-Qaeda's affiliate in Syria, Jabhat al-Nusra, were responsible for systematic and widespread violations including targeting civilians, kidnapping and executions.'

'It must be really harrowing,' people would say to me of reporting on the migrant crisis. It was, of course. Yet, seeing this migration up close was also strangely uplifting, because there was hope. You could see it written on people's faces, catch it in the spring in their step. There was resilience, too.

That morning, walking along that piece of old railway track, I drank in the sheer strength of the human spirit, and it took my breath away.

IT TURNS OUT they were right to rush. On a balmy evening a week or two later, as cameraman Brant Cumming and I filmed at the spot on the tracks where Serbia ended and Hungary began, soldiers rolled out the final sections of razor wire to seal off the route. Europe was locking down.

Over the next few days, small groups managed to breach the fence, but Hungary was no longer willing to let migrants cross through its territory on the march north, or even to aid them at the frontier. There were ugly scenes when Hungarian police used tear gas and water cannon to force back migrants who were angry and frustrated at having come so far only to have the door closed in their face.

But no sooner did one crossing close than another opened. As the clashes erupted near Horgoš, a steady stream of migrants had already begun arriving at Serbia's border with Croatia to try their luck there. The bizarre game of cat and mouse continued through Europe's historic summer.

The rolling out of the razor wire felt like a turning point. As autumn turned to winter, the migrants kept coming, but their situation got more desperate, the conditions markedly worse. Getting to northern Europe proved much harder, and many migrants got stuck along the way, some of them for years.

In Hungary, they were detained and fingerprinted, some were beaten; on Lesbos a refugee camp, Moria, became a prison where migrants faced conditions described as living hell; and on the Greek–Macedonian border hundreds of migrants who had waded through a river were forced by security officials back across the raging waters to the desolation of the muddy Idomeni camp, a refugee no man's land.

Locals were getting frustrated, too, but the kindness of strangers was still remarkable. At Idomeni we filmed while an elderly man invited a group of migrants, who'd been sent back across the river, to his home for a warm meal. They had no common language, but the man's family had been refugees themselves and he understood them. He, his wife and a neighbour fussed around them, trying to meet their requests for bread to accompany the stew they had cooked for them, and for dry socks.

The writing was on the wall though. By March 2016, the European Union had reached an agreement with Turkey under which all arriving migrants would be returned. Its blunt terms said that for every Syrian returned to Turkey, another would be resettled within the EU, as if the individuals didn't matter at all. Despite Angela Merkel's earlier assurances, Europe no longer had this.

I was back on Lesbos again, this time with cameraman Alessandro Pavone, as the new deal came into force. I regret not getting the contact details of a young couple we spoke to, both doctors, who got off a boat from Turkey early on the morning it took effect. I watched as they were shepherded onto a bus for Moria, the camp I had witnessed being turned into a fortress. Thinking back, I see their faces pressed up against the bus window, anxiously peering out, but I might have imagined this detail. I always wondered what happened to them. Maybe it's better not to know.

As Alessandro and I landed in Athens on our way back to London, we turned on our phones. News of a terrorist attack in Brussels was emerging, with thirty-two people dead and hundreds injured in bombings at the airport and at a metro station, just months after terrorists in Paris killed one hundred and thirty people.

Our colleagues from London were on their way; the decision was made to send us in too. I was dog-tired, but I felt the familiar rush of adrenaline and wouldn't have wanted it any other way. Unable to fly into Belgium, we headed to Paris, picked up a car and drove at speed to Brussels in time to make it into the evening coverage in Australia. Never underestimate the power of an Italian at the wheel.

The news had moved on, the plight of the migrants already yesterday's headline. My time as ABC Europe correspondent was also coming to an end.

When you get home from covering those stories, you hug your kids tight. You ask yourself: knowing what I know now, if it were me, what would I have done? Would I have taken the risk and paid the smuggler and bundled my babies in that flimsy boat in the hope of a better, a safer life?

The answer I keep coming back to terrifies me.

Of course I would.

Wouldn't you?

Yet fleeing is only part of the story. Almost all of those trekking through Europe that summer had left friends and family behind, not knowing when or if they would see them again. That's true of the millions who have left Ukraine or been internally displaced there, too.

I wonder about Anna's father. The woman we met in Lviv who told us Mariupol was no more said he had stayed behind. He had managed to make contact with her at some point on her long journey to Lviv. 'He says they are still shooting,' Anna said simply.

I wonder too if Oksana has managed to find out what happened to her mother. Did the old woman survive, or was she among the thousands of civilians thought to have been killed or to have perished in Mariupol, a once beautiful and thriving port?

At the time of writing, the true scale of the horrors of Mariupol are yet to be exposed. I feel we all need to brace for that moment.

What of Oskana's girls? Of the little one who clung so tightly to her mother as she spoke to us but smiled sweetly up at me as I became excited to hear her name was Varvara, Russian for Barbara. I can't remember ever meeting anyone under the age of about fifty who's called Barbara, but perhaps in Ukraine the name is still popular.

Her sister Sofia was thirteen years old, just a year older than my own daughter, safe at home in Washington. As Sofia talked quietly about seeing cars explode, I noticed how oily her hair was. Somehow that small detail was what it took for it to really hit me that this vulnerable young girl had been spirited across her city, to spend days in a basement, hiding from those who might kill or rape her, or both. After all that, Sofia emerged to embark on a frightening journey out of her hometown, which, when we met her, was far from over.

Perhaps it never really will be.

In the end, the exodus is only a beginning.

Barbara Miller was the ABC's Europe correspondent from 2013 to 2016. She began her journalistic career with Austria's national broadcaster ORF, before joining the BBC World Service in London. She is the ABC's North America correspondent and undertook a short assignment to Ukraine for the ABC in March 2022

2
KATE GERAGHTY: SOMEWHERE NORTH-EAST OF KYIV

Ukraine 2022
The Sydney Morning Herald
by Trevor Watson

With Anthony Galloway (*SMH/The Age*), Ukraine 2022.

MULTI-AWARD-WINNING photojournalist Kate Geraghty captured Ukraine's fierce resistance to invading Russian forces and mothers fleeing with their children across the Polish frontier on assignment in the war-torn country for *The Sydney Morning Herald*, and *The Age* in Melbourne. Geraghty's powerful images told very personal stories of an enormous tragedy: 'kindergarten teacher, Katya, leaves her homeland for the sake of her four young sons; Alina from Hostomel waits at a checkpoint, her face drained of emotion; Oxana serves tea to refugees as they pass her home; a young couple embrace, perhaps for the last time, on a Kyiv railway platform'.

'Kate is an extraordinary photojournalist,' says the *Herald*'s managing photo editor, Mags King. 'She is tireless in her pursuit. Her photos are the result of meticulous research, understanding her subjects and years of dedication to telling these stories.'

With a Ukraine date line and under a headline that reads, 'I was born here, I will die here: tears and desperation at the crossroads of war,' Geraghty's Ukraine by-line ran as prominently as that of reporter Antony Galloway.

During her most recent Ukraine tour, Geraghty crisscrossed the young republic, from Lviv in the east to Kharkiv – close to the Russian border – on to the disputed Donbas region and the capital, Kyiv. 'I've never before seen a nation mobilise like Ukraine,' she said. 'In every town there were volunteers, collecting and distributing supplies to people driven from their homes. They made camouflage nets, trained civilians in trauma medicine like how to use a tourniquet and provided meals for volunteers and soldiers. We visited a hospital in Kharkiv where outside you hear constant incoming and outgoing fire and yet inside the hospital it was a quiet, organised and professional environment.'

Geraghty also spent time with Ukrainian troops at the frontline. With the war continuing to rage, she is reluctant to disclose precisely where she went. 'There had been a battle a few days before we arrived at one location north-east of Kyiv,' Geraghty says. 'We watched Ukrainian emergency services retrieving the bodies of six Russian soldiers that were to be used in an exchange for two live Ukrainian POWs.' Geraghty then talked about leaving the area ahead of a Russian attack. 'We had to leave this frontline position quickly as the commander received a call saying the Russians had launched missiles in our direction. Later we found out that three Ukrainian soldiers had been killed in that area.'

Despite the near-overwhelming odds ranged against them, morale among members of Ukraine's highly professional military is high, Geraghty says. 'Drawings and letters from schoolchildren adorn the walls of the Ukrainian military's forward positions thanking them for protecting their country.'

Her most recent assignment gave Geraghty an opportunity to return to the disputed Donetsk region, which is internationally recognised as a part of Ukraine but is ruled, at least in part, by the pro-Russian Donetsk People's Republic. 'We spent time in towns and villages under Ukraine control, like Kramatorsk, Avdiyivka, Krasnohorivka, Kamyanka, some of which have now been given evacuation orders,' she says. 'Here we reported on the impact of eight years' conflict in the area. People urged their fellow Ukrainians to be strong. If they were strong, they would prevail. Some people said they didn't want the rest of their country to experience what they had experienced in eight years of war.'

Unlike many of her colleagues who develop a toughened exterior to protect themselves from the surrounding human disaster, Geraghty never loses sight of the horror faced by real people.

'It's so incredibly important to be aware of the responsibility we have to report and document that horror, so that people can see what other people are going through,' she says.

She will never forget an eighteen-year-old Iraqi named Abdulrahman Abdulaaly who was severely wounded during the battle to retake the city of Mosul from ISIS forces. 'He was bandaged basically from head to toe, eighty per cent of his body was burnt,' Geraghty says. 'His mother was there when we took his photograph. He was to become her third son lost to ISIS.'

Geraghty's respect for her photographic subjects and commitment to her profession shows long before an assignment begins. 'I find myself really involved in the preparation, the research and the story,' she says. 'I look at the place I am going to, the security logistics, the people and their history. I also think that learning a language so that you can greet people in their own language is important.' Geraghty speaks enough Arabic to get by.

Over the past two decades, Geraghty has been honoured with eight prestigious Walkley Awards including the ultimate Gold Walkley for outstanding news coverage, which was shared with a colleague. In 2021, Geraghty won Nikon Photo of the Year. Her career has been an enormous success and continues to be so.

But her pathway was not always assured. Geraghty was working for the Albury–Wodonga-based *The Border Mail* when pro-Indonesian militias unleashed a wave of violence in an effort to thwart the results of an independence referendum in East Timor, now Timor Leste, in 1999. When her newspaper refused to send her to the troubled island, Geraghty took leave and covered the story anyway.

In 2003, she was assigned by her new employer, *The Sydney Morning Herald*, to cover the United States–led invasion of Iraq, but only after the paper's then photo editor, Mike Bowers, took personal responsibility for her safety. Bowers says he was 'astonished' that management initially pushed back when he recommended Geraghty for the job.

'I was warned that it would be on my head if anything happened to her,' Bowers now recalls. 'Of course, it was a terrible story. People were worried about gas, Weapons of Mass Destruction and so on. But I had no doubt that Kate was better than anyone else I could possibly have sent. I had made sure that Kate was well trained. She had been on difficult assignment training courses, and I made her promise to wear her flak jacket at all times.' Her coverage of the battle for West Mosul won an International Photography Award.

The list of world-shaping stories that she has covered includes the 2002 Bali bombings and the 2004 Boxing Day tsunami; Cambodia; Afghanistan; South Sudan; the 2006 war in Lebanon; the 2010 Gaza flotilla; and Myanmar. She was assigned to Ukraine for the first time in 2014 to cover Russian incursions into the Donetsk region, the annexation of Crimea and the downing of Malaysian Airlines passenger plane MH17, with the loss of all onboard.

So, has Geraghty's gender helped or hindered her work in the field? 'Being female in places like Afghanistan meant that I had access to women, whereas the male reporter that I was with on occasion didn't have the same access,' she says. 'I am sometimes afforded a kind of neutral gender. I can sit and eat with the men and yet go out the back and talk with the women. Regarding security, I've never had an issue being female in conflict. In fact, I have been treated with more respect in some countries than I am paid here.'

And, despite twenty years of combat photography, Geraghty has not lost the respect that she has for the people she captures with her camera, as was evidenced by her coverage of the horror in Ukraine. 'Inside a Kharkiv hospital, a family waits for a wounded boy to wake up' reads the headline. It's followed by another prominent Geraghty byline. And then come the images: unconscious nine-year-old Volodymyr Baklanov, who was badly hurt in the same hail of gunfire that killed his mother, lies tranquilly in bed, the only sign of injury a small scratch on his nose; the boy's wrist tethered to the bed with a bandage to stop him flailing around when he wakes; his uncle Sergei, who saw his sister-in-law shot dead, sitting vigil over the child.

3
THE FALL OF THE SOVIET EMPIRE: LESSONS FOR PUTIN

Monica Attard
Moscow 1989–1995
ABC

Attard (second from left) with friends at the edge of Soviet society.

I T'S UNLIKELY THAT in 1970, when I was twelve, I could have imagined myself covering the collapse of an empire. Nor could I have dreamt that fifty-one years later, my passion for Russia would still be alive, if battered by its barbaric invasion of its neighbour, Ukraine, in February 2022.

But back then, when I was a young girl, I did dream of being a foreign correspondent; in particular, a foreign correspondent in what was then the Soviet Union. From that romantic notion to doomscrolling social media for news on the latest atrocity in Ukraine is quite the narrative arc.

As far back into my childhood as I can recall, there were dinnertime conversations about how brutal capitalism could be, how Joseph Stalin had saved Europe from fascism – and my favourite story of all, how the brave Soviet experiment with socialism would reap the benefits of communism at some point, sometime, in the future. A new world, in the nirvana of time and place, where all human beings would live as equals! My father was from war-torn Malta, and he was a 'believer', at least in a better world. He remained that way to the end. And when he encouraged me to go the Soviet Union for the first time in 1983, I was wearing his rose-coloured glasses. Everything seemed to be on the way to nirvana. Even the empty shops and the long queues for offcuts of substandard meat or clothes shops that sold thousands of copies of just one item of clothing in the same size and the same colour. This, I reasoned, was a place sacrificing something – life – for something better. In 2022, after thirty years of Russia's integration into the global economic and financial system, that long-lost world of deficits – the word Russians used for everything not available – was ancient history. But by March 2022 the nirvana of nascent capitalism born in the 1990s had abruptly and eerily been shut down, thanks to the deep and wide sanctions imposed by the West on an invading belligerent Russia. It's been a long road from nothing to something to uncertainty. The world is yet to see whether Russians will again rise against a ruler whose voracious appetite for land and blood has returned them to an Orwellian nightmare.

In 1983, when I first travelled to Russia in the dead of winter, Orwell was hovering in my mind. Although nothing I saw could have been further from my own reality, I reasoned there was *purpose*. The driver sent to ferry me and a friend from the then only international airport in the capital was such a welcoming touch, I thought. The driver was of course associated with the UPDK, the Directorate for Service to the Diplomatic Corps, an agency of the Foreign Affairs Ministry charged with looking over the shoulder of any and all foreigners who dared then visit for leisure or work. UPDK still does much the same job, if now under commercial auspices, though as Russia's President Vladimir Putin tightens the noose around the freedoms won by his own people, the agency may well return to its darker days. But back in 1983 there was still, for me, romance to the Russian capital. The streets from Sheremetyevo Airport to the city centre were virtually empty, because cars were in deficit, and the trip took a brisk fifteen minutes. Magic, I thought – no traffic.

Arriving at the decrepit and now demolished Intourist Hotel on what was then Gorky Street, it was like being in the twilight zone. These two young female foreigners couldn't figure out what all the men and women hovering at the front of the hotel were up to. Maybe they were there to greet us? How friendly, I thought. It turns out they were awaiting tourists of the male variety and businessmen to proffer the wares of what we discovered was a highly lucrative trade in sex work.

Inside, surly desk workers looked over our documents and briskly marched off with our passports, which was a momentarily discombobulating feeling. Though when they returned minutes later with our passports in hand, I thought – how efficient! All foreigners, still to this day, need to have their passports registered with UPDK, as though our arrival at the airport and delivery to Intourist hadn't already been clocked.

A rickety lift took us to our floor, where a babushka sat on a chair in the hallway, arms comfortably perched over her bosom, scowling at us for reasons unclear. Still, I thought kindly of her; it was icy cold outside and this poor woman had to come to work. Looking out our hotel window overlooking Gorky Street, we spied large long red banners with Lenin's image fluttering in the wind. 'That must be the Lenin Museum,' we decided. This place is going to be easy to navigate, I thought.

The next day, we decided to put our lives on the line and make our way across Gorky Street through foot-high snow underpinned by ice. Gorky Street was what in Australia we'd call a highway – six lanes wide and connecting the heart of the city centre, across from the Kremlin, to the outer reaches of the city. We hadn't seen the underpass to allow foot traffic to avoid the car traffic, which led to our first brush with the law. In the end, taking pity on us, the *militsiya*, or local police, accompanied us to the underpass and across the road, from where we emerged – like magic – just below the fluttering Lenin banners.

Sadly, a near hour-long effort to cross the road didn't get us to the Lenin Museum. As we looked up Gorky Street, there were Lenin banners fluttering everywhere. Most were worse for wear – much like the rest of the city as it turned out – but flutter they did as if to say, 'Welcome to the land where we all sing from the same song sheet.' Only briefly in the scheme of time has this turned out to be untrue. The thirty years between 1991 when the old order collapsed and 2022 when it threatens to rise again was, perhaps, the nirvana.

BACK WHEN I was a child, being a foreign correspondent seemed like
the best job in the world, particularly for a kid from the inner western
Sydney suburbs at a time when travel was expensive and rare. I didn't
see the inside of an aeroplane until I was seventeen. But as a child, I
imagined the vest-wearing, bespectacled, notepad-carrying reporter
in fields of war, penning stories for faraway Australia, hungry for news
from the world out there, far, far away from our marooned island
nation. And so it came to pass for this dreaming migrant child, carrying
the burden common to my socio-economic and racial class of low
expectation. Just minus the vest. But it didn't come easily.

I had spent years in newsrooms, commercial and the ABC, spiriting
myself over to the then Soviet Republic of Russia each year on my
annual break to poke around and observe. I'd been travelling in and
out of the USSR, the Union of Soviet Socialist Republics, since that
first trip in 1983. Friends in Paris who, as young university students
on exchange to Moscow's State University, had met some like-minded
Russians, led me to a woman who would become my lifelong friend.
Natasha Yakovleva was a film archivist with the state archives. She died
recently, so trips to Moscow now feel empty. Back in 1985 when I
met Natasha, she was as curious about me as I was about her, and
surreptitiously she showed me the weird and wonderful underbelly of
this intriguing city, about which, oddly, I felt I understood less and less
with each visit.

By 1989, the ABC was ready to open a Moscow bureau and post its
first correspondent. I was devastated when the job didn't come my way,
though when the second position did later that year, I was happy not
to have been the first correspondent in. Establishing a physical bureau,
navigating the vagaries of UPDK and hiring support staff while filing
on a big story would have been a herculean effort for a then young,
single female.

Soviet society was thought by its members to be matriarchal. And
in the sense that women carried the major burdens of life, including
family life, in a country of constant deficits, perhaps it was. But men,
like everywhere else, in every significant aspect of life outside the home,
held all the power. Operating as a foreign correspondent in this environment was often confusing. My questions were always entertained,
but I was invariably considered exotic for having asked. My desire
to understand the place was always welcomed but my curiosity was

considered, by some, a little unbecoming for a woman. The one saving grace for me was that socialism had given the Soviet people a strong sense that everyone was in the same sinking boat – men, women and children. There was an affordance of empathy for hardships suffered and help when help was needed. That made a difference in reporting the place.

The demise of the Soviet Union was slow, burning with disappointment and rage and, of course, with anticipation. By the time I arrived as a correspondent, it was well and truly underway, though the end couldn't have been imagined. Politically and geo-strategically isolated, the Kremlin plastered over the long and obvious economic disasters while holding out the promise of better days to come. And coercion was the tool of choice to ensure people maintained the faith, much as now in 2022, even if the faith is no longer communism but nationalism.

Mikhail Gorbachev came along in the mid 1980s. *Perestroika* (political and economic reinvention) and *glasnost* (openness) gave people the right to think for themselves about how they wanted to live and work. But it enraged the bureaucrats and the hard left of the Soviet Communist Party. As a result, it wasn't a smooth, seamless transition from *diktat* to free thinking, and it brought societal schisms – some of which were entirely predictable, some of which were not. There were those who feared freer thinking would let loose the hounds of capitalism, which would kill off the achievements of their forebears whose blood and hard work had built the Soviet industrial base and, of course, rip away the sureties their lives were built on. There were those who thought just a little freedom would do the job of making people feel valued and hopeful of a better life, and give them the chance to do something for themselves, outside the regime's boundaries, to make their lives better. And there were those who wanted the chains to be thrown off completely. Add to that potent mix fourteen largely resentful republics outside of Russia (the most politically and economically important republic of them all) and the result was years of social upheaval, from the Kremlin to the most far-flung corners of the Soviet empire. The reverberation from that upheaval, the breaking apart of a seventy-year-old federation of states built on dogma and held together by coercion and fate, is what the world now sees playing out in Ukraine.

By 1989, when I arrived in Moscow as a correspondent, even the most fearful regularly took to the streets in protests for and against

Gorbachev's rule. There would be tens of thousands, sometimes even a million or more people, crushing into each other, carrying each other along with sheer body weight, overseen by scores of KGB and *militsiya*. We saw this again on the streets of Russia's big cities in 2022 as people protested Russia's invasion of its neighbour, only this time the protests were smaller in number, people were instantly arrested, and they were entirely unified in what they wanted – no war. Back in the late 1980s and early 1990s, the protests were almost confused; some wanted a break put on reform, others wanted more and faster reform. There were uprisings against rulers and parliaments across the fifteen Soviet republics, the most frightening of them being when local Soviet officials defended their political fortresses with force, though relatively few were killed. As punishment, the food-producing republics and their subjects who wanted freedom from Moscow imposed food blockades on the capital. Deficits of cars, furniture and clothes produced by decades of a malfunctioning economy suddenly seemed quaint, even preferable.

Throughout it all, I had a group of Russian friends holding my hand, taking me to the edges of Soviet society, where I could see how people were experiencing the teetering of an empire. Some of them are still holding my hand to help me understand what rage and fury brought their country to invade its neighbour. When the USSR finally collapsed in December 1991, I again felt as I had when I first travelled there in 1983: I was in the land of the brave. Their new world was something neither they nor their forebears could ever have imagined. Now, in 2022, it all seems threatened.

THE ODD THING about Russia's relationship with women was the strange contradiction at its heart. While women had and have no real power, they simultaneously had and have all the power. They cleared those underground crossings of ice and snow in labour they were physically unsuited for. They were prevalent among university graduates in medicine and engineering, even if that led to a downgrading in the salary and status of both professions. They rarely appeared on politician roll calls, yet their influence was evident in politics. And, most certainly, the influence of women's thinking, needs and demands was evident in the manoeuvrings of local communities. There was a respect, and it was not secret. When it came to journalism, some of the toughest were women. Anna Politkovskaya is a name still recognised in the West. Her fearless reporting of the war Russia waged against the semi-autonomous republic of Chechnya as it tried to break away from Moscow remains a high point of independent journalism in a country that has never been easy, and where it now appears to have been snuffed out completely by a new law penalising journalists for telling the truth about the war with Ukraine. When Politkovskaya was gunned down returning to her apartment in Moscow in 2006, the Russians I knew were sad but not shocked. They expected something to happen to her. Who writes about atrocities perpetrated by the Kremlin without consequence?

Politkovskaya's murder – and the murder and harassment of dozens of journalists, activists and politicians since 2006 – put paid to any notion that media in Putin's Russia was free in the sense we understand media freedom in the West. But like all those killed or harassed, Politkovskaya was respected, heard. The Kremlin might wish to forget her and her reporting, but many haven't. To this day, no one sits at her desk at *Novaya Gazeta*. (In March 2022, following two warnings from the censor, the paper suspended its operations until, it said, the end of Moscow's so-called 'special military operation' in Ukraine.) Still, the retort I hear most often about this assassination is – why didn't she just stick to issues that were safe to cover, issues which women should cover? There's that odd relationship with women, again.

INTO THIS I waded, in my early thirties, single, very excited to be on my first posting and covering what appeared to me then to be the most consequential story in the world. The USSR was in its death throes. Mikhail Sergeyevich Gorbachev was tussling for authority with Boris Yeltsin, and on the streets, Russians were rooting for both men. The hard left of the Communist Party was keeping a watchful, anxious eye on the new liberties granted: the ability to trade; the new television programs which questioned; the protests which, while overseen by a still operative KGB, demonstrated the newest freedom of all – the right to protest. Even though many in my circle thought that if communism was going to survive, it would need more than a little miracle, no one thought it would collapse. The system was corrupt and few showed any real loyalty to it. But the system did provide free health care, education and accommodation. Cradle to grave security was a big deal.

Russians also knew that the nirvana Lenin had promised, Stalin had corrupted and Brezhnev, Andropov and Chernenko had failed to revive was gone – as an idea as much as an achievable destination. But life without the Communist Party was still unthinkable.

The new buzzword was 'biznez'. Making do in a nation of deficits was no longer cutting it. Even the class of people who proudly maintained 'they pretend to pay us, we pretend to work' were looking to find ways to do their own thing. My local state cafe, which rarely had anything but diluted coffee to offer its customers, and from which its manager, Galia, made a paltry amount of money each month, suddenly changed. Galia was an imposing figure: tall, graceful and gracious, and most of all, determined. She decided to offer the locals something new – real coffee, food and service. With her blonde beehive perched atop her strikingly Slavic face, Galia tapped into her contacts in the caviar industry, sourcing bucketloads of the stuff, red and black. When word spread, the customers came, queuing around the block to buy a slice or two of bread with caviar, and Turkish coffee that tasted real. She was in business for a good six months before the cafe was firebombed. The era of mafia had taken hold, with thugs whose only way of doing 'biznez' was to extort. Galia refused to pay for protection and her business was annihilated. This was life as the Communist Party lost control.

While danger was everywhere for those Russians trying to make a go of the new trade freedoms, fear of it was abating among others. By 1990, just six months after Russians experienced their first dance with democracy with the election of President Boris Yeltsin, young people were making their voices heard. They would gather on street corners to deride the 'Party mafia' that guarded its own turf and operated protection rackets to ensure only a new class of post-communist entrepreneurs could live well. People weren't afraid to talk about the issues anymore. On television, *Vzglyad*, or Outlook, was a talk show hosted by the immensely popular Alexander Lyubimov, the son of a well-known spy. Looking back now from Putin's Russia, this was a high point of media freedom. Lyubimov openly discussed with guests the ills of Soviet communism, what people wanted from government, how they would get it, what Gorbachev was doing right and wrong, how the feud between Yeltsin, President of the Russian

Republic, and Gorbachev, the last leader of the Soviet Union, might hinder progress towards a capitalism-based nirvana. In 1990, my friends could barely believe what they were watching. Now, in 2022, even using the word 'war' to describe the Russian invasion of Ukraine is penalised. As I spend nights doomscrolling on the war with Ukraine, I wonder how Lyubimov feels about the gains he forged being squashed so comprehensively?

As a correspondent, I would often hit the streets back then to test the limits of the newfound intolerance of the regime, and the reactions, while mixed, had one idea in common. Living as they had was no longer possible; personal freedom couldn't be the price for cradle to grave security. Of course, few ordinary folk followed their desire for more freedom and a better life in a functioning economy to its logical conclusion. They thought the old structures could be reformed, renewed, revitalised. Certainly no one I knew thought the old structures might actually collapse under the weight of the reforms. Not even Mikhail Gorbachev.

And so, as 1990 ushered in a newly empowered Boris Yeltsin, who held court at the Russian parliament, oddly named the White House, the demands for more grew louder and louder – led by the non-Russian republics. The Communist Party was becoming very tetchy indeed.

Enter Viktor Alksnis. Of Latvian heritage and a one-time colonel in the Soviet Air Force, Alksnis was an extremely hardline member of the Supreme Soviet of the USSR and one of the founders of the equally hardline anti-reform Soyuz group within it. Soyuz had been giving Gorbachev grief for more than a year before the Baltic states were granted independence in September of 1991. Alksnis was the most vocal of them. He was a fascinating man; his grandfather had been arrested and then executed during the Stalin purges, his grandmother spent years in a gulag and his father was condemned to a lifetime of discrimination as the son of an enemy of the people. Yet he not only defended the Soviet Union, he was prepared to see blood spilled to maintain it. In any event, in June of 1991, he was angry enough to speak to any foreign correspondent who asked for an interview.

I'm not sure whether when he agreed to speak to me, he understood I was female. But he sounded genuinely shocked when I phoned him. I remember physically reacting when he said in the course of the interview that the military and intelligence apparatus would need to act against Mikhail Gorbachev, and soon, if any republics other than the Baltic ones decided to push further with their demands for independence.

'What might that look like?' I asked.

'Ask Gorbachev,' he responded. 'He knows.'

Gorbachev, for his part, shrugged off the threats coming from 'the man with epaulets on his shoulders', as his then foreign minister, Eduard Shevardnadze, called Alksnis, and continued to tread the line between keeping the party calm and keeping people believing in a better tomorrow, which would prove to be politically fatal. It's the same line Vladimir Putin is now treading – keeping his cadres calm in the face of overwhelming sanctions which have cut Russia economically adrift, and having people believe, through propaganda, that tomorrow will be better.

On 19 August 1991 Russia – and the world – woke to startling news. Gorbachev had been put under house arrest while holidaying with his family in Crimea. In the dead of night, a group of eleven men (of course) had hastily put together a State Committee on the State of Emergency (GKChP) to return the USSR to its 'natural' pre-Gorbachev state. Led by the KGB chief, Vladimir Kryuchkov, the committee declared that the Soviet Union was falling apart. It said Gorbachev had refused to return order to the country and the protesters had eroded the authority of the state; extremism had taken hold. The GKChP encircled Moscow with tanks, and by morning, the capital had erupted in fury, fear and concern for Gorbachev, who was by then incommunicado.

On 24 February 2022, when Vladimir Putin sent Russian tanks across the border into the Donbas region of Ukraine, proclaiming his intent to rid Russia's neighbour of its extremists and Nazis, I thought of what Mikhail Gorbachev had said about the Emergency Committee many years after the 1991 coup: 'I said to them they must be mad if they think the country would simply follow another dictatorship. People are not that tired.' Russian shelling may yet break the Ukrainian resolve to fight. But it won't be soon. Putin is now assessing how much fight the Ukrainians have in them and how many urban Russians still have memories of 1991 coursing through their veins. The difference: Gorbachev was largely unwilling to turn his military against his people. Putin is different.

In 1991, like in 2022, Russians were stunned that the hardliners would mount a coup. My friend Natasha pithily noted at the time, 'They can't just roll out the tanks and hope for the best. There are Mercedes-Benzes in Tajikistan, for God's sake!' Fast forward to 2022, when another friend wrote to me, 'Surely Putin doesn't think he can just roll out the tanks and hope Ukraine will crumble. They are a democracy.' History is a cruel beast that should never be ignored.

When, in August 1991, the centre of Moscow was occupied by its own military, with columns of tanks rumbling through its main streets and soldiers armed with assault rifles fending off angry citizens, Muscovites screamed for sanity to prevail. 'Go home to your mother,' was the most frequent refrain. 'Do you know what you are doing?' was another. And a memory seared into my mind: an old man waving a picture of Gorbachev, yelling at soldiers: 'If you follow blindly, you'll end up blinded, just like Gorbachev. But remember, you've been free for six years now. Turn your tank away and go get Gorbachev.' While there was animosity towards Gorbachev for failing to deliver on his reforms, he was preferable to the putschists.

I felt safe, mostly. But never safer than when I scrambled onto a tank to speak with a group of soldiers in their early twenties. They looked terrified, like they wanted to jump off the vehicle and go home. Today in Ukraine, some young Russian conscripts have been doing just that – refusing to use force to overcome the Ukrainians who've stood in their path. Not enough of them have yet decided to defy their leaders to turn the tide, but the war is still young.

Through three days of heartache, confusion, mayhem, destruction, defiance, resilience and hope, Russians and the world were united – the GKChP must fail. Little did anyone know that its resolve to turn back the tide would be eroded by internal disorder. Defence minister Dmitry Yazov and KGB chief Kryuchkov were at odds while the other committee members, overwhelmed by their own anxieties, drank themselves into a stupor. They had all failed to understand how *perestroika* and *glasnost* had changed their own people. By day three, their efforts to end the Gorbachev era looked shambolic. Their so-called 'constitutional transfer of power' was over before it had begun. It was the defence minister's wife who summed it up: 'Dima, who are these people you have gotten mixed up with? Call Gorbachev,' she begged. Her husband reportedly wept over his desk. Writing this, I wonder if the current Russian defence minister's wife has urged him to stop the destruction of large swathes of Ukraine.

The grave errors the putschists had committed were evident – Boris Yeltsin, the leader of the defiant, had not been arrested, the TV tower had not been captured, allowing media to broadcast the truth, mass arrests had not taken place. Vladimir Putin, a student of history, has no doubt studied the dying moments of the August 1991 putsch. He has not committed the same mistakes in Ukraine.

Monica Attard was a correspondent in Russia from December 1989 until the beginning of 1995. She covered the collapse of the Soviet Union, including the chaotic aftermath of Boris Yeltsin's brief rule. Monica has five Walkley awards, including gold, as well as an Order of Australia for services to journalism. Her book *Russia: Which Way Paradise?* was published in 1998. She is now on Vladimir Putin's list of Australians banned from Russia because of their position on the Ukraine invasion.

4
THE FACE COLLECTORS OF TECHNO-AUTHORITARIAN CHINA

Cate Cadell
Beijing 2014–2021
Reuters

Still in love with China.

OF ALL THE places I visited in China, a sleepy rural village in Henan's Jia County seemed the least likely to hold unnerving insights into China's vast hi-tech surveillance network. The small hamlet was made up of rows of pale mud-brick courtyard houses that melted into fields of green wheat. Our car threw up thick yellow dust as we drove into town in the summer of 2019, dodging chickens and bouncing through potholes. The homes were eerily quiet. At first glance, it appeared the only inhabitants were the small buck-toothed guard dogs who stirred just long enough to give us a disapproving side-eye.

The trip was last minute. Less than twenty-four hours earlier, I'd been sitting in the back of a noisy Beijing eatery when I got a patchy call from my dad. He broke the news that my grandmother had died suddenly. As a foreign correspondent, I'm no stranger to the feeling of my two lives clashing suddenly and unceremoniously, but I felt this one especially acutely.

I grew up on a patch of black soil in Tambar Springs, in rural New South Wales, among farmers whose lives couldn't have been more different from those of the families eating chongqing noodles around me. I spent my childhood catching yabbies, mustering cattle on dusty ponies and wrestling two brothers in the airy hundred-year-old converted sheep shed we still call home. School meant twenty kids of all ages sharing a weatherboard classroom surrounded by gum trees. In Beijing, I'd routinely pass more people on the way to work than I'd met in the first ten years of my life.

It was moments like this when I realised just how far from home I was. Despite an early rural life devoid of crowds and technology, I ended up spending my twenties as a foreign correspondent covering politics, surveillance and censorship in China.

Walking home through the twisting alleys of Beijing's hutongs, I began plotting what I'd do for three days until my flight home for the funeral. The trip to Jia County had been in the works for weeks, and somehow spending a few days in China's wheat country felt marginally closer to home than my bustling hutong, which is how video journalist Irene Wang and I found ourselves 800 kilometres from Beijing the next day, wandering through what appeared to be an abandoned village.

As we made our way towards the town square, we finally found the missing villagers. In the midday heat, around sixty elderly Chinese people formed a line that snaked over the square and into an alley beside a farmhouse. In Beijing, it was not unusual to see a sea of white-haired retirees in the park on Sunday, but in this small village, there was a buzz of excitement around the gathering. They'd brought canes and small fold-out stools, and chattered loudly in the local dialect while shelling small mountains of sunflower seeds.

A young harried-looking man with a squeaky toy-sized megaphone paced up the line and down the line, yelling: 'Line up, line up, LINE UP!' Nearby – guarded by the most buck-toothed, pot-bellied dog of all – was a small tower of prizes: fat plastic bottles of cooking oil and shiny boxes of pots, kettles and cutlery sets.

In the alley by the farmhouse was what looked like a bizarre outdoor photography studio. Three tall black tripods, each with a smartphone attached with zip ties, stood facing the blank wall of a neighbouring farmyard. Trailing behind each tripod were wires leading to a large, expensive-looking computer setup perched on a rickety desk.

The man with the squeaky red megaphone yelled, 'NEXT!' A woman in her early seventies, at the front of the line, nervously shuffled in front of the first tripod, where she was handed a comically large set of sunglasses. She put them on, covering half her face in a way that made her look vaguely beetle-like. As she fidgeted, the smartphone began filming, and her face appeared on the computer screen.

'Look left!' barked a man from behind the computer. The woman snapped her head to one side. 'A bit slower. Now right!' The woman's gaze panned slowly across the alley to the right. She repeated the movements on command – right and left, up and down – before finishing with a wild, flourishing circular neck movement. 'Good. Next one,' the man finally said, as the woman gingerly handed back the sunglasses. She was then bustled over to the stack of prizes, where she exchanged a ticket for a jug of cooking oil.

At the second tripod, another elderly woman was handed an eerie printed image of a stranger's face that had the eyes and nose cut out. As the smartphone camera rolled, she held the unsettling mask up and poked her nose through it. On command, she darted her eyes rapidly back and forth, remaining otherwise perfectly still. 'Next ... NEXT!' blared the squeaky red megaphone. The troupe of villagers shuffled up. Just down the road, a pig grunted in an indoor sty.

To an outsider, the scene would've been entirely baffling. To me, it was a perfect example of what made China equal parts fascinating and deeply disturbing. The villagers were a small but key part of the biggest human surveillance experiment on the planet: they were selling their faces to train facial recognition algorithms in return for cooking oil.

'The largest projects have tens of thousands of people, all of whom live in this area,' said Liu Yangfeng, CEO at Qianji Data Co Ltd, the local company based in Pingdingshan that was running the project.

Dressed smartly in suit pants and a white collared shirt that was one size too small, Liu hovered nervously around the cameras, checking the photos and periodically wandering over into a nearby vegetable patch to take a seemingly never-ending stream of phone calls. In the rural setting, he looked almost as out of place as I did.

He was one of many who capitalised on the fast-growing demand for data sets used to train AI algorithms, including facial recognition. The booming industry had sprouted almost overnight. He steered us into a nearby farmhouse, its walls bare save for a large, tattered poster of Mao Zedong. The floor space was cluttered with rows of tables with blank monitors. 'Here is one of the places we train people to do the data labelling,' he said. He was coy about who he collected data for, but said his clients included the government as well as some of the country's largest tech companies.

I started chatting to the old folk in line. My years of studying Mandarin were no match for the local dialect, but I managed to find one woman two weeks out from her hundredth birthday. China is one of very few places on the planet where a one-hundred-year-old woman would, unfazed, find herself participating in an AI data collection project in a rural village square on a Wednesday afternoon. Most of the crowd were born before Communist China existed and had lived through the bloodshed of the Cultural Revolution. Virtually none owned a smartphone, but gifting their faces to artificial intelligence seemed mundane to them. Apparently Irene and I were the only ones there who thought it was newsworthy.

A woman in her fifties, one of the few who spoke standard Mandarin, stopped to talk to us after her turn wearing a pair of shiny black glasses for the camera. 'I just saw many people come here and it seemed like fun, so I decided to join,' she says. She's less clear about what she thinks they'll use her face for. She makes a long, low humming noise and looks briefly back towards the cameras. 'I know it's about artificial intelligence,' she says, pausing for a moment. 'Other than that, I don't know.'

Wandering past the villagers, I saw paper notices stuck to walls and posts advertising the project with a Chinese phrase that has the same ring as 'come one, come all!' I thought about my own granny back home and was struck again by the utter strangeness of my job and the country I found myself in. I tried to imagine what Granny would say if a man in a tight white collared shirt came to our village and asked to take photos of her in sunglasses to train facial recognition algorithms. Nothing kind, probably.

In the courtyard, the sound of an ear-splitting horn rang out, accompanied by a fierce drumming noise. A frustrated Irene shut her camera off and waited for the noise to pass. Liu apologised. 'It's the third day of a funeral for a local woman,' he told us, pointing to a crowd of smiling mourners marching two streets over, draped head to toe in long white gowns and wearing pointed hoods. Entranced, I followed them up the hill to the door of a farmhouse where a giant bow-shaped coffin sat in a leafy courtyard. A cranky-looking snapping turtle hovered by the door.

Somehow I'd found my way to an old lady's funeral among the wheat fields as planned – just on the wrong side of the planet. The cheerful mourners finally noticed me and invited me to blow on the funeral trumpet. I politely declined. Instead, I joined a team of men who – grunting and heaving – carried the giant coffin out the door and into the backyard, where a huge hole had been dug. Burial grounds are sparse in China, and I knew enough to know that this burial was illegal. They'd likely need to pay thousands of yuan in penalty fees for the privilege. But if they did, no one seemed to mind.

Heading back down through the village to the farmhouse, still reeling from my first experience of a Chinese burial, I met up with a mildly dejected Liu as another ancient woman stepped up to the tripod. He then uttered a phrase that would never make sense anywhere else: 'That funeral is why there's so few people at my AI project today.'

ALMOST EXACTLY A year before I arrived in Beijing in 2014, Xi Jinping came to power. At the time, I had little knowledge of China, or the story I'd end up devoting eight years of my life to. As Xi was busy solidifying alliances and jostling through the upper ranks of the Communist Party on his way to the top job, I was at university in Sydney, figuring out how to live in a city for the first time.

At first, I struggled dismally to keep up with the cohort in my journalism classes, most of whom had networks of people in the city they could call on for story ideas. But by the end of my first month in journalism school, I was sure of one thing: I wanted to be a foreign correspondent.

During my time at university, I spent almost as much time overseas as I did in Australia. I worked double shifts, waitressing in the evenings and dosing methadone at a clinic in Enmore in the pre-dawn hours. As soon as I saved up enough money, I'd go to any country with a newspaper that would hire me. When I was nineteen, I spent four months in the minus 40 degrees centigrade winter of Mongolia as a writer and subeditor at *The UB Post* in Ulaanbaatar. A year later, I did a similar stint at a newspaper in Myanmar's Yangon. I quickly figured out that going to places where no one else wanted to go was a sure-fire way of getting work, and in the fluid world of roving foreign correspondents in Asia, being a bumbling country kid was a non-issue. Back in Sydney, I picked up Chinese classes. Not, at the time, out of any love for the country, but because I had a sense, by then, that it would be one of the biggest stories of our generation.

What I didn't realise when I arrived in China was that it was on the precipice of a fresh digital authoritarian revolution. I had assumed I would spend a few years covering Beijing's opening to the world as a major economic power. Instead, I covered re-education camps, mass surveillance, a trade war and roughly a hundred government press conferences peppered with increasingly vitriolic, though undeniably creative, insults towards Australia and the West.

A shrewd technocrat, Xi was quick to understand the role China's technological prowess could play in cementing party authority. He swiftly created – and headed – the Cyberspace Administration of China, the body responsible for tightly censoring China's internet. By 2016, China's largest tech companies were facing mass penalties and enforced service outages for failing to follow the rules. Social media companies I covered went from hiring dozens of in-house censors to hiring thousands at a time, filling office buildings with entry-level workers whose only role was to sift through the masses of potentially sensitive online content. The remaining foreign news outlets and social media sites visible in China went dark. Xi fortified China's real-name identification system, linking SIM cards to national ID numbers, erasing anonymity from the internet. Unseen to most internet users, a mass industry of digital 'public opinion analysts' came online, aided by advances in big data and machine learning, and began crawling the internet on behalf of police and other government bodies to monitor and snuff out dissent before it began. Within a few short years, Xi had transformed China's internet into the world's biggest digital laboratory for authoritarian governance.

IT WAS IN this techno-authoritarian wave that a facial recognition mania costing tens of billions of dollars began. Government policies with sci-fi names like Skynet and Sharp Eyes laid out ambitious plans to blanket the country with cameras linked to police stations that shared data nationally. The vision was clear: just like on the internet, anonymity could be erased in real life. With accurate facial recognition, police could identify, categorise and follow a single person among 1.4 billion Chinese citizens.

As the projects rolled out, lauded by state media, those of us living and working in China had little insight into just how effective these systems were. Years of reporting on technology in China had taught me that if something sounds too much like science fiction, it often is just that. And the country's famously opaque legal system offered few insights into how Skynet and Sharp Eyes were working on the ground. But the projects fascinated me. And over the years, I delved into them any way I could, including collecting a cache of thousands of purchase orders from police that laid out requirements for surveillance systems.

These documents brought into horrifying clarity the intended use of facial recognition in China. Local police describe vast automated networks of hundreds or even thousands of cameras in their area alone that not only scan the identities of passers-by and identify fugitives but create automated alarm systems giving authorities the location of people, based on a vast array of 'criminal type' blacklists, including ethnic Uighurs and Tibetans, former drug users, people with mental health issues and known protesters.

One 2018 purchase order from Beijing reads: 'The real-time video image information can be used to classify outsiders and criminals with specific behavior characteristics, such as Uighurs; It can identify the characteristics of outsiders and criminals, including age, gender, whether they have a fringe or whether they wear glasses.'

The police description of Xinjiang's Uighurs, Tibetans and people with mental illnesses as inherently criminal is near universal, as in this 2018 purchase request for a facial recognition system from police in China's southern Guangxi province: 'Early warnings for specific personnel can be set, such as automatic warnings for Xinjiang Uighur people. It must be able to establish key personnel databases (including … terrorist-related people, Xinjiang people and mentally ill people.)'.

An order for a system supporting 1500 facial recognition cameras in Beijing's Chaoyang District lays out parameters for what must be identifiable for each person captured on camera, including 'whether people are wearing masks, glasses, the style of glasses as well as types of face structure information, including whether they have a beard … It must recall ID number, name, alias, organisation, gender, age, nationality (including Uighur), date of birth and household address.'

Some systems describe extra functions that use facial recognition for predictive policing. This 2018 purchase request from police in the Xiqing District of China's Tianjin city requests a system worth A\$4 million that sounds alarms to local police when people are captured behaving 'suspiciously', including returning to a public space repeatedly or being out late at night: 'People who have high-risk behaviors are regarded as key personnel. When their number of high-risk behaviors is higher than the system preset value, the system will generate an alarm … When a person repeatedly appears in a certain key area, they are regarded as a suspect. Similarly, there are high-risk time periods like between 12 midnight and 5 am. When people appear in key areas repeatedly during those times, their face information will be saved to the blacklist database and an alarm will be generated.'

The technology has become standard in government universities, prisons and hospitals. Often it includes tailored requirements, set by the purchaser. One A\$124,000 facial recognition system purchased in 2019 by a Chongqing vocational school monitors when its students are sleeping: 'Student information must include, but is not limited to, the grade, name, student number, major, class number, mobile phone number, ethnicity, gender, ID number, class counselor, dormitory bed number … It records the individual ID information of students and keeps record of when they go to bed and wake up.'

In my own neighbourhood, it felt like the transition came almost overnight. While there had always been a smattering of surveillance cameras in Beijing, streets were suddenly featuring fresh new models. Having reported on the companies behind each camera, I could recognise them on sight. I thought of it as a grim version of bird spotting. There was the common CCTV brand camera, visible throughout smaller streets; the svelte Dahua box, popular on city intersections and train stations; and a bulbous top-of-the-line Hikvision contraption, originally confined to spaces like Tiananmen Square, but common throughout Beijing by the time I left, including one by the entrance of my own hutong house.

Estimates of the number of facial recognition cameras in China range from 200 million to over 600 million as of 2020, but it's not clear how many have advanced facial recognition capabilities. At times, experiences like the one in Jia County made China's surveillance feel novel, but that faded as I gradually began to think of China as my second home. More and more, it felt oppressive.

In the lobby of a dingy hotel in west Beijing, another Chinese entrepreneur once showed me footage of a very different data collecting project. On a cell phone with a long crack across the screen, he showed me a video of two men walking briskly towards each other and hugging. A second video showed the same two men having what appeared to be a very real fight. Like Liu, the man was creating content to train AI image recognition. His only client at the time was the police. The image recognition project was designed to automatically identify the different ways that people touched each other in public and raise alarms about problematic behaviour. The idea that hugging someone incorrectly could potentially alert police left a knot in the pit of my stomach.

I never returned to Jia County but, out of curiosity, I searched my cache of documents in the weeks after I left China. I found the county had purchased a A\$370,000 facial recognition surveillance system eighteen months before our trip. Like other similar documents, it described technology to alert police to Uighurs in the area. It also called for a function to 'label the attributes of the captured person, including age, gender, ethnicity, whether or not they're wearing sunglasses'.

IN APRIL 2021, photographer Tom Peter and I were trudging through a swampy ditch below a massive white-walled prison south of Ürümqi in Xinjiang. Stopping every few moments to listen for movement, we crawled through the bushes and up the bank towards the prison wall.

After two weeks of being constantly tailed and harassed by a menagerie of plain-clothes police, we were looking forward to winding the project up and heading home. The prison was hauntingly large, one of many built across Xinjiang since the beginning of a mass incarceration drive that has seen an estimated one million Uighurs detained since 2016 as part of a sweeping anti-terrorism drive.

High on the prison walls, armed guards from the People's Armed Police (PAP), China's internal paramilitary unit, patrolled between watchtowers. There was no chance of an interview here. Our goal was to snap some good photos and head back to Urumqi for a beer and a rest before planning our trip home. As we slowly moved further around the back of the prison, undetected, we were shocked to find a number of villagers fishing in a small pond. Relieved by the sight of civilians in the sparse, empty district, we let our guard down, snapping pictures of the prison from the water's edge. With our photos taken and no tail in sight, we set out on a dusty track back towards the road, circling the other side of the prison.

But no sooner had we turned the corner than two women in paramilitary uniforms appeared. After some terse back and forth, we attempted to leave. A rumble began behind a doorway to our right. All at once, six paramilitary soldiers in full fatigues burst out, wielding long, thick green wooden batons and running at full speed in a line formation towards us. One by one, they slid to a halt in a semicircle around us, trapping us against the side of the prison.

Over the next ninety minutes, we stood against the wall as a cycle of PAP and police officers questioned us. At one point, a police officer urged us to sign a handwritten note saying we'd taken photos of a military installation – a potentially serious crime in China. Eventually, after deleting our photos, we were released, tired and thirsty, to head back to Urumqi.

It was one of many adrenaline-fuelled moments we'd experienced during two weeks in Xinjiang in April 2021, on my last major reporting trip in China.

I could already feel my time in China coming to a close. The country had shuttered its borders during the pandemic and expelled over a dozen journalists. Months earlier, the last two reporters working for Australian outlets left the country following a dramatic diplomatic stand-off that forced them to shelter in the embassy for five days. I was one of the four remaining accredited Australian journalists in Beijing working for non-Australian outlets, and for my last year in China, I lived with a small black emergency suitcase by the front door, in case

I needed to leave without having time to pack. But despite the rocky ending to my time in China, I managed to fall deeply in love with the country and the job that took me there.

Cate Cadell was based in Beijing from 2014 to 2021, where she covered technology and, later, politics as a correspondent for Reuters news. She is currently covering China on the national security desk at *The Washington Post*, based in Washington DC. She began her career in Asia, reporting for newspapers in Mongolia and Myanmar.

5
DISPATCHES FROM AFGHANISTAN: 'BETTER WRITE AN OBIT'

Anna Coren
Kabul 2022
CNN

In Afghanistan with US Special Forces.

'Afghanistan has a way of getting under your skin. Once you go there, we hold you, keep you close to our hearts and don't let you go.'

– Mahbouba Seraj, Afghan women's rights activist, January 2022

I'VE ALWAYS STRUGGLED to explain my love affair with Afghanistan, a country that is a world away from my reality. Was it the people I met and the lifelong friendships I've formed; the mountains I never tire of looking at; or the rugged beauty that exists in an often inhospitable environment? Was it the story that drew me back, the story of this forgotten war, these forgotten people, their suffering and their sense of hopelessness? Or was it the betrayal and abandonment of a generation of girls and women who had been promised by foreign governments and good intentioned people for twenty years that it was their right to dream of a better future, only for it to be ripped away overnight? Whatever it was, this country was under my skin, just as my dear friend Mahbouba said.

My experiences in Afghanistan were never just fleeting moments, like other assignments with CNN where correspondents hit the ground for breaking news, filing packages in between never-ending live shots, before moving on to the next story. Instead, Afghanistan stayed with me, leaving an indelible mark on my psyche. My first trip was in 2012. There had been an alarming rise in green on blue attacks: Afghan soldiers killing US and multi-nation International Security Assistance Force (ISAF) troops. The 'good war', as President Barack Obama had called it, wasn't going to plan, despite his surge of boots on the ground. US and Afghan forces were under siege from the Taliban, whose fighters were gaining territory. The world's superpower, with all its military might, was struggling to defeat these ragtag Islamic insurgents who fought in sandals. I arrived in Afghanistan – everything covered in a film of dust – hungry and eager to learn about this complicated, tribal country that empires had tried to conquer and failed. And as we now know, history would once again repeat itself.

US Special Forces Embed – March 2013
For a journalist, it's all about access. It can make or break a story. And my trip to Afghanistan in 2013 was no exception. I had been tasked with organising an embed with the US military, but it was no easy task. Opportunities for journalists to join US troops in theatre were becoming harder to come by after *Rolling Stone* magazine's exposé on the commander of ISAF and US troops in Afghanistan, US General Stanley McChrystal. In a moment of poor judgement, the highly decorated and respected war veteran voiced his true thoughts on President Obama. Shortly after the article was published, he was dismissed.

I didn't like my chances, particularly when the US military public relations officer explained my options were limited, and asked if I wanted to go out with the engineers and film the construction of roads and other infrastructure. I politely declined. Their work was of course important, but not the access I was looking for. Then, a few days later, he called and said it was my lucky day. A US Special Forces team had seen my request and agreed to allow my crew and me to tag along.

We left Bagram Air Base late at night and flew to Camp Palmerton in Kapisa Province in eastern Afghanistan. There was heavy fighting nearby, so the Black Hawk circled until we were finally allowed to land in the darkness. Greeting us at this remote outpost were members of Operational Detachment Alpha (ODA) 3112 of the US Special Forces. These Green Berets had been based there for the past several months as part of a counterinsurgency strategy to eliminate the 'bad guys', of which there were many, while trying to win the hearts and minds of weary local villagers who were resentful of their presence and tired of this endless war.

Our hosts and key Special Forces operatives were Red Beard, Dr Sniper and Blondie (pseudonyms I will give these members of ODA 3112), young, fit, bearded warriors who were intelligent and compassionate, and had leadership qualities I hadn't seen in other US soldiers I'd met. I remember thinking that if all the fighters in this war were men of their calibre, then maybe it would be over. But this was an unwinnable war, and in their hearts these brave men knew that.

On our final day with ODA 3112, we woke early to join an operation in a local village at the bottom of the valley at the base of the mountains of the Hindu Kush. The unit had received intelligence of a weapons cache in the home of a Taliban suspect. When we arrived, the mud dwelling, surrounded by fields of sprouting crops, was empty, except for a few guns and munitions. But within minutes, the sound of gunfire rang out in the distance. Suddenly ODA 3112 raced in the direction of the gunfire, sprinting across the open fields. Cameraman Mark Phillips, security guard Jock and I ran closely behind, following blindly, adrenaline pumping through our bodies. US Special Forces don't just fight back; they hunt down the enemy.

We saw a mud-walled compound in a clump of tall trees several hundred metres away. We ran to it and crouched against its high walls, taking cover and catching our breath. It was the start of spring and there was no foliage on the bare branches of the overarching trees. In a few months, the green canopy would make it the perfect hiding place for Taliban, or for us. But now, we were exposed. As we tried to get our breath back, bullets whizzed over our heads. 'Fuck,' Mark yelled.

He'd heard that sound before in the many conflict zones he'd covered in his career. For me, I'd never heard a bullet fly past so close. Machine gunfire was coming from three directions. I should have been frightened, but there was no time. We were with the US Special Forces and, even though the enemy had us in their sights, I felt protected. We made a dash around the next corner of the compound and caught up with some of the unit who were taking cover in a low-lying ditch surrounded by sparse undergrowth. I looked up. Another open field was ahead of us.

Blondie, one of the high-ranking SF operatives, yelled at his subordinates, 'Alright, so this is what we're gonna do. We'll continue up this fucking riverbed till we get to the left side. We want Haroon and them flanking with us. Ok. Let's roll.' We sprinted again, across recently planted fields, between mounds of soil piled high into columns. The villagers were nowhere to be seen. Were they hiding in their homes listening to the fighting raging beyond the high mud walls that were supposed to provide a sanctuary from the unfolding chaos outside? Or were they harbouring the Islamic insurgents? We knew there was a Taliban stronghold at the base of the mountains close by, but perhaps they had infiltrated the village or at least had sympathisers … which was happening right across Afghanistan.

An Apache helicopter gunship was called in and began circling the valley, looking for the Taliban fighters. Spent cartridges littered the ground where they had staged their final attack, the only remnants of an enemy that had seemingly vanished, blending into the community and the landscape. Red Beard, the SF commander, told me at the end of the ninety-minute battle, 'You know, I admire their resiliency and their conviction, for sure. There is a degree of mutual respect. But it doesn't mean we want to kill them any less.'

Suddenly it was over. And the invincibility I had felt, the coat of armour I'd been wearing, suddenly slipped away as reality set in. We had to walk several kilometres back to the MRAP (mine resistant ambush protected) vehicles and navigate the fields, the dirt paths and roads under the midday sun. With every step I took, I kept saying to myself, 'I still have a leg. I still have a leg.' Over and over again. IEDs (improvised explosive devices) and land mines terrified me. But we were lucky that day. We all returned with our limbs intact and our minds sound.

America's longest war would claim the lives of almost 2500 US soldiers, 1144 coalition forces and 66,000 Afghan military and police. More than 45,000 Afghan civilians were also killed; at least half of them were women and children.

When the US withdrew from Afghanistan, I asked Commander Red Beard for his thoughts. We had kept in touch over the years, and he was still on active duty. This is what he told me. Perhaps it was a premonition.

> After toppling the Taliban, as many have said before me, it was never a war we could win militarily. Our Western hubris set the wrong conditions from the beginning and allowed us to press on without ever really adapting our approach to what we all seemed to understand on the ground. That said, with the circumstances under which we are leaving, it's hard for it not to feel like failure, and victory for bad actors who, for all of our flaws and mismanagement of the effort, will almost certainly slaughter thousands and destabilize the country, region and world. I don't envy the American President, confronted with making this decision, and I don't envy anyone in the country. I have a bad feeling that we will witness atrocities in the months to come and we are far from being done fighting AQ [al-Qaeda] and the Taliban in Afghanistan, whether it is weeks, months, or years from now.

Commandos Execution – July 2021

It had been seven years since I'd last visited Afghanistan and a lot had changed in my life. I had gone from a globetrotting CNN International correspondent based in Hong Kong to becoming the proud mother of twin boys and marrying the love of my life. I had worked out a healthy balance between motherhood and still having a career without being weeks away on assignment. But now the US was pulling out of Afghanistan after twenty years of war and I wanted to be there to cover a story that had fascinated me for so long. I lobbied for the assignment and emailed CNN's then boss, Jeff Zucker, in New York. My pitch worked and within three weeks I was back on the ground in Kabul.

Within days of arriving, US forces announced their withdrawal from Bagram Air Base, the nerve centre of America's war operations.

They flew out overnight without telling their Afghan partners. It was obvious they were packing up; US President Joe Biden had made it perfectly clear in April that America's war was winding up, but no one on the Afghan side knew exactly when that would be. Without the Americans and the coalition forces, the people of Afghanistan who'd been living under the rights and freedoms of a democracy knew their country was in imminent danger of collapse. The Taliban was seizing territory and gaining ground at lightning speed. US Intelligence estimated that in the worst-case scenario, the Afghan government would fall within six months. What they didn't understand was the level of disillusionment with Afghan president Ashraf Ghani's corrupt government. The Afghan military, who hadn't been paid for months, were choosing to lay down their weapons and walk away rather than fight for a government no one believed was worth dying for.

The Afghan commandos, however, were a different breed. They were trained by US Special Forces and weren't your ordinary grunts. They were the cream of the crop, loyal to their commanders, and they believed it was their duty to defend their country. They were also stretched thin and dying at an alarming rate. The commandos were now the last line of defence in the fight for their country's survival.

My crew and I came across a shocking video on social media. As we watched it, I asked my friend and local fixer Basir if he'd seen it. He looked at me with horror, saying, 'I have never seen this footage before.'

It begins with the sound of shouting as Afghan commandos walk out of a building with hands in the air. 'Surrender, commandos, surrender,' yells a Talib. After two hours of fighting, all ammunition spent, the commandos are surrounded. But the rules of war don't exist on this battlefield. They file out, knowing they are a prize for the insurgents. Within seconds, the Taliban open fire, screaming, 'Allahu akbar.' A villager pleads with the Taliban to stop shooting, asking, 'How are you Pashtun and you're killing Afghans?' All twenty-two members of the Afghan special forces are executed.

Basir called a journalist contact in Faryab Province in northern Afghanistan where the massacre took place and asked him to investigate. The Taliban had taken control of much of the province and the journalist needed to be very careful making inquiries. He found five independent eyewitnesses who all confirmed the events that had taken place. 'The commandos called for air and ground support, but none came,' said a local resident. 'Then they surrendered. But the Taliban just shot them.'

Our story caused an international outcry. The US State Department said our report 'depicts horrifying scenes. The killing – in this case, the slaughter – of unarmed individuals is – it's an atrocious act, it's an outrageous sight, and of course we condemn it.' Amnesty International accused the Taliban of committing war crimes and said, 'This evidence suggests that the Taliban's persistent claims to have changed their ways are predicated on a lie and completely undermines their claims that they will respect human rights in the peace process.'

Our report had shown the Taliban for who they really were. But the next morning when I went down for breakfast in the safe house where we were staying, one of the other guests, a US analyst focusing on all things Taliban and al-Qaeda, asked if I'd seen the Taliban's response to my story on Twitter. I had not. He proceeded to tell me that they had gone on the PR offensive, declaring my story fake news and claiming that the footage was government propaganda. They issued a statement in multiple languages stating they had never executed surrendering commandos. He warned me, 'Anna, you need to get ahead of this. They are trying to discredit your story and change the narrative. You need to respond.' I make no apologies for the fact that I hate social media and rarely use it except to post my stories and I wasn't about to get into a Twitter war with the Taliban. I called my bosses, who said that my next live hit would be my official rebuttal and that it would be posted on the CNN website. I went to the rooftop where our live location was set up and delivered my rebuttal.

We stand by our story one hundred per cent. Five eyewitnesses to the massacre spoke to us and risked their lives in doing so. Our story is a huge embarrassment to the Taliban. They're trying to pretend they are an alternate governing body, that they've changed, evolved, modernised. They are due to hold peace talks with a high-level delegation from the Afghan government in the coming days in Doha, Qatar, but this video proves that it's all a lie – they are still the same brutal, violent, primeval group they were twenty years ago.

My cameraman, Sanjiv Talreja, looked up from the camera after the live cross and said, 'I think we should prepare our obits.' We both burst out laughing.

The next morning we were due to fly to Kandahar Air Base in the country's south to embed with an Afghan commando unit. Bags were packed and we were ready to go. But our security detail, Daoud, was on the phone and gestured for us to wait. We weren't going anywhere. Afghan Intelligence had informed him that there was a photo of me circulating among the Taliban. Certain members of the group were not pleased with my rebuttal and accusations. Whether it was a scare tactic or something more sinister, CNN wasn't prepared to find out. Management decided I was leaving the country on the next flight out. Less than a month later, Kabul fell; the Taliban entered the capital without firing a bullet.

Evacuation – August 2021

I watched from Hong Kong confused, shocked and angry as Kabul fell on 15 August 2021. How was this allowed to happen? How did Afghanistan fall so quickly? How did the Afghan president flee his own country? What happened to the 300,000 Afghan soldiers who had been trained and equipped? How did America's longest war end up with the Taliban back in power? And how did this US$2.26 trillion experiment go so spectacularly wrong?

I was on the phone to Basir as the Taliban rolled into the capital. I have never heard him so alarmed. I was deeply concerned. What would happen to my dear friend and his family? And all the people who had worked for the US government, military and foreign companies?

In the frantic weeks that followed, CNN managed to evacuate Basir and his family to Turkey, where he's awaiting Special Immigrant Visa (SIV) approval to go to the United States. We also rescued two Afghan military interpreters whose stories I covered. Luckily, once inside Hamid Karzai International Airport, they found themselves in the right queue, boarding the right plane, and are now living new lives in the United States. But for the few we could help, there was an ocean of people who were trapped in this landlocked country with no way of escape. The impact was especially great on women. Overnight, they had gone from having jobs, careers, being integral members of civil society and government to being stripped of their rights and voice and confined to their homes.

Word that I'd helped Afghans escape the country quickly spread and I was inundated with messages and calls begging and pleading for help. But that window had closed. When an ISIS-K suicide bomber blew himself up outside Abbey Gate at Kabul airport, killing thirteen US service members, the American evacuation went into overdrive. All airport gates were shut and no more civilians were allowed to enter. Those already inside the airport and on the tarmac were the last Afghans to leave before it was wheels up for the remaining handful of US troops on 30 August 2021, a day ahead of schedule. America's twenty-year war was officially over.

There was one message that haunted me. A woman contacted me in the weeks after the Americans left, and what she said encapsulated what all the Afghan women I knew were feeling. 'Since the regime changed, all my world is three rooms of my home. Sometimes I become so tired I feel I can't breathe easily. I feel there is not enough oxygen in the house. I feel oxygen has left us and left Afghanistan. Now these three rooms are my shopping markets, ice cream shop, my office I used to go to before. Now I just go from room to room to ease my heavy heart.' These educated, smart, talented women who had dreamed of a better future were now prisoners in their own homes.

Return – March 2022

Purpose in life is often elusive to so many of us and Mahbouba Seraj had struggled with it for most of her life. She'd spent decades away from Afghanistan, her country of birth, after fleeing the Communists in 1978 and her life in the United States was comfortable and convenient, but meaningless. One evening while watching the news in her home in Santa Fe, New Mexico, in early 2001, she saw a story that would change the course of her life.

In Kabul's Ghazi soccer stadium, a woman in a burqa kneels down on the grass at the goal posts. A Talib points a gun into the back of her head. She turns to look at the sun through the mesh of the burqa covering her eyes before turning back. The Talib towering above her pulls the trigger; her body slumps to the ground.

The execution of this mother of seven for the murder of her abusive husband made Mahbouba scream. For a moment, she didn't know who was making that blood curdling sound. Those images had awakened something inside her that had been lying dormant for too long. In 2003, she would pack up her life and move back to Kabul. She was finally home and ready to help her people.

For almost twenty years Mahbouba has worked tirelessly for the girls and women of Afghanistan. She was one of many female voices breaking through this patriarchal society, a chorus demanding to be heard. There was power and authority that came with operating as a bloc to open shelters, pass legislation to improve women's rights and create a tolerance in a society that traditionally had repressed the female population. But that all came to a screeching halt when the Taliban returned to Kabul. Everyone wanted to flee. Everyone, except Mahbouba Seraj.

'I received calls, hundreds of calls, that day. Honestly, from the army, the Germans, the Americans, people at the airport, everybody. Miss Seraj, you're an Afghan American? Yes, I am. You have an American passport? Yes, I do. When do you want us to come and pick you up? No, thank you. I'm not going anywhere.'

It was her determination and resilience that inspired me to get on a plane and return to Kabul, seven months after the fall to the Taliban, and film a documentary about this seventy-three-year-old women's rights activist. As she relays those chaotic days, her white and brown–spotted rescue dog Bullet, whose ears and tail were cut off by a previous owner, lies contentedly at her feet in her office in Kabul. 'Why didn't you leave?' I ask her. Without hesitation, she replies, 'In my mind I did not think that was the answer to anything. What about Afghanistan? Who was going to be here? Who was actually going to be witnessing what is happening here? Somebody had to be the voice of reason here, honestly. And that's what I thought I would be. I would be the voice of reason for the people of Afghanistan, for the women of Afghanistan.'

Her shelter, which cares for dozens of women who have survived horrific domestic and sexual violence, is the only facility still operating in Taliban-controlled Afghanistan. There used to be almost thirty shelters dotted around the country, but they have all since closed, fearing a rebuke from the Taliban, which believes they are a front for brothels and prostitution. Mahbouba walks into the shelter and is showered with hugs and kisses from the women and their children. The newcomers hold her hand, wanting to share their stories of how Mahbouba saved them from the ugly, evil world outside.

A twenty-four-year-old woman from Badghis Province, one of the poorest in Afghanistan, has been living at the shelter for the past year. She motions to me that she wants to tell her story. She wants me to understand what Mahbouba has done for her. She sits quietly on the carpet and fidgets with the edge of her headscarf, before taking a big, deep breath.

At the age of seven, she was married off to an eighty-year-old man as a child bride. As abhorrent as the practice is, the husband of a child bride is supposed to wait until the girl reaches puberty before having sex. That wasn't the case for this little girl. 'He tied my legs, he tied my hands and then he raped me. I lost a lot of blood that night and they took me to hospital.' After a couple of days in the hospital, she was brought home, and the nightly rapes continued. 'He was always beating me and saying why haven't I given birth to a baby. I married you to give me babies.' After a year the now eight-year-old was returned to her family. The old man didn't want her. She was useless, damaged goods.

Her brothers wanted to stone her to death because her husband had left her. She ran away and was taken in by a shelter and has lived a life of refuge ever since. 'I'm very grateful to Ms Seraj. She saved my life and stopped the Taliban from closing the shelter. She's like a big mountain in front of me.'

Mahbouba is a mountain, weathering all storms with her conviction and tenacity, and her unwavering sense of purpose, protecting a battered and traumatised country that remains in her heart, and in mine.

Anna Coren is an international correspondent for CNN. She has won multiple Asian Television Awards, a Royal Television Award for coverage of the Hong Kong protests and a Gracie from the Alliance for Women in Media Foundation for her work on CNN, which she joined in 2008. She is the mother of twins.

6
HIGH VALUE TARGET: RUNNING FROM THE TALIBAN

Lynne O'Donnell
Kabul 2001–2021
AP, AFP, various

Kandahar Province, Afghanistan 2014.

M Y HEAD AND heart pounded in unison as I hiked along a narrow path through wheat fields lit only by the stars floating in the velvet-black sky above remote, rural northern Afghanistan. I hooked my right arm through the left elbow of my friend and colleague Massoud Hossaini and pulled him close to my side as I picked my way over the ridges and potholes that stood out as darker patches on the shadowless track before us.

Behind, the crack-crack-crack of automatic gunfire was getting louder. And, I was sure, closer. We were escaping a Taliban ambush – high value targets of a vicious insurgency. This night could finally, I thought, be my last.

Ahead, Salima Mazari and her husband, Ali Ahmad, were doing the same as me and Massoud, arms locked as they set the pace across what was to them familiar terrain. Step after step, I planted my feet where Salima had just lifted hers. Massoud, camera and video gear in his backpack, could hardly see in the darkness; I kept him on his feet.

As the gunfire intensified, cracking around us, beams of light appeared to our left. I started, a sharp intake of breath as my guts tightened; fear is a sign of intelligent life. The torches weren't the insurgents', as I'd thought for that jolting half-second. Local militia loyal to Salima – the female district governor and local wartime leader I'd come to interview – were shadowing us and communicating between themselves. On we marched in silence, the gunfire following us. Now and then, the AK-47 cracks were broken by booms – rocket-propelled grenades? I can't wish myself not here, I thought. I just have to go with it, keep my head, hold onto Massoud, and hope this isn't the night I run out of lives.

BY THEN, IN June 2021, I had been covering war, in Afghanistan and elsewhere, for almost twenty years. I was in the city of Mazar-i-Sharif when America bombed the Taliban from power in October 2001, less than a month after the al-Qaeda attacks on the United States that killed almost 3000 people. The Taliban's suggestible mullahs and maulvis had given Osama bin Laden, al-Qaeda's manipulative and hate-filled leader, a haven and hospitality while he was planning the attacks that changed the course of world history. Their removal from power, ending the five years of misery and poverty and fear their regime had inflicted on Afghanistan's enervated population, was revenge for collusion in that atrocity.

I was in Afghanistan in August 2021 when the Americans left, eager and relieved to end their 'forever war', and the Taliban returned victorious. It was just six weeks after their gunmen had chased me through the farmland of Charkint District, in the breadbasket province of Balkh not far from the country's northern border. Soon after that heart-thumping night, having let this quarry slip to safety, the Taliban declared me a 'high value target' (HVT). I left Kabul on 15 August 2021 on the last commercial flight, just hours before their gunmen retook control of the capital and the country, and I was told not to return. 'Do not come to Afghanistan,' was the unequivocal message from one of the group's senior leaders. It was a message I thought I'd be wise to heed.

What seemed to have clinched my HVT status was a story I had written for *Foreign Policy* magazine that nailed down the true nature of the Islamist group and their deep, illogical, unfathomable and unmovable hatred of women. I had told the world just what fate the Taliban had planned for women when – for by then, there was no longer any question of if – they reconquered Afghanistan. As they took territory in their inexhaustible advance, the Taliban were rounding up the women and girls of villages and towns, and 'marrying' them, for that's the euphemism, to their fighting boys and men. In effect, the women under Taliban rule were being forced into slavery. Sex slavery.

After forty years of war in Afghanistan, women account for considerably more than half the population of around 38 million, the gender imbalance skewed by tens, possibly hundreds of thousands of battlefield deaths. As my reporting foretold, women under the returning Taliban were to be wiped out of public life and condemned to be the ejaculate vessels of the conquerors – herded like cattle, to be distributed to the foot soldiers of terrorism as reward for their loyalty.

This isn't random. It's an extreme, conservative concept that informs Taliban ideology, allowing a victorious army to claim everything in conquered territory, including the human beings, as the spoils, the plunder, the booty of war: *ghanimat*, as it is called in Arabic. According to this principle, the women are regarded only as *kaneez*, handmaidens or slave girls. The language says it all.

THE AFGHAN REPUBLIC was disintegrating before my eyes. Everywhere I went across the country in the final three months of the war, I found government forces in retreat, under fire, besieged; cut off from logistical supply lines, with no food, no water, no ammunition; surrendering, deserting, crossing lines; and, in the final few weeks, bereft of the only real edge they'd had in this war, air cover, as the United States withdrew the contractors who were keeping the jet bombers and helicopter gunships flying.

The Taliban were taking the country from the outside in, closing off border crossings, overrunning districts, surrounding provincial capitals.

That they had a strategy at all came as a surprise to many. For most of the past two decades, the insurgency had appeared ragtag, dependent on pot-shot firefights with foreign soldiers; children strapped with suicide vests to kill and terrorise civilians; and useful fools to ram cars and trucks packed with explosives into targets that ranged from military bases and government offices to embassies and hospitals.

Now, in the hot northern summer of 2021, the influence of the Pakistani military, which had bankrolled, armed and advised the Taliban since 2001, was taking on a devastating clarity. Senior advisors directed the battles fought by teenage cannon fodder drawn from the thousands of madrasahs in western Pakistan's Pashtun belt. Sent over the border to reinforce the ever-intensifying fight, these young men were integral to the Taliban's ultimate success. A zombie army of brainwashed children and young men streamed unhindered through the gates at Spin Boldak, the crossing into Kandahar from Pakistan's Balochistan Province, to fight the godless forces in Afghanistan.

The Taliban victory was terrifyingly imminent, enabled by an American president ignorant of the progress that Afghanistan had made since 2001 and dismissive of the consequences of unilateral withdrawal. US president Donald Trump had betrayed the government and people of Afghanistan, signing a deal with the Taliban on 29 February 2020, effectively handing them their victory. War was ending and all members of the international alliance which had held the country together for twenty years were racing for the exits.

It was a shameful treachery. The man who would follow Trump knew that. Yet, US President Joe Biden decided, in April 2021, to honour the Trump–Taliban deal and continue the drawdown to zero. America's leaders believed there was nothing left to fight for; America's partners were just glad to be relieved of their obligation to stay. The foreign policy priorities of the new US administration were now focused on Russia and China – and leaving a potentially chaotic South Asia to them appeared to be part of the bigger picture of containment.

Afghanistan's US$80 billion military saw their Western comrades, partners and mentors leave, and they no longer had a reason to fight. Fighting forces melted away; the young men who remained on the frontlines did so only to protect their own families and land from Taliban predation. They had long since ceased to fight for the government. President Ashraf Ghani proved himself unworthy of their sacrifice when he boarded a chopper on 15 August and flew to Uzbekistan. From that moment, the Islamic Republic of Afghanistan was no more.

But, in the final death throes, ordinary people had shown their determination to hold on to what the republic had given them. Contrary to what many people believe, the largesse of the international backers had brought Afghanistan schools, hospitals, roads, telecommunications, a free media, a constitution, an awareness of democracy, an appreciation of the outside world. Life expectancy and literacy grew; maternal and infant mortality shrank. Yet it also brought eye-watering corruption that saw politicians, officials, warlords and drug dealers amass fortunes that dwarf the economies of some small countries. Ghani's government was seen as venal and grasping, the man himself as stupid and self-interested, the likely loser of the two elections that gave him office.

In many parts of the country, with encouragement, arms and funding from the intelligence service, people had banded together, often under the leadership of local warlords, to form folk militia, fighting alongside the security forces in a desperate last stand. I believed then that had President Biden left a counterterrorism and mentoring force in situ, these militias could have tipped the balance for the republic. They fought with heart, and they fought to win. In some places, they held off the Taliban onslaught; in others, they pushed them out, albeit, as it turned out, temporarily.

It was into one of these areas, in the Amrod valley in Afghanistan's central highlands, that Massoud and I drove, in a heavily armoured police convoy provided to us by the governor of Bamyan Province, Mohammad Tahir Zohair, to see and hear for ourselves the story of Taliban assault, takeover and retreat under fire. It was July 2021, a few weeks after we were chased for our lives through Charkint 330 kilometres to the north, and less than a month before I would leave Afghanistan. Here, in the township of Sayghan, we uncovered the truth of the Taliban's profoundly brutal misogyny.

IT WAS A drive, of course, through astounding landscape – by turns arid, undulating mountains, and lush, fertile agricultural land. Just 60 kilometres from Bamyan's provincial capital, also called Bamyan, it could have been a trip to another planet. In our body armour and helmets, sitting in the back of the up-armoured police utility vehicle,

Massoud and I felt secure enough. In the front passenger seat, a police officer nodded off, his gun upright between the front seats. In the back of the ute, two armed cops sat on fold-down seats, hawk-eyes on the road behind and the golden mountains that rose and fell around us. We were heading off the grid. No one knew where we were. No one would know what had happened to us, if anything did. It was Massoud's perfect place – the absolute middle of nowhere.

Along the way, rocky ravines gave way to orchards and crops. Goats, sheep and donkeys grazed between fruit trees and beside fields of wheat, barley and potatoes; Bamyan is famous for its potatoes. The people of the Shia Hazara minority dominate the province's population, though this valley was dominated by Sunni Tajiks. The economic divisions were clear by the time we reached Sayghan: Hazaras farmed the land, Tajiks ran the town. First stop was tea with the local police chief, fresh apricots and boiled sweets, a chat about the security situation, then back out the gate and into town. Sayghan, in July 2021, was one of the strangest places I've ever been.

Sayghan consisted of one single concrete road, a dual carriageway split down the middle by a narrow median strip and lined on each side by deep open drains, like almost every city street in the country. Single-storey shops on either side of Sayghan High Street seemed to have been built one at a time, with no consistency in style, and leaning to one side or another, against their neighbour. Some were open, most were not. Two men sitting among the sacks of grain and spices in a produce store were licking ice-cream cones that looked like they'd just been handed through the window of a Mr Whippy van. 'We're celebrating,' said one. 'We beat the Taliban.'

Along the street, men and boys sat on chairs outside the few shops that were open, drinking tea, gossiping, fixing motorbikes, or watching us as they nudged each other, pointed and giggled. Each was dressed in a shalwar kameez of a different, gorgeous colour. Magenta, cyan, pistachio, chocolate, turquoise, rust, peach, mustard, mint, sage, nutmeg, coffee, with matching or contrasting waistcoats. Men's fashion in the summer of 2021 was all about colour. Gone were the intricate traditional hand-embroidered tunics in muted tones. They had been undercut on price by mass-produced Chinese goods. Here in Sayghan, the colours almost vibrated against the eye-watering glare of the parched-white concrete road.

There was not a woman to be seen.

We walked the eerie length of the street, followed by a rainbow of boys, teenagers and men, and an escort of armed police in khaki fatigues. We stopped at a shop stocked with phone accessories and plastic flowers and went in to chat to the handsome, smiling man behind the counter. We were soon joined by another couple of men, also handsome and smiling, and the conversation moved from the traditionally polite introductions to the battle for Sayghan and the Taliban's war on women.

It was 14 July 2021 when the Islamists fought their way into the valley with little opposition. The government's forces were late to the scene, their advance slowed by mines that the Taliban had planted on the only road in. The local militia were quickly overwhelmed. The Taliban overran Sayghan in just a couple of hours, and immediately set up committees to consolidate their takeover. One group looted the stores, warehouses and fuel storage depots; another group set about levying a 'tax' of about US$100 per resident, an enormous amount of money anywhere in Afghanistan, but especially in these small remote townships. They ransacked homes, seized weapons and food, and stole livestock. They terrorised the residents, who cowered in their homes behind high mud walls and heavy wooden gates on the rutted dirt roads running off the High Street.

With the town locked down, the Taliban then ordered the mullahs to use the mosques' loudspeakers, which call the faithful to prayer five times a day, to order every household to hand over details of all their women and girls, listing them by name, age and marital status. Not only that, they were ordered to provide details about who the women were married to, specifically identifying those married to men who had joined the republic's armed forces, and which of them were widowed. They wanted any videos that those soldiers or police fighting on the frontlines may have sent to their wives on their smartphones. The Taliban sent their gunmen door to door to search every room of every house. They searched the wardrobes and cupboards to determine how many women and girls lived in each house, how old they were, where they were. They went through their clothes, touching them, pulling them out to size them up. They violated the sanctity of every home, the privacy of every resident. It was a gross transgression in a country where outside the cities, and often inside them, women generally do not meet with men they are not related to or do not know through family connections. The home itself is sacrosanct; the family's private quarters where the women dwell inviolable.

The Taliban's reign of terror in Sayghan had begun, and its first targets were the women. It quickly became clear, the handsome men told me, their smiles long faded, that the Taliban intended to round up the future wives of their fighters. The women of Sayghan – their wives, daughters, sisters, aunts, cousins – were to be systematically kidnapped and condemned to a captive life as sex slaves.

Sayghan panicked. Baes Sakhizada, a twenty-eight-year-old maths teacher who had joined us in the shop, invited me and Massoud back to his home to meet his wife, sister and niece. He'd been married only a couple of months, and the room he and Nafisa shared was small, cosy and spotless; the only decoration was a wall-hanging with three red and white hearts and the word 'love'. Baes gave me a shy smile of pride and adoration when I took a photo of him and Nafisa sitting on the carpet beneath it. Nafisa stared at the floor, reliving her personal nightmare as Baes's sister, Basira, told me her story.

Rumours had circulated for months about the fate of women in districts that fell to the Taliban; now they knew the rumours were true.

The women began to leave Sayghan. In the dead of night, they packed what they could carry, crept out of town and kept on going, eventually building to an exodus that choked the roads on the other side of the valley. They walked to nearby villages; they hired cars to drive them to neighbouring provinces. Nafisa, Basira and their nineteen-year-old cousin Tammana made the 240-kilometre journey to the capital, Kabul. There, they huddled, traumatised by what was happening in their hometown, terrified that it would catch up with them in Kabul, that this was what awaited their entire country if the insurgents could not be beaten back.

And beaten back they were, in a fierce firefight with militias and armed police that lasted just two hours. The Taliban had held Sayghan for four days, from 14 to 18 July. I arrived in the valley on 22 July, to find a population shaken and shocked, the men still swapping details of the fight to dislodge the insurgents, and many of the women who had fled yet to return. Those who had, like Nafisa, Basira and Tammana, were visibly disturbed and still in shock. They spoke of sleepless nights, and of the nightmares that stalked their dreams when they did sleep. Their biggest fear was the Taliban's return: now they knew their fate. They spoke to us, barely coherently, on camera, but only after covering their faces but for their eyes, to conceal their identity. While the men were relieved and clearly thought they'd escaped the worst, the women were not so confident that the Taliban would not return. Theirs had been a closer call.

FOR WOMEN EVERYWHERE, it is a fate worse than death: we know that women just like us are tricked, kidnapped, and forced or sold into sex slavery by gangsters who see people trafficking and prostitution merely as profit opportunities, alongside drugs, the organs and limbs of exotic animals, and antiquities. Women are the contraband, the commodities, of multibillion-dollar criminal enterprises. For the women of Afghanistan in 2021, one of the world's biggest drugs cartel, the Taliban, was rapidly advancing across the country with the aim of toppling the government that had been supported and funded by the Western alliance for twenty years. The aim was to reinstall an ultra-Islamist government and, using the cloak of religion and the ignorance of its henchmen, to eradicate all forms of modernity, including any notions of gender equality and the rights of women to be recognised and protected by law. To the Taliban, women are chattels, to be kept indoors for the use and comfort of men, of far less value than their guns. As flawed and as corrupt as the Western occupation, democratic experiment and war on the Taliban had been, all hope for lasting progress that had infused two generations of Afghan men and women since the Islamists were blasted from power in 2001 was about to be snuffed out.

By the time my report from Sayghan was published, on 23 July, the Taliban were already doling out handmaidens, the swag of victory, to their fighters in regions under their control, close to Afghanistan's northern borders with the Central Asian nations of the former Soviet Union. For weeks, as the insurgents rolled out their battlefield strategy, firstly taking border posts to seal the country, followed by the territory surrounding provincial capitals, there were rumours about the fate of women trapped in this new brutality. But as media outlets were taken over or closed down by the advancing Taliban, and with journalists fleeing search-and-kill squads, there could be no credible confirmation. Until, that is, my story with Massoud's photographs appeared in *Foreign Policy*. It was, as Massoud likes to say, 'like a bomb going off'.

For revealing the truth, I was trolled, attacked and threatened by the Taliban's online army of sympathisers the world over, including Australia. English teacher Timothy Weeks was kidnapped soon after arriving in Kabul in 2016 and held by the militants for three years. After being freed, thanks to the American government, Weeks became a Taliban apologist, and used his Twitter account to warn me that I would 'be held accountable' for my apparently 'merciless quest to demonise the Taliban'. I was accused of making it all up, of fabricating the quotes, of being an anti-Taliban stooge of the Ghani government and the American 'occupiers'. Massoud had doctored the photos. We had been the victims of a conspiracy. Everything I wrote was lies.

I was now a high value target and the Taliban wanted me dead.

The Taliban reaction to the revelations of their sex slavery policy was almost as revealing as the story itself. The abuse that followed was relentless, but by protesting too much, the Taliban simply confirmed it: women were to be enslaved for the sexual use of militant fighters. Like the 'comfort women' kidnapped and enslaved for the gratification of Japanese soldiers across Asia during World War II, women across Afghanistan were of no use for anything else. Lumpen meaty holes for the masturbatory convenience of men brainwashed to believe that this was the only purpose for which their god put women on earth.

The pressure was immense, the gaslighting so effective that I began to doubt the efficacy of my work and to consider that perhaps I had indeed been taken in. And this was despite the fact that everything had been taped, filmed, checked and verified. Some of the people quoted in the story got in touch to say they were also being threatened and harassed because of the subject matter. Not for the first time, Massoud and I suggested they accuse us of taking what they'd said out of context, had been mistaken, or even that I'd made it up. It was vital for their own safety that they paint me as a liar. I didn't mind; we all knew the truth.

AFGHANISTAN CONSISTENTLY RATES among the worst places in the world for women and girls. Since the Taliban returned to power, the progress of twenty years has been wiped out as girls and women have once again been locked out of education and work, and forced under the hijab and into their homes. The world has stood by either silently, like China and Russia, or impotently, like Australia, Britain and the United States. United Nations (UN) representatives have paid lip service to the restoration of human rights while paying the Taliban for their on-the-ground security in Afghanistan. In the midst of a starvation crisis, their agencies are ceding a large portion of taxpayer-funded food aid, meant to ease the appalling misery, to the Islamists.

When the Taliban were removed from power in 2001, many women emerged from the confines of their homes blinking like koalas waking from a long nap up a gum tree. Many others were afraid to venture outside their homes in case the Taliban were still lurking. More still had never been allowed outside their homes and would remain there, trapped within the confines of local and tribal practices that purport to honour women by imprisoning them and denying them access to education.

The constitution that followed the military intervention and international interference in the appointment of the post-Taliban government guaranteed women equality and safety from violence. It was aspirational and admirable, a multi-generational project that was making some inroads into modernising attitudes towards women and their place in society. There are those who question the impact that all the noise about women's rights had on the men who saw themselves as guardians of their women's honour; some people I know believe that the Western zeal to prise women from the clutches of custom triggered a reactionary response that pushed them deeper into it. What cannot be denied is that many millions of women and girls did find their voice during those twenty years; they went to school and university, found jobs, started businesses, travelled. In the months after the Taliban returned, they took to the streets and social media to use their voices to call for their rights to be restored. They scream; no one listens. Out on the streets, where they are beaten, detained, disappeared and sometimes killed, certainly gang-raped, for calling for their freedoms, they are alone; not even their own men stand up for them. The world and Afghan men were and continue to be shamefully and shamelessly silent as the handmaid's tale has become reality before our eyes.

WHEN I WAS first posted to Kabul as a correspondent and bureau chief, I had no real understanding of how women were regarded and treated in Afghanistan. I understood misogyny from my personal perspective, the fact that the world is run by mediocre, middle-class, middle-aged, and mostly white, men who are threatened by able women. The trajectory of my career had been stalled on many occasions by men who clearly felt threatened by me, though it took me a long time to come to that realisation. I once mentioned to my mother, as I looked back on yet another episode in which men had used and abused me to boost their own careers, 'You know, I think it might be because I'm a woman.' 'Honey,' she replied, 'I've been watching you for all these years, and it is always because you're a woman.'

For twenty years, the taxpayers of the West poured money into programs that purported to improve the lives of Afghanistan's women. I sometimes laugh that as a citizen of Australia, Britain and the Republic of Ireland, working for an American news organisation and living in Afghanistan paying value-added tax on everything I bought, I was hit five ways. But it isn't very funny. Hillary Clinton and Laura Bush urged the world to get behind the 2001 invasion by highlighting the way the Taliban had disappeared women. Horrific photographs surfaced anew showing women, anonymous in the all-covering burqa, on their knees in sports stadiums filled with men, being shot in the head by a Talib with an AK-47 for such crimes as having sex outside marriage. We were, ostensibly, in Afghanistan for the women.

The United States Congress set up a watchdog called the Special Inspector General for Afghanistan Reconstruction, or SIGAR, for the sole purpose of tracking US money as it flowed into the country. It found that, overall, about one-third of almost a trillion dollars was lost, unaccounted for, wasted, stolen. The US government's departments of State and Defence, and the Agency for International Development poured almost a billion dollars into programs just for women and girls, for their education, their health, their political awareness. Then there were the untold millions from other countries, charities and organisations that set up programs, rented houses and offices, bought armoured cars and employed people – internationals on huge packages, locals on salaries they could expect in New York, London, Melbourne, Hong Kong. These excesses just screwed the economy of what is still one of the poorest countries on earth.

I met some of the women running these programs; many of them had never ventured beyond the confines of their homes, cars and offices. After being called a 'c**t' by two young Afghan men as I sat in traffic in my car with the window open, I thought I'd write a story on street harassment of women. I discussed it with a girlfriend, who told me about the time she was walking in a shopping district, head covered, of course, in a long tunic over loose trousers. Young men walking towards her had hissed: 'vagina vagina vagina'.

I went to interview the head of a US-funded women's charity, who had been employed because she spoke English and had a degree from an American university. We sat in her office in a typical Kabul house, which at that time would have cost upwards of US$40,000 a month to rent, and were brought tea and sweets by a servant while her driver kept the car running downstairs as she was about to head home. I asked her about street harassment. She told me women should be careful about what they wear or they'd bring it on themselves.

In March 2014, the artist Kubra Khademi took refuge in my home amid a weeks-long barrage of death threats that followed a public performance that aimed to highlight the prevalence of sexual harassment. She'd made a metal suit of armour in the shape of a woman's body and wore it to walk through a district where she had been sexually molested a few years earlier. Her first experience of being inappropriately touched had been as a child and she had wished then that her clothes were made of steel to protect her from the unwanted touches of strange men. After her public walk, she was forced to move out of her home, and then out of a friend's home and into mine for her own safety.

While Kubra was with me, a woman named Farkhunda Malikzada was set upon inside a mosque by a mob of men and women who believed she had tried to burn a Koran. She hadn't. But she had berated a man selling fake charms to vulnerable women and he had in turn accused her of setting fire to the Muslim scripture. The crowd beat her for hours, dragged her onto a road and ran over her, dropped a massive rock on her head, and then threw her onto the bank of the Kabul River and set her alight. The most senior imam in Kabul told Friday worshippers that she'd got what was coming to her. The police said she was mentally ill. In fact, she was the beloved daughter of an educated middle-class family; she wore full hijab by choice and was a scholar of Islam. Her family endured death threats and eventually resettled in Germany. Kubra moved to France.

There is nothing much left to show for the billions of dollars that the Western alliance spent trying to make Afghanistan a modern country, with rights for all. On 15 August 2021, it all just disappeared. It's gone. Almost like it never happened. Afghanistan is not now and has not for a long time been a country for women. But at least they can point to those twenty years of Western-funded development and say there was progress, and there was hope. Now there is none. I saw it coming, and told the world. No one can say they weren't warned.

Lynne O'Donnell is the only journalist who witnessed the beginning and the end of the West's twenty-first century adventure in Afghanistan. She was present when the Taliban were bombed from power in 2001, and when they returned in 2021. She was bureau chief in Kabul for the Associated Press (AP) and Agence France-Presse (AFP) between 2009 and 2017. She was based in China with Reuters and *The Australian* for more than a decade, and has covered war, conflict and terrorism since the 9/11 attacks on the United States. Her book on the Iraq war, *High Tea in Mosul: The True Story of Two Englishwomen in War-torn Iraq*, was published in 2007. Her next book, *From the Frontline: Women Reporting on War 1899–2020*, will be published by Hurst.

7
THE LAST CORRESPONDENT
IN THE BEIJING BUREAU

Kirsty Needham
Hong Kong 2019
The Sydney Morning Herald, The Age

On the turbulent streets of Hong Kong 2019.

THE LIGHTNING CRACKED across the Taipei night sky as I watched the colossal storm from my hotel. The window in my room was so clear and wide I could have been watching the spectacle on flatscreen TV. It was late. As the China correspondent for an Australian newspaper, I often worked late to beat the time zone. Three hours behind Sydney, my habit on the road was to work past midnight to serve up stories ready baked and fresh for the Australian morning.

I was here, and not at home in Beijing, because the thirtieth anniversary of the Tiananmen Square massacre loomed in a few weeks. It would be near impossible to interview survivors in the city where it happened. State security surveilled our bureau and it was forbidden for

Beijingers to publicly acknowledge those tragic events. So, I had flown to Taipei on Friday without letting my Chinese colleagues know I was leaving. We had agreed when I started my posting two years earlier that there were things they didn't want to be told; it was the simplest way to avoid being grilled on sensitive details by security officials.

Two charismatic leaders of the 1989 Tiananmen student protest movement, Wu'er Kaixi and Wang Dan had spoken that morning, Saturday, at a small and tightly guarded conference at a Taipei university. With them were exiled Chinese historians, a former People's Liberation Army (PLA) soldier, who described cleaning up the bloodied square, and a student who had lost his legs when he was dragged under a tank. They were still searching for the truth: what was the real number of deaths, and who gave the orders to fire? Mainland Chinese students and journalists were in the audience. When the organisers cautioned anyone travelling from Beijing to stay off-camera from the livestream, several dived under their chairs.

My mobile rang as I watched the night sky. It was my mother. There was another lightning crack as she told me my father had died. I was fortunate to be in Taipei, where overseas phone calls to foreign journalists connected seamlessly, unlike Beijing, where my newspaper editors and parents often couldn't get through to me. I had seen Dad a week ago on a trip back to Sydney, made suddenly and alone, leaving my seven-year-old son in school in China. It was one more impossibility I faced as the Beijing correspondent – being with Dad, who had brain cancer, to say goodbye at the end.

These are the hard calculations made by a foreign correspondent pulled between ageing parents and a young family on different continents. After a decade coveting the post and studying the Chinese language, I found myself in the Beijing bureau as a forty-six-year-old mother.

Stretched taut between personal responsibilities and the job, I like to think I didn't snap, but became a highly tuned instrument: I wrote stories with the frenetic energy of a woman who knew how precious time was, determined to capture this moment when China was centre stage.

WHILE I HAD gone to Taipei to interview Wu'er Kaixi, I always planned to be in Hong Kong on 4 June, the only place on Chinese soil where a Tiananmen Square vigil could be held. Every year, tens of thousands of Hong Kongers gathered in Victoria Park to commemorate with candles. It was an important symbol of how this city, handed back to China in 1997, remained different.

I arrived there from Sydney with a suitcase full of black clothes; my son and husband returning to Beijing after Dad's funeral on a separate flight. At that point, I had no idea I would spend the rest of the year ping-ponging between Hong Kong, soon to explode in angry protests, and my family.

I juggled the Tiananmen anniversary story with Hong Kong Chief Executive Carrie Lam's speech to an Australian business dinner, then the next day sped across the world's longest sea bridge to Macau in a casino tycoon's Tesla for an exclusive interview about a billion-dollar merger. But within a short space of time, the only Hong Kong coverage the newspapers wanted was of the protests that were to paralyse the former Crown colony.

I had spent hours talking to people at the 4 June candlelight vigil and found many Hong Kongers who were also Australians. In the lead-up to the 1997 handover of the city from Britain to China, thousands of people had migrated to Australia in fear of the communists. When those fears weren't realised and China pursued economic reform, many returned to Hong Kong with young families, believing it to be safe.

But now in interview after interview that night, people told me that a legal change proposed by Lam's government had revived the old fear. The changes would allow Hong Kong citizens to be extradited to mainland China to face trial. Hong Kong's separate status, and its legal system, was being eroded, they said. Next Sunday there would be a march bigger than the Tiananmen vigil, they predicted, because Hong Kong people needed to stop this law.

I flew back to Beijing, glad to see my son, who put a brave face on in my absence. The news filtered through on social media on Sunday night that a million people had surged onto Hong Kong streets. The Chinese government prohibited mainland television from broadcasting the images, but I knew I would have to return to the Territory, and quickly.

I was outside Hong Kong's parliament on Wednesday 12 June, as tens of thousands of students surrounded the building, prompting Lam to suspend debate on the extradition bill. Church groups sang

'Hallelujah'. A few hours later, all hell broke loose. Riot police fired rubber bullets and unleashed 150 rounds of tear gas, more than they had fired in the entirety of the 2014 Umbrella democracy protests. It was the first time I had tasted tear gas. I was surprised by the burning sensation on my arms and face. A block away, after running blind in a fog, I sat in the gutter spluttering, trying to catch a regular breath.

The forceful response from police that day was a tipping point. Instead of cowing the students, it prompted a community-wide back-lash against Lam's government. A million marched again the next Sunday. Their protest was peaceful and they picked up the rubbish as they went. The self-restraint in this public show of defiance – no smashed glass, no violence – made front-page news globally.

Maggie, forty, who grew up in Sydney before returning to Hong Kong, was walking with her five-year-old son on a scooter.

'I want to have confidence in Carrie Lam, but I am changing my mind. Why doesn't she stop the law? What pushes the people to stay on the street and protest since June 12 is she didn't listen to the people,' she told me in the dripping humidity.

As the months passed and the government refused to back down, the level of force used by both police and hardline protesters escalated. The use of tear gas, rubber bullets, water cannon, and finally live bullets from the police was met with rocks, poles, Molotov cocktails, even arrows.

Lam withdrew the extradition bill in September, but by then it was too late. The protesters now had five demands, with the alleged brutal-ity meted by police to the thousands who had been arrested, a major grievance. People had seen the batons flying, and the blood spilled in once pristine subway stations and glossy shopping malls – middle-class Hong Kong's happy place – live on TV in their lounge rooms, as regular programming was replaced by protest news livestreams.

Buses were pulled over by police and black-clad protesters arrested. School students were lined up in subway stations to have their bags checked. I wrote about three children removed from the care of their parents by police after being caught at an outdoor screening of the Netflix film *Winter on Fire: Ukraine's Fight for Freedom*. The court was told each had a mask, not yet banned, but viewed by police as protester gear, and a laser pointer in their backpack. The parents of one fifteen-year-old boy went to the High Court to win back custody, arguing that he had been told to carry a mask as protection from the tear gas billowing through the city.

I gravitated to the backlines of the increasingly violent night-time protests in search of context for my news reports – filed in real-time on my smartphone for an online audience. I found lawyers, bankers, public servants out there. Church volunteers, medics and retailers.

Amid the choking tear gas clouds in the narrow side streets of Mong Kok or Wan Chai, there were also the mothers. Often they would have their backs pressed to the walls of shuttered shops as the 'raptors', the special tactical squad, charged past firing rubber bullets at fleeing youth. These women were poorly protected: a paper mask, sandals. We journalists wore military grade gas protection.

'Why are you here?' I asked. Night after night, their answers cut through the government's allegations of 'foreign interference' behind the protests. 'I'm not strong enough to be on the frontline,' they would typically reply. 'But we support the protesters.' Some believed their presence on the streets might somehow restrain the violence. This was wildly optimistic, as tear gas canisters exploded out of rifles at head height, and Molotov cocktails set alight store hoardings.

Teresa, fifty-eight, told me: 'When I was young I was too busy raising my family, and the communists got away with so many things. I regret I didn't do anything. Nowadays the young value their freedom.'

I was at the Chinese University of Hong Kong, out in the lush green hills of the New Territories, for the start of the universities strike. Tina, a lecturer and parent of a teenage protester, welled up as she watched thousands of students pouring into the campus, carrying banners. 'I am so impressed when I see so many students here. I can't fight the police at my age,' she said, and added that she condoned the violence. A fiery battle to stop riot police entering the university in November would see the institution's president tear gassed as he stood on a bridge trying to mediate a truce.

There was a flood of disinformation on social media, which meant that I needed to do as much eyewitness reporting as possible. Sometimes I buddied up with another journalist. Mostly I was alone on the streets at night. I wore visible press ID, a high-vis yellow vest and a helmet, and talked to protesters or police before holding up my smartphone to record at close range. The 'frontliners' I interviewed were wary of being identified, even though most wore gas masks. I had seen instances of other media confronted by angry groups on alert for 'government spies'.

I don't speak Cantonese, Hong Kong's language. But being able to speak Mandarin, the official language of the mainland, helped when talking to older Hong Kong residents who came down from their apartments to watch the fiery chaos. I could assure them that I wasn't a blonde 'American spy', as pro-Beijing newspapers were portraying Western reporters, and that I wanted to hear their views.

I refrained from using Mandarin when speaking to protesters after a university student on the subway on 12 June cautioned me to remove the mainland's simplified Chinese characters for journalist on my helmet. Language was a battleground, and students refused to use Beijing's words and script. Mainland Chinese journalists working for Western media had a rough time on the streets.

I saw police booed and heckled by bystanders as residents across the city became increasingly angry over their heavy-handed tactics

Unhappy with the international media coverage, which it alleged favoured the protesters, the Hong Kong government planned a live television forum to amplify the voice of what it thought was the 'silent majority'. It was a public relations disaster for Lam. A small audience selected in a ballot could ask any question of her on camera. Her interlocutors were so critical that Chinese state TV cut its broadcast. From inside the event venue, I could hear the chants of protesters gathering outside. Lam, surrounded by protesters, was unable to exit for hours.

The most important safety rule for me personally was to send an email every hour I was on the street to a designated person on a news desk 7000 kilometres away. As the late shift in Sydney clocked off, desk staff in Paris, London or New York would pick up the baton until I was back at my hotel. Often, I couldn't afford the distraction of typing an email while evading the water cannon, so I pre-typed the message, set a timed alarm, and hit send when it rang.

As the violence worsened, media companies began hiring security guards to accompany reporters on the streets. After the first live bullet was fired by police in October, hitting a protester, many kept bulletproof vests on standby. Our newspaper had two, but they were in Syria. My gas mask was upgraded to one with ballistic eye protection – this was my biggest concern, after an Indonesian journalist was blinded by police firing rubber bullets. With my mask on, I could work for hours, and felt safe – it was a more prized accessory than any shoes, dress or bling I had ever bought from a fashion boutique.

As a one-person bureau, keeping balance in our news coverage meant dashing in the rain across the city between press conferences held by police, by Lam, by the opposition parties and by the iconic young face of the movement – though avowedly not the leader this time – Joshua Wong. Just twenty-two years old, Wong had been repeatedly jailed by Hong Kong authorities for his role in the 2014 Umbrella protests over China's plans to alter the Territory's electoral system. The demonstrations and sit-ins had paralysed the centre of the city for months.

Wong was still in prison when the million-strong marches against the extradition bill began in March 2019. This was proof, opposition parties claimed, that this was truly a people's movement, without a designated leadership. Prominent pro-democracy figures explained that protesters used a social media forum to freely exchange ideas on tactics, with the most popular winning the day. While there was no leader for the authorities to arrest and jail, this, of course, also meant there was no clear leader for the government or police to negotiate with.

I was impressed by the ferociously independent Hong Kong press corps, demanding answers from Lam and her ministers and police chiefs. To me, coming from Beijing, where media access to government officials was tightly restricted, it was a tremendous display of freedom. During those press conferences, Lam and her officials often retorted that such aggressive questioning by media demonstrated her point that 'One country, two systems' – China's guarantee that Hong Kong would maintain its economic and administrative systems for fifty years after the Territory's handover, including press freedom – was alive. As riot police roamed the parliamentary corridors ahead of an October announcement of emergency powers and a mask ban, Lam's media relations team refused to accept my mainland China press pass, hurriedly offered as identification to gain entry to the press conference. 'We have One country, two systems here,' the young official told me sternly, and asked to see my Australian passport instead.

I managed to speak to the most popular pro-democracy politician, Roy 'God' Kwong, a romance novelist, by joining his signing queue at the Hong Kong Book Fair. Kwong had attracted a record half a million votes when elected to the Legislative Council, and polling now showed that his popularity had soared even further as he dashed between protesters and police on the frontline, seeking calm. 'He writes love stories telling girls what to do with their broken hearts, but he also does so much for us in the protest movement. He is so fast, whenever there is trouble, he is there,' Cherry, thirty-two, told me in the book queue.

Kwong's political career would end dramatically in 2021. Under new national security laws imposed by Beijing, fifty-three pro-democracy politicians were arrested for participating in a preselection ballot for forthcoming elections. The power of the new laws was demonstrated when 200 police raided a pro-democracy newspaper and arrested its owner, and the organisers of the 4 June candlelight vigil were charged with subversion.

Looking back, those frantic, dangerous days before the crackdown were a high-water mark for the city's press freedom.

Like many China correspondents that year, I constantly shuttled between a Hong Kong hotel room and my home in Beijing. It would have been simpler to stay in Hong Kong for the duration of the protest story, but months were passing by, and we had children in China. I felt like a ping-pong ball some days, bounced at high velocity between two worlds.

I flew home to Beijing from Hong Kong one Monday to cover the Chinese Communist Party's seventieth anniversary military parade on 1 October, only to be immediately informed by officials that our media passes to the event had been cancelled on security grounds. Beijing was locked down to allow the movement of tanks, and hypersonic and intercontinental ballistic missiles, so I resigned myself to watching the parade on TV. As evening fell, the news desk in Australia urgently contacted me to say a student had been shot by police with a live bullet in Hong Kong. We could see nothing in Beijing, where the Great Firewall was aggressively blocking internet content. I was on the 3.30 am flight back to Hong Kong.

TV colleagues with identifiable equipment were often grilled at the border by Chinese officials, who inspected their smartphones and computers for footage of protesters. As a newspaper reporter, I flew under the radar. I carried my helmet and gas mask in my carry-on luggage, the latter dismantled into indistinguishable shapes for the airport's security scanner.

When home, I would throw my tear gas-soaked clothes in the washing machine and say little about where I had been to my son. I had to silo my life in Beijing and my work in Hong Kong. In Hong Kong, boys his age in school uniform were stopped and searched by police.

In Beijing, what was happening in Hong Kong was labelled terrorism by black hands.

This was the only story told by state media. Even in apartment blocks designated for foreigners, which had access to the BBC World News, the TV screen would go black at the first mention of Hong Kong.

Our Chinese friends had only government-sourced information, and this coloured their views. At children's parties, I was careful about what I told Chinese parents curious about my work. In the diplomatic compound where we lived, there were also differing views, with many neighbours from Central Asian and African countries allied to Beijing's expanding Belt and Road trade routes. Friends warned me the compound spies were in overdrive, sidling up to a European journalist in the gym, for example, to quiz his views on Hong Kong, and on separatism in general, and to enquire about his travel plans. As with the Taiwan trip, I didn't discuss my Hong Kong reporting with Chinese colleagues in the bureau office.

That year, I would more frequently see the other China correspondents on Hong Kong's streets than in the bars or cafes of Beijing. Many were women, and we compared notes on what we were missing. A European journalist was anxious about her teenage daughter's dental surgery. 'I should be there,' she said. Waiting for luggage at the airport carousel in Beijing, a Scandinavian correspondent told me she had missed her daughter's first day of high school. Sharing the guilt made it bearable. There were a dozen European, Asian and American women correspondents in Beijing, my age or older, with children. This was a change for me from the newsrooms in Sydney and Melbourne, where young men strutted the foreign policy and defence rounds. In the embassies in Beijing, too, there was a rising proportion of female diplomats with families – in the Australian diplomatic corps, where the ambassador, foreign affairs department chief and the minister were all women, this was the result of a drive to achieve gender equity.

The flipside was a growing number of male spouses trailing us, most unable to work because of visa restrictions. My husband joined the blokes doing the school run and organising play dates, comparing notes on homework schedules, before regrouping in craft breweries after nightfall.

A quiet truth underpinning the success of the 'band of craft brew brothers' on the home front was the Beijing ayi, the auntie or house-keeper. It was expected that all foreign families would employ an ayi, and ours was a rock of reliability. No matter how short my travel notice, I knew my son would get to school, and eat. After classes, he would roam the vast interior gardens of our Soviet-era apartment compound with friends who negotiated games of tag and bike races in a mix of English, French, Russian, Japanese, Spanish and Chinese. On the weekend, my son and husband would explore Beijing's wonderland of military, police, plane and natural science museums, ancient temples and parks. Surely they were too busy to miss me.

ON THE NIGHT of 17 November, thousands of protesters at the Polytechnic University in Kowloon were gripped with fear after Hong Kong police issued a statement threatening to use live fire. The street outside the campus had been a scene of pitched battles between the police water cannon and medieval catapults firing flaming rocks. A People's Liberation Army barracks was metres away. I felt I couldn't leave: the international media with cameras needed to be here to witness any use of lethal force.

Hundreds of protesters, student journalists, medics and church volunteers had already been arrested trying to leave the cordon that police had drawn around the university. Anyone arrested would be charged with rioting and face ten years jail, they said. For days, arrows had been fired down from the campus at the entrance to the Cross Harbour Tunnel and toll booths were bombed, crippling a major transport route to Hong Kong Island.

Now protesters were feverishly building brick walls to block the narrow passageways into the heart of the campus. They said they were defending themselves from police incursion. I hoped to god there would not be a fire, because there would be no quick way out.

In courtyards, where the slogan 'Liberty or Death' was sprayed on walls, teams assembled crude bombs by mixing chemicals from science labs. Beer was poured into toilets and the precious glass bottles recycled on Molotov cocktail production lines. Six-packs of bombs were sent up to the campus perimeter. I saw hundreds stacked on footbridges overlooking major roads. Young women with bows and arrows stood guard. A statue of Sun Yat-sen, the founding father of China's first republic, was kitted out with facemask and goggles.

These students said the bombs were their response to the police attack on the Chinese University of Hong Kong that week. To me, it seemed a deep paranoia had set in. By Sunday afternoon, the protesters faced police water cannon on the street outside in a kind of medieval siege; two large catapults on a university balcony pelted rocks down onto the police position. At the PLA barracks, literally a stone's throw away, uniformed soldiers stared out through the trees, but the students didn't dare attack it.

I teamed up with the Australian Broadcasting Corporation crew for safety. Chasing catapult images, we ventured up through a maze of ruined classrooms filled with choking tear gas that had penetrated broken windows, and across carpet soaked with water from triggered sprinkler systems. Half a dozen reporters filming behind the catapult soon raced back inside as it backfired. I grabbed water bottles to douse their shocked faces, splattered in unknown red liquid.

Outside on the street again, the light was fading and for the first time in the six months of covering the protests, I was scared. A lot was changing quickly. The road was crowded with thousands of people pushing in different directions. I could feel the heat from the Molotov cocktails and tear gas canisters exploding on the bridge close behind me. Social media showed a police armoured vehicle ablaze after it tried to push through the protester lines on the bridge. The volunteer medics and church groups who vowed to stay at the campus to monitor developments that night genuinely feared that history could echo with the nearby PLA again violently putting down student protests, this time in Hong Kong.

I couldn't see the ABC crew and didn't want to leave the police cordon on my own, because of the threat of arrest. I looked around for the safest place. I had been trained to find an elevated position. A dark granite staircase led up to a balcony on the building opposite the university's main entrance. It looked like it would give protection from shots fired from above, or from the street. The ABC team and a handful of other international media and human rights observers made the same choice.

The riot police swept in before dawn, at 5.20 am, when every-one was exhausted. At the first loud crack, the ABC's cameraman motioned for me to get down on the balcony floor. Police snipers atop the museum building next to us were firing down. We were anxious to know if these rifle cracks were rubber bullets, or the live fire threatened earlier. Many more police rushed down the side street, dark shadows who could barely be seen in the smoke, except for the green lights they wore to identify each other. The surprised protesters tried to rush inside the campus. I saw some dragged away. Trees caught fire as tear gas canisters exploded. Students threw Molotov cocktails in retaliation.

I ventured down the staircase when dawn broke. There was no sign of the protesters here, but the main entrance to the campus was ablaze. I felt sick, thinking of the narrow brick passageways inside and so many homemade bombs. Fire fighters arrived much later. There were shell casings from rubber bullets strewn across the road, and a pair of abandoned goggles floated in a pool of blood.

'Do not fire directly at persons as serious injury or death could occur' was printed in large letters on a spent canister of unknown variety.

Explosions continued as the fire ignited the students' bomb stock-piles. A loud chant erupted from the PLA barracks, but the Chinese soldiers stayed inside its gates. I had been wearing a full-face rubber gas mask almost continually for twenty-three hours and the skin on my face was red and sore. But taking it off would meaning inhaling the fiery tear gas that hung in the air.

The battery on my phone was in its final gasps; my power bank was sucked dry, and we had no water or food. We needed to leave. But we were concerned about the police cordon and threats of arrest for anyone not carrying correct media accreditation. Images were circulating on social media of rows of students, NGOs, human rights observers and volunteer medics with hands cable-tied behind their backs. There were two student journalists left with us on the balcony, one working as a translator and the other as a photographer for international media. They feared they would be arrested. We walked out as a group.

The national broadcaster in Australia rang to request a live radio interview for their morning program. I agreed to take the call, but flagged the situation, not least the dying phone battery. The inter-view began as we approached the police. It continued, live to air, an Australian radio audience listening in, as a police officer asked me to open my bag, hand over my passport and stand up against a wall. He searched my items and was concerned by the Beijing press pass, saying he needed to consult someone higher up. My details were recorded, another data point in the tally of a thousand rioters and black hands that police later announced had been detained leaving the university. We all left.

The Polytechnic siege continued, with dramatic escape attempts down drains, 300 children escorted out by school principals, and 280 injured protesters leaving in ambulances.

Then, exhausted by violence, protesters left the surrounding streets. Attention switched to the ballot box. District council elections a week later powerfully answered the question of what Hong Kong people thought about the protests. In an unprecedented result, pro-democracy candidates won control of all eighteen of Hong Kong's councils, as 3 million people in a city of 7 million voted in the direct ballot.

A fortnight later in Beijing, I packed up my family and returned to Sydney, at the end of a three-year posting. A global pandemic that would close borders was silently seeding, but we didn't know it. Diplomatic tensions between Australia and China would worsen. Forty-six years after *The Sydney Morning Herald* was one of the first international media outlets to open in communist China, I was the last correspondent to turn out the lights in the Beijing bureau.

Kirsty Needham was China correspondent for *The Sydney Morning Herald* and *The Age* newspapers from 2017 to 2019. Her book *A Season in Red: My Great Leap Forward into the New China*, published in 2006, is about her time as a foreign expert English language polisher at *China Daily* in Beijing. The Beijing bureau was forced to close in December 2019 after Kirsty left, when the Chinese government declined to issue a visa to the next correspondent, and the Australian Government advised correspondents to leave China due to safety concerns amid a diplomatic dispute. She now writes about diplomacy for an international news agency.

8
THE ACCIDENTAL CORRESPONDENT

Tracey Holmes
China, Middle East 2001–2012
ABC, CNN, CGTN

At the controversial Beijing Winter Olympics 2022.

F ROM THE MOON, the world is a pretty small place. From out there it would be hard to imagine the multitude of differences that at times threaten to completely derail us on planet earth. It would be hard to imagine that people, all so similar, could see each other and treat each other so differently. Ideology. Culture. History. Religion. Politics. The accident of birth. It all plays a part. It is only through hearing the stories of others that we might begin to understand and reconcile the differences between us. That's part of a correspondent's job.

Let's be frank. My husband, Stan Grant, is the correspondent. I went along for the ride, and became one myself.

As CNN moved Stan from Sydney to Hong Kong to Beijing to the United Arab Emirates (UAE) and back to Beijing, we'd get the kids settled at their new schools and I would begin the search for work. Sometimes this work was for consumption back home for the ABC or

SBS, other times it was for local audiences, such as those who tuned into Dubai Eye or RTHK (Radio Television Hong Kong). Mostly, though, it was for global audiences whom you could not neatly fit into one box or another; these were the audiences of CNN International and China Central Television, now known as CGTN (China Global Television Network).

Stan was elsewhere much of the time. The kids and I watched the news to see where he was and which disaster he was trying to make sense of in the always fraught, often dangerous, complex world that others live in: one that is so removed from us here in peaceful, democratic Australia, where we are protected from the outside world by the vast ocean around us.

Bus bombings in Israel, tsunamis and earthquakes throughout Asia, wars in Afghanistan and Iraq remain mostly foreign to us. Sometimes Stan was closer to home, but still not with us as he documented daily life in the cities of China, Mongolia and North Korea. Occasionally my work would take me away too. Every now and then, our overseas assignments overlapped for a few days.

'Hi, what's for dinner?' one of the kids would ask over the phone from Beijing.

'I don't know, I'm in South Korea,' I remember replying during one trip.

'Oh, where's Dad?'

'In Iraq.'

We didn't abandon them. There were always arrangements made: sleepovers at friends' places, or one of two dedicated grandmothers would fly in to bridge the gap. If it was school holiday time, the older two boys would fly back to Australia to visit their mother, while our youngest son would head to my mum's place. Their childhood wasn't normal, but it taught them the world was a colourful place with differences that could divide, but equally with similarities that could unite. Moving frequently into the unknown was an adventure full of excitement, not fear; the world became a place of wonder.

From Shek O Beach in Hong Kong, to the streets of Beijing, Abu Dhabi and Dubai, the kids discovered they were fluent in the world's only international language – sport. It was the icebreaker wherever we went. Kicking a football was the same in any country, only the players changed. Our sons' friends were from everywhere – Chinese locals to

German expats, a Muslim child from Kazakhstan, a Jewish boy from Israel, and other Australians too.

Like our kids, my childhood was also one of change. I grew up with surfie counter-culture parents who roved the world. From my parents and their anti-establishment friends from all over, I heard about military regimes, dictatorships and corrupt governments. Perhaps it was inevitable that I would navigate towards a career that involved collecting the stories of others. More than anything, it has been luck, accidental timing, and the path initially paved by my parents that saw me end up doing what I do, reporting from wherever I find myself.

The world of my childhood included the whites-only beaches in Durban and camping trips through Zulu townships, to remote bays where the waves had not yet been hijacked by South Africa's cruel apartheid policies. Later I lived with a Hawaiian family, caretakers of an old Chinese graveyard on the outskirts of Honolulu. A short walk across a small bridge over the Pauoa Stream took me to a side entrance of my elementary school, where the motto was, in part, 'Stand Up, Be Heard!'

My classmates were mostly Hawaiian and Japanese. There were regular alarms as earthquakes randomly rattled the buildings. We were taught to dive under our desks with our hands over our heads. The road that wound past the school, and my home, ended at the Punchbowl Crater, where veterans from four wars were buried at the National Memorial Cemetery of the Pacific. One of those remembered there was Gerry Aikau, the son of the family we lived with. They had taken us in like long-lost relatives, teaching us Hawaiian ways, and the spirit of Aloha that is so much more than a slogan on a tourist's postcard.

Later, as fate would have it, my husband's work would take me overseas again: to live in a fishing village at the foot of a national park in Hong Kong; then to a new development across the road from one of the poorest hutongs on the outskirts of fast-growing Beijing; next followed Abu Dhabi where, in a former palace, you could eat gold-leaf chocolate cake served by migrant workers who lived in hellhole conditions, with their passports confiscated and controlled by their employers.

I have been told I am a contrarian. I don't believe I am. Certainly many of my stories don't align with the popular narrative, and I've often joked I must have either been a salmon in my past life or I am preparing to be one in the future, given the frequency with which

I have found myself swimming upstream, against the current of the news narrative.

Here are two quick anecdotes that might help explain the lens through which the world appears to me.

Somebody once asked me at a black-tie function if I could direct them to a particular guest. I gave clear directions to his table and described with clarity what he was wearing; he was easily identifiable by his brightly coloured tie and pocket square. Much later I bumped into the person who had asked for directions. 'Why didn't you just say the black guy; it would have been easier than looking at all the pocket squares,' she said with a laugh. To be honest, his skin colour was not something I had given any thought to. It's not that I am blind to colour, but since my childhood there has always been such a mix of people from different places that other identifiers have become important in distinguishing one from another.

There is also a story that has stayed with me from my childhood, one that I overheard. I reflect on it often as I consider how journalists are viewed when they parachute into foreign locations and immediately try to make sense of where they are and whatever it is that is making headlines that day.

A white schoolteacher in South Africa wanted to make a difference: teaching the kids in one of the many black townships locked out of the white mainstream, if they would have him. He gradually worked through the mistrust and became an accepted part of the community. Years later, he joined a street march demanding change to the political and structural system that locked black South Africans out of the opportunities only given to whites. The protesters came face to face with police and a contingent of counter protesters. It quicky turned violent. In the mayhem, the schoolteacher was presumed to be from the other side. He was beaten to death.

The idea of 'the other side' fascinates me. Mostly I have come to see that the other is not so different to us: just people living their lives in the circumstances they were born into, hoping for work, security and a life for their children that is better than their own. We cannot change the colour we are, nor our histories or our heritage. But life has shown me each of us is so much more than our colour. Each of us becomes the total of our experiences, those experiences shaping how we see the world around us.

My mum and dad were surfers at a critical time in surfing history. In the late 1960s and early 1970s, the alternative hippie lifestyle was flirting with global adventure and a shift to competitive professionalism. My dad made surfboards; my mum made clothes. They were at the forefront of an industry set to explode. They both worked, they both surfed, they both travelled − individually and together − to compete. I did not grow up in a family with a pronounced division along gender lines; much of what I saw my dad do, my mum could do too. When we moved back to Australia and settled into 'the system', the experience of my formative years crashed head on into one where males and females were like train tracks − heading to the same place but always at a distance from each other.

THERE ARE ONLY two places where representatives from every country on earth come together, the United Nations and the Olympic Games. The International Olympic Committee (IOC) has observer status at the UN, and boasts more member states. Taiwan and Hong Kong have their own teams at the Olympic Games, separate to the People's Republic of China. Palestine is also recognised, as are American Samoa, British Virgin Islands, Cayman Islands, New Caledonia and others.

Each Olympic Games is a perfect snapshot of our world, a slice of history at a particular moment in time. The way sports are contested tells you much about the people of a nation. Australian sporting teams have a reputation of never-say-die, of always rising to the challenge even when lacking the technical skills of their opponents; they are considered physical in nature with a can-do attitude. The politics around a sporting event explains the world in the clearest of terms. China's President Xi Jinping shaking hands with Russia's Vladimir Putin at the Opening Ceremony of the 2022 Beijing Winter Olympics in February while Western heads of state boycotted the event told us very clearly what we needed to know just weeks out from Putin's widely condemned invasion of Ukraine.

I have covered fourteen Olympic Games, each of them revealing the pressure points that exist on our planet and how different nations respond to them. In the way a high-school biology student might slice a cross-section of a specimen to view under a microscope, much of my storytelling from elsewhere has been informed by my observations of the world seen up close at every Olympics, as the world gathers together for that short moment in time.

When I first became aware of this thing, this place, this occasion called the Olympics, I lived in South Africa, a country that had banned television. It wasn't the only ban. The country itself was banned from almost all global sport. Television only arrived in South Africa in 1976, and all broadcasting was under the auspices of the South African Broadcasting Corporation (SABC), which did as much to keep the news out as it did to let it in. In a history of the broadcaster, former prime minister Hendrik Verwoerd is quoted comparing television with atomic bombs and poison gas, while Albert Hertzog, a former minister for Posts and Telegraphs, said TV would come to South Africa over his dead body, as it would show races mixing and make non-white Africans dissatisfied with their lot.

It is no wonder my first love was radio. There was no alternative. It is still my favourite reporting medium today. Audio is a doorway to the world that is deeply personal; it involves only the speaker and the listener. Radio requires an imagination, it exudes empathy, it teaches the listener to pick up the smallest intonations or shifts in the voice, taking the listener on a rollercoaster ride of emotions. Power leaps out from it, but, just as easily, the timid and often unheard can find a space that gives them voice. It is not surprising that while many in the media industry have been predicting the demise of radio, there has been exponential growth in the new storytelling format, podcasting. A podcast is just a takeaway version of radio.

The crackling archived broadcasts of man landing on the moon, or the voice of Hitler on a loudspeaker in front of thousands of frenzied supporters, are radio waves that remain embedded in my mind. Once heard, they become like the rings of a tree trunk, the scars of history that remind the internal body of the external world that once was.

I don't know when I first heard the powerful and maniacal voice of Hitler on radio, but I know it made me want to know more. Accounts of Berlin 1936 introduced me to the Olympic Games. Dubbed the Nazi Games, Hitler's public relations campaign to prove the dominance of the Aryan race came unstuck when the USA's Jesse Owens won four gold medals with Hitler watching, angry and embarrassed, from the stands.

Political enthusiasts who dismiss sport as irrelevant, childish games are missing out on the most fascinating, all-consuming, global politics of all. Presidents and prime ministers of all persuasions seek to be photographed with winners. The messaging is clear. Associate yourself with a human specimen that is the best in the world and, hopefully, in the minds of the public, some of their supremacy rubs off. Liberal democracies and authoritarian states alike invest in sport – training athletes, building facilities and spending millions, even billions, in bidding for and hosting major international events.

The sports industry is valued at around US$600 billion. Australia exports its sporting know-how to countries interested in building their own industries. Turn up at any centre of excellence, any major event, and from the physiotherapists to the drug testers, the CEOs to entertainment producers, you will hear Australian accents. Australia's reputation as a sporting nation is not just because we win our fair share of world titles and gold medals, it's because we know how to stage events from initial planning and risk management through to the legacy programs associated with business and tourism.

Australia and Greece are supposedly the only two countries that have competed at every summer Olympic Games since they were revived from the Ancient Games in 1896, although, at the Moscow Games of 1980 the handful of Australians who competed did so as individuals, marching under the Olympic flag rather than the Australian flag. Then prime minister, Malcolm Fraser, supported US president Jimmy Carter's call to boycott Moscow after the Soviet invasion of Afghanistan.

That war in Afghanistan lasted a decade, with more tragedy to follow. The government was overthrown in 1992, followed by the rise of the Taliban, an invasion by US-led forces after 9/11 in 2001, through to 2021, with the final withdrawal of US, British, French and Australian troops as Kabul fell, again, to the Taliban. Frantic scenes of locals holding onto the wings of military aircraft as they taxied down the runway for a final time shocked the world.

The COVID-delayed Tokyo Olympics had just ended on 8 August 2021. Afghanistan's team of five – one female athlete and four males – were on their way home, or to other competitions, when news broke that their capital was under threat. The Paralympic Games were days away and two athletes were due to fly to Tokyo from Kabul. I had just flown back into Sydney after the Games. I contacted the London-based chef de mission for the Afghanistan Paralympic team from my quarantine hotel room. In an interview for my ABC podcast The Ticket,

I asked him what was happening with his two athletes – Zakia Khudadadi, a female taekwondo athlete, and Hossain Rasouli, a male sprinter. He was desperate, confused and feeling helpless. His athletes were pleading for help, but he had no idea what to do. The chaos at Kabul airport and the lack of security made it virtually impossible for his athletes to leave the country.

The interview was heard by a group of former athletes and others in the sports industry who now work as human rights lawyers, immigration advocates, and security experts with military contacts. They each got in touch, offering to do what they could. Together they pulled off a miracle. Not only did Zakia and Hossain make it to the Tokyo Paralympic Games but hundreds of other athletes, mostly female, were also rescued from Kabul. Many of them are now settled temporarily in Australia, including the Afghanistan women's national football team, who have been welcomed and supported by the football community in Victoria. This is the best of humanity. This is what the international language of sport can do.

Moscow was not the first Olympic city to be boycotted. That honour belongs to Melbourne and its 1956 Olympics. Eight nations stayed away for different reasons. Israel, the UK and France had invaded Egypt after it nationalised the Suez Canal; Lebanon, Iraq and Cambodia joined Egypt in refusing the invitation to Melbourne. The Soviet Union had invaded Hungary; the Netherlands, Spain and Switzerland withdrew from the Games, protesting the Soviet Union's presence – interestingly Hungary did not. When the Soviet and Hungarian teams met in the Olympic water polo tournament, there was blood in the water as players came to blows. China also withdrew from Melbourne, protesting the team from Taiwan.

Mexico City 1968 gave the world arguably the most recognisable image in sports history – the bowed heads and raised black-gloved fists of Americans Tommie Smith and John Carlos, with Australia's Peter Norman, on the medal dais protesting on behalf of the black civil rights movement. For their efforts, the Americans were expelled from the team and struggled to find employment for years after. Norman was never selected for another Australian team despite being the number one ranked 200 metre runner.

People today would find it hard to believe that there was a time when North Korea was richer than South Korea – two countries that remain officially at war. When South Korea was granted hosting rights for the 1988 Summer Olympics, it was a dictatorship. By the time the Games were staged, they had become the world's newest democracy. Thirty years later, when South Korea hosted the 2018 Pyeongchang Winter Olympics, a combined north–south Korean women's ice hockey team came together under American coach Sarah Murray. The story of that team extended well beyond the sports pages.

It is the intersection of politics, humanity, sociology and psychology that sport provides that has consumed much of my journalism. Global issues, cultural clashes, economic differences all collide in the international sports arena. That is something Australia's former foreign affairs minister, Julie Bishop, was always conscious of. When the diplomatic ice needed to be cracked, it was often the gift of a signed, framed sporting jersey that did it. It's a tactic that others now use with Australia.

In February 2022, Beijing made history. It became the first city in the world to host both a summer and winter Olympic Games.

Ahead of the Opening Ceremony of the 2008 Summer Olympic Games, then President of China, Hu Jintao, hosted a luncheon for visiting heads of state and other dignitaries. At it were American President George W. Bush, Australian Prime Minister Kevin Rudd, French President Nicolas Sarkozy, Israeli President Shimon Peres, Japanese Prime Minister Yasuo Fukuda, even Taiwan's honorary head of the Kuomintang, Lien Chan. Vladimir Putin, Prime Minister of Russia at the time, was also a guest.

Fourteen years later, revealing how much geo–political relationships had changed, only one nation from that list had a representative attending the Winter Olympics Opening Ceremony: Vladimir Putin, now Russian President. The others stayed away, some publicly declaring a political boycott, others blaming COVID.

Days after the Beijing 2022 Winter Games had ended, and before the Paralympic Games had begun, Putin's troops invaded Ukraine. It wasn't the first time he'd mixed duties at the Games with an invasion of a foreign territory.

During 2008, Russia and Georgia were officially at war as the Beijing Summer Games began. Traditionally, shooting medals are the first to be presented at a Summer Olympics. I do not remember who won the gold medal in the women's 10 metre air pistol event, but I can tell you who won silver and bronze, because the medal presentation made headlines around the world. Russia's Natalia Paderina earned the silver medal, ahead of Nino Salukvadze of Georgia, who collected bronze.

Only days before the event, there had been rumours the Georgian team would withdraw from the Games, protesting Russia's presence in Beijing and the invasion at home. With the IOC always keen for a show of unity above politics, frantic negotiations behind the scenes saw the thirty-five member team from Georgia remain.

News archives tell the story of Paderina and Salukvadze embracing on the medal dais. Speaking to journalists afterwards, Salukvadze said, 'If the world were to draw any lessons from what I did, there would never be any wars. We live in the twenty-first century, after all. We shouldn't really stoop so low to wage wars against each other.'

Six years later, while hosting the Sochi 2014 Winter Olympics, Russia invaded eastern Ukraine and annexed Crimea. That conflict was still unresolved and was threatening to escalate significantly at the time of the Beijing 2022 Winter Olympics. Reflecting the changed landscape politically, relations between some athletes and sporting bodies had also significantly shifted. There was no Paderina–Salukvadze moment in Beijing. During his competition in the men's skeleton event, Ukrainian athlete Vladyslav Heraskevych unveiled a sign that read 'No War In Ukraine'. The self-declared 'politically neutral' IOC did not sanction the athlete, as many had expected: the Olympic Charter's Rule 50 forbids any kind of demonstration at Olympic venues. In announcing Heraskevych would not be sanctioned, IOC spokesman Mark Adams told the world's media, 'We all want peace.' It was a rare instance where the IOC publicly revealed it had taken a side.

Unlike Georgia's Salukvadze in 2008, Ukraine's Heraskevych took a much harder line. After the Games and following Russia's full-scale attack on his homeland, Heraskevych wrote an open letter to the IOC president, Thomas Bach, calling for all Russian athletes to be banned from international sport. The athlete did not hear back. But not long after, the IOC issued a statement calling on all sports bodies, where possible, to ban all athletes and officials who represented Russia, in line with the economic and financial sanctions imposed on Russia by most Western governments.

'I just want to bring peace to the world,' Heraskevych told me. 'I believe the IOC supports me in that.' Russia's invasion of Ukraine was a breach of the Olympic charter, Heraskevych said, and all Russian athletes should pay. 'Every athlete represents their own country … this is a very strong propaganda tool … 'cause they use these athletes as heroes on the geopolitical map.'

Heraskevych said there were many Russian athletes who supported Putin's war on Ukraine. He did not speak of the many who at great personal risk had spoken against the war and had offered their support to Ukraine in media interviews and on their social media accounts. He suggested if Russian athletes were allowed to compete, it would give the impression the sports world supported violence, and asked why should they be allowed to compete when Ukrainian athletes were at home fighting for their country?

'Athletes are the face of their country,' he said. He is right. Often, they are the best face, the diplomatic face, the other frontline in a world that can come together in peace rather than war.

Australia is facing one of the biggest challenges in its history. A new Cold War era has begun. The US and China are at odds. China is on the way to surpassing the US as the globe's largest economy. Militarily we are on the side of the US, yet our largest trading partner is China. During 2021 and before the federal election in 2022, Australian Government ministers could not pick up the phone and talk to their equals in China. The old Cold War saw a thaw in relationships when US president Richard Nixon sent a team of table tennis players to China in what is famously known as 'ping-pong diplomacy'. This time around, it is China making the moves towards a possible thaw in relations.

China has sent a new ambassador to Canberra to try to re-open old doors. Xiao Qian is using sport as one method to revive the relationship. Following the Olympic and Paralympic Games in February and March of 2022, the ambassador held a 'welcome back' function at the Chinese Embassy in Canberra for representatives of the Australian Olympic and Paralympic teams. It was not a story in the Australian media though.

Journalism has changed. Perhaps it's the influence of social media and the desire to 'stand out'. Reporting is often one-sided and driven by political ideology. Rather than helping the public understand the complexities and the nuances of the world we live in, coverage today is as divided as the ruling classes that govern us. It pains me to think that journalists of the future will not enjoy the opportunities that my husband and I and others of our generation have had.

TO HAVE LIVED with and among people who neither look like me nor speak my language is a rare privilege. To have had a career that is built on sharing the stories of others is both hugely rewarding and incredibly challenging. Everybody's truth is different. Whose truth should I tell? Am I reflecting it honestly or are my own preconceived ideas interfering? There is the constant voice in the back of my head to observe, not judge … then there is the reaction of the audience, many of whom think what others say is what I believe. The hope is, ultimately, that each story chips away at the divide between what we commonly refer to as 'us and them'.

Our youngest son once asked me, when he was about three, whether I was alive when the world was black and white. He'd seen some old photos in an album and was struck by the lack of colour in days gone by. Too often we in the media still report the world through a black and white lens.

The decision by my surfing parents to abandon the few items they owned and all the family they had to head off on an adventure aged twenty and twenty-four, would not only shape my childhood but heavily influence my career. We hopped on a boat just before my third birthday that looked to my young eyes like it could have been the *Titanic*. It was enormous. It appeared larger than any building, with more rooms and balconies than I'd ever seen. It was called the *Galileo Galilei*. It was built to bring immigrants from Italy to Australia during the sixties before being refashioned into a cruise ship during the eighties. It featured in a Bollywood drama in the nineties and then sank in the Malacca Strait after an onboard fire. Unlike with the *Titanic*, all passengers and crew were rescued.

The Holmes family jumped ashore in Durban, South Africa. Why there? Because Mum and Dad heard the surf was good. It was prior to South Africa's expulsion from the International Olympic Committee, and its decades long absence from international sport.

Our house in Goble Road, in the Durban suburb of Morningside, was filled with people of all shapes, sizes and colours, who spoke words I could not understand. When I could understand them, they were in accents I had not previously heard. They ate different food, they danced to different music, and told stories of other places more far-flung than the one we had come from. It wasn't by accident that my obsession at the time was with one of my dad's records, 'People Are Strange' by The Doors.

As pioneers in an anti-establishment counterculture, my parents were at the cutting edge as a renegade, hippie pastime transitioned into a competitive, semi-professional sport. Surfers from around the world came to compete in what has become the world's longest-running professional event, known back then as the Gunston 500, now called the Ballito Pro. The competitors from all points on the globe would gather at our place for the parties, some even stayed for extended periods as guests. This was a pattern that was to repeat as we moved, years later, to Hawaii, and then back to Australia. There was a never-ending stream of visitors staying at our place – from Brazil, Peru, Hawaii, Japan, South Africa … you name the place, we knew a surfer from there.

Conversations weren't just about weather patterns and ocean currents; they were of political challenges, human struggles, and stories of discovery. Others were about the Hawaiians, people from a kingdom that had never ceded its sovereignty and yet had become the fiftieth state of America; others still were about a people called the Incas and the trail to Machu Picchu. I would lie in bed listening to the adult conversations that could be heard through the walls and fall asleep with my imagination full. I was a white kid in a country of black people subjected to a cruel regime that separated people by colour, a regime so afraid of letting the masses know what was happening elsewhere in the world that television was banned.

Thirty years later, sitting around the large work desk with my Chinese colleagues at China Central Television, it was as though I was caught in a time warp. The large TV screen at the end of the table was always switched to CNN. The constant stream of voices and accents telling stories from all pockets of the globe was only ever stopped when the China correspondent appeared. Each time it happened, I would imagine a 24/7 operation inside the large concrete State Security Building on Dong Chang'an Avenue, near Tiananmen Square, where some low-ranking employee would follow instructions to pull the plug, only reinserting it once the China story had finished and the broadcast had moved on. It made for some strange silences in an otherwise noisy office when it happened several times a day. My colleagues all knew CNN's China correspondent was my husband.

For all they knew, he might as well have been reporting on a foreign land. But he wasn't. It was their country, their lives, told in ways they were unable to. While Stan worked for the globe's biggest, and at the time most respected, international news network, I was seeing China from within, listening to how they told their own stories for an international audience that mostly did not watch and did not care.

As the nineteenth century American philosopher Henry David Thoreau wrote, 'It's not what you look at that matters, it's what you see.' The challenge for all of us is to see what is there; not what our pre-conceived notions are looking for.

Tracey Holmes has lived and worked in Hong Kong, Beijing, Abu Dhabi and Dubai, working for organisations including the ABC, CNN and CGTN. Currently based in Sydney, she is widely regarded as one of Australia's leading sports journalists and program presenters. Tracey is known for bringing a unique perspective to the state of the world through the prism of sport.

PART TWO
MAKING HISTORY

'Where in the world would I rather be than on the frontline of history?'

– Lynsey Addario, photojournalist

A single bomb dropped on the Japanese city of Hiroshima on 6 August 1945 changed the course of history. Australian women covered WWII and its shocking aftermath and the events and issues that shaped the post-war era.

While the Cold War gave rise to hot-war proxies across Asia and assorted skirmishes in Africa and South America, the news focus in recent decades has moved to the Middle East: civil war in Lebanon, the Arab–Israeli conflict, a land for the Palestinians, the Arab Spring and war in Iraq.

The complex war in Syria between the forces of President Bashar al-Assad and opposition forces including ISIS continues to play out.

9
LORRAINE STUMM: A CORRESPONDENT WHO SAW TOO MUCH

Hiroshima 1945
London *Daily Mirror*
by Melissa Roberts

THE WAR HAD been over for a matter of days when Australia's first female accredited war correspondent, Lorraine Stumm, filed her world scoop. She had tracked down and interviewed the first known western survivor of the atomic bomb at Hiroshima, a blast that would put an end to the long and savage conflict in the Pacific and change the world forever.

Stumm flew over Hiroshima with a group of correspondents, and later wrote of the experience. 'The usual journalists' banter in the aircraft stopped as we neared the city, we were all so silent. I will never forget what it was like. I had expected rubble and the devastation, but nothing prepared me for the piles of bodies, clearly recognisable, and the bitter desolation of a once prosperous community. This [silence] continued even when we touched down. No-one said a word.'

But it was her interview with Father Wilhelm Kleinsorge as he lay in his hospital bed, suffering from radiation poisoning, that gave her readers the first real insight into what had taken place.

'Father Kleinsorge described walking barefoot through devastated Hiroshima for hours after the bombing,' Stumm filed. He had been reading at his presbytery, just 500 metres from ground zero, when he saw a flash.

'I don't remember hearing any explosion or how I came from the second floor to the ground floor, but when I did, I found that our house was the only one left standing as far as I could see,' Stumm quoted Kleinsorge as saying. 'It was black as night. Six people, four brother priests, one student and one servant collected together, and we dug out the wife and daughter of the caretaker from under the wreckage. Fires had broken out all over Hiroshima. They raged at us from every direction. We had small splinter-like wounds all over our bodies. In the afternoon a whirlwind sprang up which made the sky pitch black and drove many people into the river, where they drowned. People were wandering about with their whole faces one large blister from the searing effect of the bomb. Only forty out of six hundred schoolgirls at the Methodist college survived; three hundred little girls at the government school were killed instantly. Thousands of young soldiers in training at barracks were slaughtered. I walked for two hours and only saw two hundred people alive.'

'Two days after the bombing, Japanese military forces entered Hiroshima and collected 200,000 bodies for cremation. In addition to those killed outright, many more died through lack of medical attention as every hospital had been destroyed,' Stumm reported.

WITH A BA, a diploma of journalism and some casual sports reporting experience at the *Brisbane Telegraph* under her belt, Stumm had followed her boyfriend, Harley, to London, where he was training to become a Royal Airforce pilot and she aimed to be a reporter.

Unfortunately, it was 'harder to get into Fleet Street than to rob the bank of England,' she would later write in her autobiography, *I Saw Too Much*. So, in 1936, she 'crashed in' to the night editor's office at the *Daily Mirror* and plied him with a judicious mix of charm, truth and falsehood.

'He asked me, can you do interviews? Never having done such a thing in my life, I promptly replied, yes.' To her amazement, he gave her a month's trial, which would end up taking her across the world to cover the story of the century.

I was as green as grass for I'd never known what real work was like until I joined the *Daily Mirror*. However, it didn't take long to realise that my job was one that demanded the qualifications of a Scotland

Yard sleuth, combined with the acumen of an astute lawyer and the bright ideas of a crack advertising agency.

In the beginning I had no technical knowledge of how a newspaper operated. What I did have, I quickly discovered, was an instinctive news sense, something I believe you cannot learn: you either have it, or you don't. In some instinctual way, I could scent, or feel my way into an important interview or recognise a good angle for a story.

And her angle was firmly tabloid. She covered crime, securing her first scoop by stalking a pathologist, charmed the leading tenor of the day into the bath to sing for a photo, interviewed movie stars like Robert Taylor and authors like George Bernard Shaw, and tailed Princesses Elizabeth and Margaret through the zoo at Regent's Park.

When war broke out, Stumm followed Harley, now her husband, to Singapore and quickly found a job on *The Malaya Tribune* as a general reporter, bringing a 'dash of Fleet Street' to South-East Asia, so much so that her first story defamed the governor, almost getting her deported.

After the birth of her baby and the Japanese shelling of Singapore, Stumm received a cable. It was her old editor at the *Mirror*. 'Delighted to know you are safe. Can you become our accredited war correspondent and start filing stories immediately?'

She became known as 'that war correspondent with a baby'. Tiny Sheridan waited outside press conferences with her amah, as her mother covered the refusal of authorities to believe that Singapore was vulnerable to Japanese attack. But Singapore did fall, and Stumm was forced back home to Brisbane, where she received another cable from the *Daily Mirror*. 'All delighted you are safe. Can you represent us at General MacArthur's HQ in Brisbane?'

The US general was the Supreme Allied Commander South-West Pacific Area, and Brisbane seethed with hundreds of thousands of US and Australian servicemen and -women. It was a city of sandbags, brown outs and bomb shelters.

Stumm wore an Australian army officer's uniform, and the flat, broad brimmed Australian women's army hat, all of which she felt was far from flattering. The American brass, complaining the hat made her look like a squashed tomato, gave her a US officers' side cap, which she wore with flair. The quality of her reporting brought her to the notice of MacArthur, who included her in an otherwise all-male reporting pack sent to Port Moresby to cover the battle against Japanese forces.

'Here at this forward area, the atmosphere tinges with excitement and grim preparedness,' she filed. 'Rugged Australian soldiers load trucks, dig roads, heave fence poles, their mahogany backs bent to the job, their Digger hats stained with the perspiration that pours off them in this humid land. Side by side with them work the Doughboys, more conventional in their fatigue suits with rolled down sleeves, some even in khakis with ties neatly tucked in at the neck.'

She worked alongside George Johnston, who would cover the war in China and go on to become one of Australia's most important authors, and Ian Morrison, the war correspondent son of Australian George Morrison, who had covered the 1900 Boxer Rebellion in China for *The Times*. Like most of the men, she operated out of the local command post, covering stories that she couldn't see firsthand, like the Battle of Kaiapit that saw Australian soldiers defeat a much larger force of Japanese with few losses, to establish an airstrip to protect the northern coastal town of Lae.

'The country around Port Moresby was so bad it was a wonder to me that troops could fight in such difficult terrain,' she would write later. 'The jeep track leading to the Kokoda Track was so rough it was a misery to ride along. But even here, Australian humour came to the fore. At the start of the Kokoda Track, a huge banner was stretched across the track which read: "Through these portals pass the best damn mosquito bait in the world." On the other side to welcome the returning troops was written: "We told you so!"'

Stumm covered the work of nurses, impressed with their courage and the hardships they faced. 'Into Moresby by plane usually come the wounded from land and sea battles. Twenty-four hours a day the girls of Moresby, Australian and American, are on the job, taking care of them,' she filed. She would later interview a group of nurses freed from Japanese captivity, who, fearing pack rape, had kept vials of morphine, ready to kill themselves.

'Even though I'd been through air raids in Singapore, New Guinea was a shock,' she wrote later. 'I remember walking down a dusty track, feeling dazed by the heat and the noise, when coming towards me was a war correspondent colleague, George Johnston. He asked me how it was all going. "It's all a bit overwhelming, suddenly finding myself in the theatre of war." He nodded sympathetically. "I know. It's a case of I saw too much.'"

As the war was ending, she took a job on *The Daily Telegraph* in Sydney. But there was one last cable to come from the *Daily Mirror*, this time asking her to go to Tokyo to cover the Japanese surrender. In a story that would be repeated for women correspondents for decades to come, the editor of the *Daily Telegraph* only agreed to let her go if she made her own way there. With no civilian flights available, Stumm called on her air force connections, who helped her in memory of her husband, Wing Commander Harley Stumm, who had been killed in action.

After the war, General MacArthur awarded Stumm the Asiatic Pacific Service Star for her services as a war correspondent in New Guinea.

10
DIANE WILLMAN: NO PLACE FOR YOUNG WOMEN

Beirut 1969–1979
ABC, CBC
by Trevor Watson

Sheltering baby Tarek from the shrapnel.

VIA UNRELIABLE AND sometimes close to inaudible telephone
circuits from Beirut, freelance correspondent Diane Willman
charted the brutal course of the religious and politically fuelled civil
war that reduced the Paris of the East to rubble in the early 1970s.

Willman's reports (often filed with baby Tarek in her arms) were a
regular feature of ABC Radio's agenda-setting morning current affairs
program, AM. The young reporter quickly became a household name.

Towards the end of one memorable report, AM's listeners were
given a very personal insight into life as a Beirut-based correspondent
and mother of a fourteen-month-old son. 'It's one thing to go out and
report a battle or an air raid and quite another to shelter in one's own
home while bombs and rockets explode all round,' Willman said on air.

'There'd be a hissing, whistling noise and then silence for about two seconds and then the crashing explosion.

'When one landed near the house, there'd be rubble and shrapnel on the roof and past the open windows,' she continued and went on to talk of her efforts to protect her infant son. 'I've wrapped my small son in a quilt and jammed a mattress into a corner as an extra buffer. And, at the height of the bombing, as mortars and rockets were whistling in on us, I covered him with my body and another quilt and turned up the radio to full blast to try and drown some of the worst explosions. After two or three hours there was a lull and we fled to a nearby basement, but now there is nowhere else to run.'

Willman was an outstanding correspondent, providing the ABC with exceptional coverage of a war that reshaped the Middle East and still reverberates today. And yet the national broadcaster, in the cruellest way, had sought to crush her ambition to become a foreign correspondent. 'We don't send women to foreign postings,' Willman was told by a Sydney-based news editor. 'What if they get married and have children? The ABC can rely on men.'

Undeterred, Willman took leave without pay from the ABC (which now prides itself on its commitment to diversity and inclusion) and headed overseas. 'I didn't know where I would end up,' she later revealed to an interviewer. 'I knew I couldn't go to places like London, Paris, or New York, because they were all places where there were regular paid correspondents. I ended up in the Middle East. I had no knowledge or understanding of the region at all, but it became clear within the first twenty-four hours that if I was ever going to make a living as a freelancer this was the place to be.'

The Canadian Broadcasting Corporation, CBC, took Willman on as a freelancer, as eventually did the very same ABC that had warned her off the fanciful idea of corresponding from abroad. Willman's reports under fire quickly made a mockery of her one-time editor's view that 'men are more reliable'.

'All of the foreign reporters in Beirut were men. There were certainly no women on their own,' she says. 'People didn't know what to make of me. Some even thought I might be a spy. But I did have novelty value that opened doors everywhere.'

On one occasion, that novelty value helped protect Willman from the brutality of the civil war as it raged on the outskirts of Tripoli.

'The fighting, I was told, was at the edge of the city at the top of a low mountain. Following directions, I eventually heard shooting. Microphone at the ready to record a wild track for my current affairs package, I walked past the last house, along an open path towards an old crusader castle. Heads appeared over the wall. The shooting stopped. Men began shouting and waving me back. Shouting was also coming from the hillside across the valley. I had walked into the middle of a firefight.

'Both sides waited courteously for me to leave. The mountains were silent. Not one voice. Not one echo. Not a single shot. But no sooner was I out of their direct line of fire than the firing resumed. My decidedly foreign bright orange, red, yellow and blue frock had probably saved my life.

'There was no survival training, no protective clothing or equipment,' she writes. 'But being different was far more useful. Curiosity value opened doors and prompted assistance in so many unlikely circumstances.'

Willman recalls one particularly prolonged battle and a tank positioning itself just outside the apartment where her small son was asleep. 'Clearly, they planned to stay. Equally clearly, I needed them to go. Downstairs and into the street I went. The tank looked empty. Polite is good, I thought. I knocked on its side and almost immediately a head popped up. After explaining I needed the tank to leave because my son was asleep and their firing would wake him, there was a quick conference inside the tank with the rest of the crew. Their leader then apologised for disturbing us and the tank rumbled off to a new position. Neither of us mentioned the inevitable consequences if the tank had gone into action; it would have become a target and incoming shells would likely fall on everything and everyone except that tank.'

In September 1970, Egypt's long-serving president Gamal Abdel Nasser Hussein, who had ruled since his 1952 overthrow of the country's monarchy, died suddenly. The media converged on Cairo for the funeral and, says Willman, to learn of Nasser's successor. 'I was sent by the American radio network I was working for at the time. The ABC was also offered coverage if it also shared the costs, but the Australian broadcaster wasn't interested. I covered the funeral itself from halfway up a tree beside the Nile to the puzzlement of the crowds below and was nominated for Best US Radio Report of the year despite my nationality.'

Willman says that among her weaknesses is a tendency 'to do something because it needs to be done and no one else will take it on'. She believes that those who refuse the task are actually the smart ones. As an example, she talks of an occasion in Beirut when she responded to a plea from a neighbour to go to a building in the city centre where the fighting was currently concentrated and retrieve two German Shepherd dogs locked in an apartment. 'Their owners had fled to Paris; the dogs had no food left and little water. Eventually I agreed, providing someone else would take the dogs and look after them. There was barely enough to feed my sixteen once-stray cats let alone two big dogs. The walk was about two kilometres through deserted streets. Eventually I found the caretaker who had a key to let me in. He goggled when told what I planned to do but could not wait to get rid of the dogs. They were just as anxious to leave and, pulling and straining to escape, we eventually made it back without a single shot being fired at us.'

Professionally, Willman says she was always amazed at how much we learn from others doing the same job. 'American correspondents invariably managed to find drama even when the event or incident was over by the time they arrived. On one occasion, at least one house on the outskirts of a southern Lebanese village had been bombed several hours before. Undeterred, a cameraman persuaded one of the villagers tending a small cooking fire to build it up until it was more smoke and flames than charcoal. He then proceeded to film the damaged village and its people through the smoke of the fire. Instant drama.'

Decades on, Willman reflects on what it was that kept her going through Lebanon's bloody civil war. 'It was sheer bloody-minded determination to do the job and to overcome obstacles on instinct,' she says. 'Adversity sometimes teaches imaginative and often creative ways to approach a problem. A pity it lurches rather than flows smoothly.'

Willman returned to Australia in 1979, with her lifelong ambition achieved. Her ten-year assignment had been tough, particularly on a freelancer's income. 'It was hand to mouth, and without the support of the Canadian national broadcaster and a US radio network it would have been impossible,' she says. 'ABC colleagues in London and Australia were wonderfully supportive and became a lifeline during some of the worst of what had become a civil war. Decades later, I still think of them with gratitude and affection.'

11
BIN LADEN AND THE LAND OF THE PURE

Amanda Hodge
Pakistan 2011
The Australian

Light and shade of Pakistan.

THE MEDIA SCRUM was so tight I barely felt the hand rummaging inside my bag. I couldn't have done anything about it anyway, my arms were pinned so closely to my sides by the crush of bodies inside the lavish Lahore compound of Pakistan's then opposition leader, Nawaz Sharif.

It was early 2009, my first trip to Pakistan as a newly minted foreign correspondent – actually, my first trip ever to Pakistan – and by the end of that press conference, attended by the city's media and hundreds of over-excited, conservative Islamic youths, I had been relieved of both wallet and passport. Hours later, in a suburban police station, my 'fixer' – a term that does no justice to the local journalists lured with US dollars into babysitting foreign correspondents – stuck close as two officers wolfishly suggested I should be locked up for carelessness. I still have the police report – promptly leaked to local media – which correctly noted my passport details but spectacularly misreported me as Eminda Ermaj.

It was a rocky introduction to a country I grew fond of in coming years, notwithstanding the late-night check-ins by intelligence agents, and regular shadowing as I stretched the limits of my visa at trouble spots around the country. Superficially, I fell in love with the beauty of Pakistan: its soaring mountains and long coastlines, the casual elegance of its people, its Mughal architecture, literary traditions, food, endangered Murree Gin, and its love of adornment on absolutely everything from shoes to trucks. On a deeper level, it was the country's light and shade that fascinated me: the courtly manners and instinctive hospitality that ran parallel to the unflinching cruelties inflicted by feudal lords upon landless labourers in the name of nationalism and religion.

My first encounter, however, proved good training for the extraordinary events that, two years later, would help derail Pakistan's shaky Western alliance.

LOOKING BACK, YOU can draw a reasonably straight line from the US military raid on a suburban compound in Abbottabad on 2 May 2011, codenamed Operation Neptune Spear, which ended the life of Osama bin Laden, to the August 2021 omnishambles that was the final withdrawal of US and allied troops from neighbouring Afghanistan.

When Pakistan's political and security establishment awoke to the news that US Navy SEALs had crossed into the country just after midnight – allegedly without official knowledge or approval – to eliminate the world's most-wanted terrorist, the ensuing two-way 'trust deficit' so often spoken of would prove to be terminal.

The United States' alliance with Pakistan – the 'Land of the Pure' carved from the bloody dissection of the subcontinent – barely survived the embarrassment to both sides of America's key ally in its war on terror being definitively outed as a harbourer of terrorists.

It was one thing to know Pakistan's shadowy Inter-Services Intelligence (ISI) agency was harbouring Afghan militants – the Taliban, Haqqani network, al-Qaeda and the entire Quetta Shura (elders' council) of militant leaders – even as US and NATO allies fought those same groups over the border. It was quite another to find that the man responsible for the 9/11 attacks on US soil that killed more than 3000 civilians was living peacefully in a garrison town a short stroll from Pakistan's most prestigious military academy and two regimental barracks.

Islamabad was slow to anger that week, apparently blindsided by the brazen operation. As communities across the world celebrated the death of a notorious terrorist chief, Pakistani officials were deeply divided over how to respond. Should they play along and claim some credit for eliminating the world's most wanted terrorist, potentially alienating millions of conservative and anti-American countrymen and -women? Or should they protest a gross breach of trust by a powerful ally and risk allegations of institutional incompetence or terrorist collusion?

In the end, Pakistan chose a wounded combination of both.

But that short window of time in which the civilian and military leadership clashed over how to handle a foreign policy disaster and potential domestic crisis was long enough for Delhi-based correspondents to scramble over the border and up into the leafy highland region that once served as cantonment for British forces. Anyone without a current Pakistani visa was sunk. Islamabad's reflex reaction was to shut down visa services to journalists clamouring to get in.

There was plenty more punishment to come, with new edicts issued every few days like angry thought bubbles. A humiliated Pakistan military demanded the US strip back its military presence. A week later, it ordered a review of its intelligence cooperation with the US. By November, the US military had been evicted from the Shamsi air base in Baluchistan, curtailing the CIA's deadly drone campaign targeting militant commanders in the Federally Administered Tribal Areas bordering Afghanistan. The critical overland supply route through which US and allied forces shuttled armaments and equipment into Afghanistan's battle theatre was also shut down.

Pakistan's capriciousness, and the unpredictability of a supply route now captive to a deteriorating Cold War–era alliance, would be a contributing factor in convincing US president Barack Obama and his successors of the futility of their role in the Afghan conflict.

Bin Laden's death also removed a key obstacle to a US withdrawal from Afghanistan, though it would be another decade before the last American military plane would leave Kabul, plunging Afghanistan and the wider region into chaos.

A CALL FROM the Sydney news desk pierced the early morning silence long before it penetrated my sleep-deprived brain with the biggest news of the decade. I weightlifted my head off the pillow, cursing the weekend's late finish, and stumbled into *The Australian's* bureau – the third bedroom of our New Delhi apartment – to find the quickest route to Abbottabad, and enough fresh detail to pull together 1800 words before my noon flight.

It's not easy to get from India to Pakistan speedily, thanks to their edgy bilateral relations, and it would take almost twenty-four hours to do so. On 2 May 2011, I joined an anxious foreign media pack travelling from Delhi airport to the far southern port city of Karachi – the only flight into Pakistan that day – back up north to Islamabad and overland to Abbottabad.

But that torturous trip would be child's play compared to the Russian roulette, that week, of getting in and out of Bilal Town, the housing estate on the edge of Abbottabad where Osama bin Laden lived and died, as a wrong-footed Pakistan security apparatus shifted into high gear.

Bin Laden's neighbours were mostly happy to talk about the mysterious occupants of the sprawling three-storey cement compound known locally as Waziristan Haveli, or Waziristan Mansion, after the Pakistan province that had become a militant hotbed for the Taliban, al-Qaeda and the Haqqani network.

'In a friendly neighbourhood, where most other houses are built close together, the compound was built in the middle of a vast field across the road from other houses. Anyone who dared lean on the wall was warned to move on,' I wrote at the time. The local kids – predictably cricket mad – offered one of the first revelations when they boasted of the cottage industry that flourished out of the paranoia of the compound's residents, who preferred to pay US$2 or $3 for every cricket ball that sailed over the five-metre perimeter wall than allow them to be retrieved.

The milkman was under instructions to leave ten litres of milk daily at the front gate but not to ring the bell. There were no phone or internet connections to the house. They burned their own rubbish and brought in their own livestock for slaughter. It was more than enough grist for Bilal Town's gossip mill. Many assumed the mysterious inhabitants were drug runners or Pakistani Taliban leaders. If anyone in that middle-class neighbourhood had speculated that the world's most wanted terrorist might be living among them, playing Mortal Kombat and pacing the veggie garden, they were not sharing those suspicions now.

How did bin Laden get away with it? The short answer, it seems, was by being a good neighbour. The longer answer is one Pakistan continues to dodge to this day. Arshad and Tariq Khan, the two brothers known locally as Big Khan and Little Khan who drove and ran chores for the bin Laden family, were said to have been kind and respectful – though Big Khan was also allegedly the key al-Qaeda courier who unwittingly led the CIA to the compound. They shared meat from animals slaughtered inside their own cattle yard with their neighbours on Muslim Eid holidays, occasionally bought sweets for the local kids and even gave away some rabbits, which a couple of neighbourhood children happily showed me on a nearby roof terrace.

America's audacious hunt for Osama bin Laden would ultimately make gripping, cinematic drama. But on the ground in Abbottabad that week, the scramble for the story of how the architect of the 9/11 attacks had managed to live such a prosaic existence undetected, with three wives, a brood of kids and a hutch of bunnies, was equal parts cinéma vérité and slapstick comedy.

Within a few days of the raid, the security noose around the neighbourhood had been pulled so tight I found myself in an absurd game of tag: running arcs through the cauliflower and wild marijuana fields on the edge of the suburb, with armed, uniformed police giving chase and yelling, 'Madam, madam!' at my back. On one occasion, I passed local kids selling scraps of genuine US Blackhawk, scavenged from the first helicopter that crashed into the compound wall as it hovered low over the property in the early hours of the morning. But there was no time for souvenirs. Unforgiving deadlines – Sydney is five hours ahead of Pakistan – meant having to run the gauntlet back into Bilal Town all over again in the late afternoon after hitching to the closest internet connection to file.

Still, local authorities, who were by now facing intense military and political pressure to chase the foreign media out of town, vacillated over how to handle the crisis. From one day to the next, you never knew if you would come up against a wall of security or a compliant local constabulary. On one such lucky day, we were allowed into a building next to the compound to get a better look. From the second floor of that hollowed-out structure, I had a clear view into the bin Laden compound and the tiny life his family had lived in the central compound, partitioned off from most of the garden, the servants' quarters and the front gate by a series of barbed wire–topped walls. All around me, travel-hardened correspondents took selfies with the bullet-marked building as backdrop.

But the mood among locals had started to sour. There was palpable anger over rumours the SEALs had shot Muslim women and children in the house – one woman had indeed been killed – and increasing scepticism over whether it was in fact bin Laden the Americans had found there.

Five days after the raid, a colleague from *The Independent* and I were detained by local police while trying to interview a man employed in 2003 to oversee construction of the compound. He had been detained earlier that week, and had since suffered a heart attack, his son told us before we were led away.

'We are only concerned for your welfare,' the local inspector told us over a relatively pleasant few hours of chai and chat, though his concern might have been more useful at 3 am the next morning when I woke to the sound of my neighbour trying to enter my room via the connecting 'family' door. It wasn't entirely unexpected. I had noticed my side of that door suspiciously unbolted on my return the previous evening and slid it back into place. The many stories shared among South Asia–based women correspondents of attempted hotel room invasions had taught me the wisdom of checking all locks before retiring. Exhausted but furious, I stormed from my room and hammered at my neighbour's door, demanding an explanation. Silence.

I was still fuming when I went to report the incident hours later at the hotel front desk, only to find two Federal Investigations Agency officers waiting to throw me out of Abbottabad. It took an hour to work out why they had singled me out (my toney New Delhi address) and another to secure a weekend reprieve by cynically deploying the near outrage of my modesty.

Official paranoia was not reserved for the crowds of foreign journalists who had descended on the town. Local police banned a long-haired and bearded local from the area for fear his resemblance to a young Osama bin Laden could stir angry passions. The friendly engineering graduate, who spoke fluent English, turned out to be the son of a retired Pakistani Army major. He also had a Taliban militant for a brother, who had only recently been released from jail.

The brother was happy to be interviewed, with one condition. I had to conduct it from behind the family's living room curtains to spare him the polluting influence of a *kafir* woman. In the end, he sat on the porch – the two of us in full view of each other through the window screen – as he raged over bin Laden's apparent connections with the CIA, Mossad and India's spy agency. The unrepentant Talib's wild conspiracy theories and extremist views spoke volumes of the radicalism that was spreading like mould from Pakistan's wild west to the chintz-filled lounge rooms of its educated and military classes.

Not even Abbottabad – where every third house was occupied by a police or army officer – was immune.

THE STEADY MARCH of extremism through a nation steeped in the ancient Sufi and Barelvi cultures of qawali devotional songs, saints and poetry had escalated in lockstep with the creeping advance of Pakistan's home-grown Taliban from the Pashtun tribal border regions with Afghanistan in 2007 into the verdant Swat Valley in the north. As the government oscillated between fighting and negotiating with those militants, terror strikes escalated across the country.

In December 2007, former Pakistan prime minister Benazir Bhutto was killed by a suicide bomber after a political rally in Rawalpindi, the very heart of the country's military establishment. Nine months later, a massive truck bomb tore through the Marriott Hotel in Islamabad, killing fifty-four people and injuring hundreds more. The government needed a solution and in early 2009 reached a settlement that would allow the enforcement of sharia law in Swat, one of Pakistan's most popular tourist destinations. It wasn't enough, and within months the Taliban had marched to within a hundred kilometres of Islamabad, terrorising residents of towns and villages from the snow-covered mountains of northern Pakistan – the Switzerland of the east – to the edge of the Pakistani plains.

The militants' seizure of Swat's main town, Mingora – where they closed down girls' schools, banned music and barbers, and hanged dissenters in the town square – shocked millions of Pakistanis. But it also

sharpened the divide between liberals who cherished the fading ambitions of the country's whiskey-swilling founding father, Muhammad
Ali Jinnah, for a pluralist democratic nation and those who yearned to
bury that vision under a cloak of Islamic conservatism.

Out of that dark time, in which two million people evacuated
to relatives' homes or baking refugee camps ahead of a massive
military operation to retake the valley, the diary of homebound
Swat schoolgirl Malala Yousafzai – serialised by the BBC under a
pseudonym – underscored the struggle for the soul of a nation.

As the military fought for control of the Swat Valley, I interviewed
many families displaced by the militant strife. Even within the most
conservative clans – where I would talk and eat with the men in the
outer areas of compounds before entering inner sanctums to speak to
the women and girls – most were aghast at what was happening to their
country and conflicted by the government's willingness to negotiate
with terrorists who were hanging ordinary citizens from light poles.

The militants were ultimately routed from the valley, but the government's hesitancy had given a whole new generation of extremists
legitimacy and momentum.

BY 2011, PAKISTAN was still cooperating in America's now decade-
long war on terror, but it was far from enthusiastic. Frustrations over
its duplicity were reaching boiling point well before the bin Laden
raid, with leaked US diplomatic cables six months earlier warning 'no
amount of money' would convince Islamabad to stop backing militants.

Long-held suspicions that the military was publicly supporting the
war on terror while covertly using US money to train and support
militant proxies in Afghanistan had by now burst into the open. To
many Americans, the US$18 billion in aid given to the Pakistani state
over a decade seemed a poor investment given how much of it had
gone to a Janus-faced military intent on ensuring India never gained a
foothold in Afghanistan.

To Pakistanis, the national humiliation of the bin Laden raid only
reinforced a popular view that the country was paying too high a
cost for its supporting role in the war on terror, and that American
dollars came with too many strings attached. Authorities had long
blamed the rising terror strikes inside the country on America's war

next door, which they believed had turned former militant proxies against them.

By the time the White House dispatched Senator John Kerry to Islamabad in mid-May 2011, the Obama administration was openly accusing its ally of aiding the Afghan Taliban insurgency. In such a febrile climate, it was inevitable the US would suspend aid as the two countries circled each other, calculating the cost of estrangement. For the US, it was the prospect of a nuclear-armed nation with escalating debt and terrorism problems spiralling out of control; for Pakistan, it was the loss of face and a deep-pocketed patron.

For one man, however, the crisis would present an unparalleled political opportunity.

Anti-American sentiment was already uncomfortably high in Pakistan thanks to the CIA's deadly drone campaign in the border regions, which killed militants but also many innocent civilians. But it soared after the Navy SEALs raid, as did Imran Khan's popularity with every fresh denunciation of bin Laden's 'cold blooded murder'. Within months, the former playboy cricketer, whose efforts to build a political career had hitherto come to little, was drawing more than 100,000 people to rallies demanding reform of a corrupt political system, closer ties to China and an end to Pakistan's participation in the war on terror.

On a flight from Islamabad to Lahore not long after the raid, I eavesdropped on a debate between wealthy English-speaking Pakistani women and businessmen across several front rows of the plane. Could Imran Khan head a government capable of brokering a truce with the US, India and Afghanistan, they wondered? A glamorous woman with a Chanel bag and colossal diamond ring interjected to suggest Pakistan needed a 'Mexican-style revolution'.

'We need to get Pakistan's best brains together and overthrow this establishment,' she said to a stunned silence. 'I mean, we can't go on like this, can we?'

A year later, as terror strikes escalated, the inconceivable had become plausible and Khan was shaping up as a wild card 2013 election winner. In an interview at his mountaintop home overlooking Lahore, the politician – by now dubbed 'Taliban Khan' for his alliance with the religious right – laid out an unapologetically conservative platform. Pakistan's Islamic militants, responsible for the deaths of thousands of fellow citizens, should be pacified with talks, not drones, he said. The country must wean itself off US aid and end its cooperation in America's war on terror.

'Amanda, I will tell you something,' he purred, leaning in close for effect. 'This will be bigger than you can ever imagine. In Pakistan a tsunami is coming. It's going to be a young population for the first time voting against the status quo.'

Ultimately, it was not Imran Khan who was swept to victory the following year on a wave of voter anger but Nawaz Sharif, who promised to rebuild relations with the US. Still, the gains Khan's Pakistan Movement for Justice party made in those polls would set him up for political victory in 2018.

MAKING SENSE OF how Osama bin Laden was ultimately hunted down, who harboured him, and who gave him up has become something of an industry in the years since that raid.

A generally accepted outline has bin Laden and his family crossing into Pakistan within weeks of the late 2001 US invasion of Afghanistan, sheltering for several years in the tribal areas before moving back and forth across the porous border and finally settling in Abbottabad in 2005, most likely with the knowledge and assistance of former or serving ISI officers.

How much the two countries cooperated in the lead-up to Operation Neptune Spear (briefly and controversially called Operation Geronimo) has never been revealed, though Pakistani commandos conducted a similar raid on a terrorist hideout in Abbottabad four months earlier to arrest Bali bomber Umar Patek. Indonesian authorities alleged the explosives expert, who trained in Pakistani militant camps before 9/11, hoped to meet bin Laden before heading to North Waziristan. Patek's arrest and subsequent interrogation – kept largely secret until after bin Laden's death – raised fresh questions. Did the Indonesian bomber provide vital information to the US mission to capture or kill bin Laden? Or was his arrest a Pakistani attempt to foil it?

I tracked down the Abbottabad house where the Indonesian militant and his Filipina wife had briefly stayed with a softly spoken civil servant, Abdul Hameed Sohail, who said he had taken them in after his twenty-year-old son found them begging for food at the local market.

They were thin and 'close to dying', Sohail said. 'I tried to communicate with them, but we could not understand each other.'

For ten days, the couple stayed in a first-floor room with a view of the Murree Hills, barely eating and receiving no visitors. Then, on 25 January, Pakistani commandos burst through the front door, guns blazing. Patek was hauled out unconscious in a fireman's hold, his wife dragged down the stairs behind him. Both were eventually extradited to Indonesia, where Patek was jailed.

That might have been the end of it for the Sohail family if the son had not also been hauled away. Local police insisted he was not in their custody, but the stricken father's attempts to locate him had failed. Anyone associated with Patek was guilty by association, just as those unlucky enough to have had more than a passing connection with the bin Laden compound, or that of a secret CIA house nearby, were swept up in a humiliation-fuelled witch hunt four months later. Official confirmation that CIA agents had been spying for months on the property from another neighbourhood house was like pouring gasoline on fire.

Among those arrested was a Pakistani doctor, Shakeel Afridi, alleged to have cooperated in a CIA operation to collect DNA from the fugitive terrorist under the guise of a hepatitis vaccination drive.

Local journalists, too, were in the eye of the storm. I met Saleem Shahzad, an Asia Times Online reporter known for his exposés of the Pakistani military, at a Gloria Jeans cafe in an upmarket Islamabad suburb the week after the raid. After receiving ISI death threats, he was nervous about the imminent release of his new book, which drew links between the militants and Pakistan's military. It hadn't stopped him reporting, nor from musing that the Saudis may have mediated bin Laden's handover to foil a 9/11 anniversary terror plot.

But like so many well-connected journalists in Pakistan trying to make sense of the hostile, sometimes conspiring forces at play there, Shahzad knew it was a perilous balancing act. On 27 May, the father of three small kids wrote a story alleging al-Qaeda was responsible for a recent attack on Pakistan's largest naval base in revenge for the refusal by authorities to release naval officers arrested for suspected links with the terror group.

Three days later, Shahzad disappeared on his way to a television interview in Islamabad. His battered body was pulled from a canal 130 kilometres from Islamabad the next morning. Australia's then High Commissioner to Pakistan, Tim George, condemned the killing, as did Hillary Clinton, US Secretary of State at the time, though no one was ever charged over his murder.

Shahzad's number is still in my phone, buried among a digital graveyard of contacts who became casualties of the military's ruinous shadow boxing with militancy. He was the thirteenth Pakistani journalist killed in eighteen months.

After bin Laden's death, Pakistan was a less friendly place for foreign journalists too. The legacy of Operation Neptune Spear was even tighter visa restrictions. The friendly tea and small talk in the blue-domed Pakistan embassy in New Delhi that had been a traditional prelude to any new visa stamp was largely dispensed with.

The *New York Times* Islamabad-based correspondent Declan Walsh would be expelled without explanation almost exactly two years later. Two photojournalist friends were pictured on the front page of a military-friendly newspaper as alleged Mossad or CIA spies. The claims were ludicrous but also a potential death sentence, as the editor (later a minister in Imran Khan's government) well knew.

For months after the raid, I worked obsessively on securing a long-term visa to Pakistan, trudging back and forth over the Punjab border under the duelling portraits of Mohandas Gandhi and Muhammad Ali Jinnah, whose failure to find common ground left enduring scars on their populations and the political landscape. I finally secured one, only for my Pakistan visits to dwindle as the 'Af/Pak story' wound down and the bigger story became the West's withdrawal from Afghanistan.

On one of my last reporting trips there, I covered the 2013 elections, a bloodbath of a campaign in which several hundred people lost their lives to terror strikes and gangsters. Still, tens of millions came out to vote, in the hope of turning their country's fortunes around.

Brave democracy, rogue nation, land of smoke and mirrors, and puppet masters – Pakistan's identity crisis continues long after mine was resolved when a middle-aged couple found my wallet and passport, by then long since cancelled, in long grass not far from where they had been stolen. They tracked me down and sent them back to me in India, with a kind note and an invitation to tea.

Amanda Hodge has been *The Australian* newspaper's South-East Asia correspondent since 2016, based largely in Jakarta, Indonesia, with some spells back in Australia during the COVID pandemic. Before that, she was *The Australian*'s South Asia correspondent, based in New Delhi from 2009–2016, where she had her daughter Dominique. She has won a Walkley Award, a UN peace prize and was the 2021 Lowy Institute media award winner.

12
SHELLS SLAMMED INTO THE EARTH: DISPATCHES FROM A SYRIAN VILLAGE

Ruth Pollard
Syria 2012
The Sydney Morning Herald

Jabal al-Akrad on the road to war.

WE HIKED INTO Syria after midnight, the sliver of a new Ramadan moon offering next to no light to guide us.

It was August 2012 and President Bashar al-Assad's brutal war against his citizens had entered its fifteenth month. Mass protests – peaceful and unarmed – that swept across the country had been met with a violent military crackdown. In turn, citizens had formed rebel brigades to defend their towns and villages. Fighting had also reached the capital, Damascus, and the second city, Aleppo.

Travelling from my base in Jerusalem, I had covered the protests in Cairo's Tahrir Square, the fall of the Libyan capital, Tripoli, and the revolution in Tunisia.

Now, in the beautiful mountains of Syria, I would shelter with a family as they were stalked by helicopter gunships and fired on by a tank. I would run from sniper fire. And I would meet the civilians – farmers, accountants, teachers, doctors, librarians, shopkeepers, web designers and bakers – who joined with Syrian army defectors in a quest to overthrow the Assad regime.

THE SYRIAN CONTACTS I'd been talking with on Skype, WhatsApp and Facebook had dwindled as the death toll climbed and those who knew they would be targeted by the regime fled. Entering Syria was a challenge for journalists. Official visas from Damascus were difficult to come by (especially if you had an Israel date line). Crossing the border illegally was the only option. I followed a route that was to become a well-worn path for reporters, fighters, refugees, medics and smugglers, through the countryside of Turkey's Hatay Province, up and over the Jabal al-Akrad (Kurd Mountain) and into Syria's Latakia region.

With me were Lebanese photographer Fadi Yeni Turk, Portuguese journalist José Manuel Rosendo of Antena 1 radio and Abed, the Syrian farmer who had agreed to guide us to the battlefield that was once his village. I cannot remember how long we walked in worried silence along the dark, rocky trail before we came to the border and the Turkish soldiers who controlled it. I kept to the back of our group, my headscarf tied in the local style, and eyes down. Abed said we were his family returning to their village. They let us pass.

We walked until we reached a road. A white van pulled up, as arranged, and we jumped in. Speeding through the night without headlights to evade Syrian army units positioned all around the mountains, the van wound through the town of Salma and into Abed's village. Surrounded by orchards, dense forest and high peaks, its beauty would have taken my breath away in better times.

The homecoming was bittersweet for thirty-eight-year-old Abed. His village had been mostly emptied of women and children, including his own family, who he'd taken to the Turkish border town of Yayladağı. There was no power or water – both had been disconnected by the regime or damaged in near-constant shelling. And his beloved apple, peach and plum trees, which his family had nurtured for generations, were in desperate need of attention.

As the sun rose, we sat in Abed's house and shared suhur, the pre-dawn meal eaten before the Fajr prayer during Ramadan, joined by a handful of male relatives who had stayed in the village to try to keep the animals alive and protect the orchards from destruction amid the bombardment.

It was early days in the battle for the strategic nearby town of Salma and the Sunni villages that surrounded it. Once a summer retreat from the coastal humidity of Latakia, Salma sits around 800 metres above sea level. Rebel forces had launched an offensive in June and took Salma a month later, giving them control over the supply route connecting the other opposition-held areas of Hama and Idlib and a vantage point overlooking government-controlled villages. This area would change hands many times in the course of Syria's war, ultimately coming under government control in 2016 with the help of Russian air strikes.

The region was also home to several hamlets dominated by members of Assad's Alawite sect, a branch of Shiite Islam. Both the town and the province of Latakia remain key Assad and Alawite strongholds.

The fragility of the opposition's hold on the area became clear at dawn on the first day as we surveyed the town. Rebel forces, including soldiers who had defected from the Syrian army, had commandeered a house in the centre of Salma, from where they ran operations. Under daily bombardment, the town's population of 70,000 had shrunk to around 5000.

Signs of mortar fire and shelling were everywhere: apartments with balconies demolished, roofs and ceilings collapsed, cars destroyed, craters marking the streets.

Few stores apart from the bakery and a basic grocery shop were open; the streets were mostly deserted. Yet each morning, a long line would form outside the Free Syrian Army (FSA) house, as men – mostly residents who were unable to leave, farmers and volunteer fighters – lined up for their daily ration of bullets and bread, both in chronically short supply. Watching over operations was the quietly spoken regional commander, Lieutenant-Colonel Abu Ahmad. Dressed neatly in military fatigues and already weary from the struggle, he was under no illusions about the challenges his forces faced in their battle for a democratic Syria.

The Free Coast Brigade commander, who had been forced out of the army over his open support of the Arab Spring revolutions in

Tunisia, Egypt and Libya, said his unit only needed one thing to over-throw Assad: more weapons. To him, the contest for Salma and its surrounds was important both strategically and politically: 'To have a hole of resistance within this province is a thorn in Assad's side.'

Brigade leaders arrived with requests for weapons and ammunition. They stayed to sit and discuss strategy. Others came with news of captured Syrian army soldiers and their supporters. Some just wanted to list their losses.

It was here, too, that the true breadth of the rebellion became apparent: the fighters were accountants, teachers, lawyers, farmers, traders, mechanics and public servants. Even a poet-cum-beekeeper who physically towered over us all was ready to fight to rid Syria of the Assads.

More than 200 rockets had fallen on the town the night we arrived, and the bombardment continued for the next few days. Even in the early morning, the repetitive boom, boom, boom of shelling echoed across the mountains. We entered a nondescript, low-rise block of flats in Salma where a small field hospital was operating in the basement. Tank shelling and mortar fire shook the ground we walked on.

After a particularly vicious round of fire, the medics, led by Rami Habib, a paediatric surgeon with Britain's National Health Service who started the clinic when he was in town visiting his parents, received word that casualties were incoming.

I prepared myself for the worst. Covered in dust, bleeding and quietly sobbing, the injured began arriving. An elderly man and his family, reeling with shock and with shrapnel wounds marking their bodies, collapsed into chairs and waited to be triaged.

Four rockets fired from a nearby Syrian army post had landed on their house as they sat in their lounge room, all but destroying the building and leaving relatives trapped inside. Even as the doctors and their assistants treated their injuries, the mortars kept thudding away, a little closer each time. I watched their faces for signs of panic; there was the occasional flinch, but the work went on.

Rami Habib was one of many dedicated doctors and medics I met over the course of the war, treating the injured at great personal risk while trying to keep up with the other day-to-day medical needs of the community they were serving. Babies had to be delivered, diabetes treated and broken bones set. Many were highly mobile, travelling in and out of Syria carrying medical supplies and other essentials, as the fighting turned from an anti-Assad rebellion into a far more sectarian conflict, fuelled by the ambitions of Iran, Russia and the Gulf states.

Inside the operating theatre, a handwritten sign pasted to the wall spoke to the desire for a new, united Syria: 'We believe the human being is the centre of the universe … [we are] offering medical care to the whole people involved on both sides of the conflict and delivering them to a safer place to receive medical care, regardless of their age, sex, ethnicity or religion.'

Tank shelling was new for me. I had covered the revolution in Libya a year previously, arriving in Tripoli just as it fell to rebel forces, as well as the surging protests in Cairo's Tahrir Square and skirmishes in the West Bank when the Israeli Defense Forces sought to crush Palestinian protests. But this was different. Habib was angry: 'This is what Assad is doing to his people,' he said as he delicately removed shrapnel from an old man's back. Others were resolute, vowing to stay in their homes and outlast their dictator.

As always, I kept a watchful eye on my colleague Fadi. A photographer and documentary maker, he grew up during the Lebanon Civil War and had worked throughout the Middle East. His manner was at once intense and controlled, he moved quietly, quickly and with enormous care, taking photographs and gently asking questions of the wounded, obviously moved by their answers. He taught me how to be in a conflict.

I am often asked what it is like to cover war as a woman. I never know how to answer. For women reporting from the frontlines, our days revolve around the most basic needs: a safe place to go to the toilet, a car and trusted driver, a supply of water and somewhere secure to sleep. Food, apart from the nuts and energy bars we carry, is mostly incidental. The work is everything. I care less about the details of the military hardware and more about how it affects people's lives; how people find the courage to rise up against a violent leader and the price that some ultimately pay.

There were no hotels in this warzone. Just modest houses along a small lane on the edge of lush farmlands. Abed welcomed us into his home and set us up in his lounge room. It was a big leap for both of us. He was a conservative, rural Muslim. I was a Western female journalist travelling with men who weren't my relatives. It was an awkward conversation, made worse by my broken Arabic. Fadi helped translate.

Eventually we came to an understanding: I would sleep on the lounge, Fadi and José would be next to me, but a respectable distance away, on mattresses on the floor. We would get by as best we could.

I slept in the clothes I wore that day in case we had to get out quickly, and it was several days more before I felt safe to take off my bra. I washed my face, cleaned my teeth and towelled down with wet wipes.

When we woke the next morning, a huge, old mulberry tree at the front of Abed's home dominated the scene outside our window. It was covered with fruit that left droplets of red-purple stains over the path and along the stone fence. His family had saved us breakfast from their suhur earlier – an omelette, tomato, cucumber, curd, cheese, bread, honey, olive oil and tea. Sitting on the floor eating together lifted our mood and provided fuel for the day ahead. That peace was quickly shattered.

The sound of helicopters suddenly overhead was chilling. We all reached for the small, old Nokia phones we were carrying, quickly removed the batteries and lay flat on our stomachs on the floor. Everyone was so quiet it was as though they were barely breathing. We listened to a helicopter gunship sweeping back and forth over the village for what seemed like an eternity, bursts of gunfire punching through the air.

We knew the Assad regime tracked the mobile phones of journalists, but we thought we'd taken all precautions. No smartphones, moving in a small car with local residents, laying low. We were aware of what had happened to journalists Marie Colvin and Remi Ochlik, who just six months previously had been killed by Syrian army artillery fire while covering the siege of Homs. The building they'd been working from was believed to have been identified using their satellite phone signals.

The attack lasted so long that I was hours late with my security check-in with the *Herald*'s foreign desk. I knew my partner back in Jerusalem would be frantic. The crisis passed and I let people know we were safe. But then the news came. One of Abed's cousins in the house just metres away had been shot through the head by a sniper as he sat on the front porch. He was deaf, and he'd been hit before he'd even felt the thudding pulse of the chopper blades above him.

He was rushed to the makeshift hospital in Salma, his family holding out hope he'd be sent into Turkey, to more sophisticated medical facilities and life-saving care, along the same route we took to enter Syria.

But he could not be saved. Another young life lost. By 2022, upwards of 400,000 have been killed in the eleven years of this conflict.

The funeral had to be before sunset. That's when the tanks shell in earnest, and nothing is off limits. Not the home of elderly farmers, and not a ceremony for the dead, either. As soon as the young man's body arrived in the village, there was a dash for the cemetery. A grave had already been dug. Friends and family crowded around his body as it lay on the tray of a pick-up truck, a single bullet through his brow, one eye purple and swollen shut from the impact. The sorrow was overwhelming: one man laid his hand on the body, others rested their hands on each other, and the boom of the shelling grew closer and closer.

Suddenly it was time. He was lowered into the ground, while men quietly wept. Then we rushed to motorcycles parked nearby to head back to the village, where we waited out another bombardment.

The curtains were drawn at Abed's house and those relatives still in Syria came to mourn. It was only the second year of the battle against the regime and already people had lost so much. This tiny village in the mountains was just a microcosm of the bigger war. Abed told me it was hard to grieve without his wife, his aunts, his sisters. Without women, the heartbreak just didn't seem real, he said.

I too missed women around me. Their absence from this village was palpable. I missed the perspective they gave, their assessment of the conflict, their humour, their affection, their biting sarcasm. As a female reporter – a sahafiya – I had grown used to having access to people and areas that were off limits to my male colleagues. I could ask questions men could not and see a slice of life that was always out of bounds for them. It provided a depth to my stories, and to my understanding of the region, and I had come to rely on these moments of truth to guide me through the unfamiliar terrain of the Arab revolutions.

As darkness arrived, we could not light candles. The faintest sign of life could bring danger. So there was just quiet talking and mourning as the Ramadan fast was broken. We were scared, but we slept – as mad as that sounds.

The attack had spooked us. We discussed leaving Syria the next day, but there were rumours of an imminent prisoner exchange. We decided to stay.

It's always a risk to extend a trip. I already felt, and Fadi and José agreed, that we were sitting ducks in this village: the only news crew in the area in a house already targeted by the regime. But we balanced that against the risk of the journey out. Might it be safer if we waited another day to see if the shelling was less intense? Our host, Abed, was also worried about travelling and was still coming to terms with the loss his family had just suffered.

Another day also meant more time to meet the rebel commanders and their brigade members who had left their day jobs to join the armed resistance. These meetings always involved a giant leap of faith. Even though this was several months before the rash of journalist kidnappings, including James Foley, John Cantlie, Theo Padnos and others – and Foley's horrific televised murder that presaged the Islamic State's assault on Syria and Iraq – such meetings were still tense and dangerous. They were even more so for local reporters trying to cover the war in their own country and raise their voices above the din of the Western media's interpretation of the conflict.

We met two rebel battalions. One group was close to Abed. Their senior officers drove us from village to village and made sure we arrived safely back home, often with a helmet full of fruit from Abed's trees. They took us to their training ground, where young men with mostly ancient weapons – including an extraordinary 1963 Dragunov sniper rifle that was almost taller than the fighter who was handling it – talked tactics and learned to fight.

The next group was a little messier. Led by a volatile man known as Abu Haytham, the East Coast Brigade held a handful of prisoners in a dark room under a mosque and were keen to trade them. Emotional and cocky, Abu Haytham was a man on a mission – and that put every-one in his orbit at risk. So, when he invited our little team to break the fast with him at his family home higher up the mountain, we agreed, but with some trepidation.

We wound our way up into the hills. For me, thoughts of delicious Levantine food and the threat of Syrian tank fire were battling it out in my mind. The journey took us to a beautiful setting among the wooded peaks and into a compound that was full of the remnants of war collected by Abu Haytham. As it got darker, he lifted the spent mortar shells above his head, like they were some kind of trophy. Missiles from Assad that had not yet killed him.

A feast followed, prepared by the fierce women in his family who had remained in the village to fuel the anti-Assad resistance. It was an uncomfortable meal. Abu Haytham's brigade seemed unhappy we were there, while he became more and more swaggering. We ate and bade them farewell, worried about the time and the journey home.

Again, we were on the road in the darkness, which is never ideal when it comes to staying safe in a conflict zone. As we slowly wound our way down the mountain, the headlights cut to avoid detection, our car slammed into the back of a water tanker parked on the shoulder. We were stunned. Terrified. We quietly got out and, in the dark, assessed the damage.

Everyone was keen to get back on the road. After some half-hearted tugging at the metal that had collapsed in onto the left-hand tyre, we attempted to drive on. But the damage was too great. The driver couldn't control the steering. We were forced to pull off the road and look again. With the dim light of an old Nokia phone, he checked the tyre.

At that moment, a Syrian army tank fired at us. Fadi, José and I were squeezed into the back seat of the small sedan. We leapt out the right side door and dived for cover. The shell slammed into the earth just in front of us. My mind was blank with fear. I tried to hold Fadi's hand. We piled back in and the driver launched into gear. He battled to keep the car on the road as we headed into Salma. We couldn't believe we were alive.

I still needed to file. Looking back, I know I shouldn't have worried.

We made it to a house that was operating as a communication centre in Salma and I managed to get a story through to the *Herald*. By then it was late and Abed decided it was too dangerous to go back to his village. We were going to try to make it to the house commandeered by the FSA, less than 200 metres away. The shelling was intensifying, as was the gunfire. We had to run for it.

I had a backpack full of computer equipment, a flak jacket and a helmet, all of which weighed around eight to ten kilos and made it difficult to move quickly. We crouched down next to a waist-height fence and headed as fast as we could towards the FSA house. Syrian army snipers were in the hills less than a kilometre away. They shot at us as we ran through the darkness and eventually made it to safety.

It was just the beginning of a very long night. The lieutenant-colonel, Abu Ahmad, ushered us inside and we joined his battalion sitting on the floor below the windows to avoid the sniper fire and shelling, which was shaking the bungalow at its foundations. That I was the only woman in a house full of male soldiers was clearly playing on Ahmad's mind. He had asked one of his guys to clean the toilet before I used it and then kicked a handful of tired young men out of a bedroom to give me some privacy.

I was too on edge to sleep. The shelling from Assad's forces was relentless. One of the medics at the makeshift hospital we had visited the day before was badly wounded right outside the house as he tried to make it inside. He was rushed across the border into Turkey, a gaping wound in his stomach draining away his lifeblood.

I moved to the doorway of the room taken by Fadi and José. We talked quietly through the fear.

Dawn broke, and as the sun rose, the shelling slowly came to an end. The queue for bread and bullets formed again outside the FSA house and battalion leaders arrived with news of the injured and dead. The crater on the road outside and damaged balconies showed just how close the war had come.

Fed up with the sporadic supply of weapons and critical shortages – every drop of fuel had to be smuggled in from Turkey, and wheat for bread flour was scarce – many fighters would eventually turn to the better-funded, more radical brigades. Some ultimately joined Islamic State. Others, like Abu Haytham, were severely injured in the fighting. He was blinded in an attack, I later learned.

Back in Salma, the prisoner swap he'd promised failed to materialise. By now, Abed was keen to get back to his family in Yayladağı, and after that harrowing night we were ready to leave too. This time we would be travelling in daylight, which would leave us vulnerable to tank fire as we wound our way around the mountain back to the Turkish border. José and I squeezed into the front seat of a small delivery truck and Fadi and Abed sat on the flat-bed tray behind us, wearing our flak jackets and helmets, a couple of FSA soldiers armed with AK–47s beside them.

I look at a photo I took of the two of them, grinning from ear to ear, and I feel their high spirits in my heart. Fear, tiredness and relief was making us all a little crazy. I look at a photo Fadi took of me as we waited beside the vehicle that would take us to safety. I was also smiling. Yet now, all I can see are my mistakes. My heavy-framed glasses and large men's watch would have been a giveaway to any border guard paying the slightest attention, even with a properly tied Syrian headscarf.

At some point close to the border, we stopped and called Abed's contacts to make sure they'd be at the meeting point in their car on the other side as planned. Then we started the difficult hike up the mountain and back into Turkey.

It was still Ramadan; everyone was fasting and it had been a long time since we'd had any food. We only had a little water and it was a baking hot mid-summer afternoon. In those short few days, Turkey had hardened its stance on the border and we had to find a way to cross undetected. We were so close to the Turkish border post we could hear the soldiers speaking. I was terrified my breathing – heavy and noisy from climbing up and down the rocky path carrying my gear – would give us away.

Just when I thought I would have to rest, we emerged out of the trees and onto the small farm that we'd been given permission to cross, what felt like a lifetime ago. We said goodbye to Abed and his cousins.

Since then, I have devoted days to trying to track him down. Several return trips to Yayladağı led nowhere. He was passionate about the Free Syrian Army's aims, he wanted Assad out and dreamt of a Syria that wasn't divided along religious lines, where his children would have the same opportunities as those of other sects. Did he give up on it all and join the 6.8 million Syrians who left their country, looking for safety and a better life? Or was his family part of the 6.7 million displaced within Syria? Maybe his ambitions hardened with all the losses he'd sustained. Maybe a more radical group won him over. I have changed Abed's name and concealed his village to protect his family.

IT'S HARD TO know just how to recover from a reporting trip like the one we'd just had. Fadi and I were sharing a room in a cheap hotel in Antakya – a gorgeous small city in Turkey's Hatay Province with a beautiful old quarter that became a hub for reporters covering Syria and the flow of refugees across the border. It was time for long showers, a big meal and beer.

We were exhausted, but the adrenaline was still pumping and there was more to do. Why would we even consider going back to Syria after the near misses of the past few days? It was our job to report on the conflict, to document the abuses and mark some of the losses. I was working on a story on prisoners of war and we knew there was a large makeshift FSA jail we could access in the town of Marea.

Fadi and I mapped out a plan, then slept. We headed for Aleppo the next day.

Ruth Pollard is an award-winning multimedia journalist based in New Delhi, where she covers politics, defence and international security across South and South-East Asia for Bloomberg. She moved to India in 2016 after specialising in conflict reporting across the Middle East and North Africa, where she focused on those affected by war and repression in Syria, Libya, Egypt, Lebanon, Turkey, Tunisia and Jordan, as well as the Israel–Palestine conflict and the refugee crisis that stretched into Europe and beyond. From 2011 to 2015 she was Middle East correspondent for *The Sydney Morning Herald* and *The Age*.

13
HOPE RESTORED IN A SYRIAN OASIS

Yaara Bou Melhem
Syria 2019
SBS, ABC

With the crew, Syria.

I REMEMBER THE exact moment my disillusionment with war report-ing from Syria began. I was lying on the side of a hill, covering my ears with my hands and watching Free Syrian Army rebels fire off homemade rockets. I had spent a gruelling day with a ragtag outfit of villagers-turned-fighters, travelling the Idlib countryside, crawling through the tunnels they used to evade Assad regime forces and visiting a bomb-making depot after being smuggled into northern Syria from Turkey overnight.

I was there as a video-journalist for SBS TV's *Dateline*, so it was just me, a camera, and a very tall ginger-bearded former Special Air Service (SAS) Afghanistan war veteran with the signature hollowed-out eyes of someone who had seen – or done – too much. He was there as security. But whenever someone asked, I called him my 'producer' and followed up with a knowing smile and a wink. It became a running joke with the rebels, who kept asking if my 'producer' carried a gun or what hobbies my 'producer' had. He warmed to the fellas as they had a go at whoever's bright idea it was to use such a ridiculous cover. The rebels, anxious at first, started to relax around him. I was glad he didn't become a problem, as security contractors sometimes do, by sticking out too much or needing to validate their exorbitant fees by war-gaming every scenario to the point where you can't do your work as a journalist.

It was nearing dusk by the time the rebels decided to test their makeshift rockets, and we were all exhausted. The leader of the group, Bilal Al Khabir, was a Syrian army deserter. He would've been about the same age as me, late twenties or a little older, and was generous with his time – and protection.

It was mid-2012, around about the same time that aid workers and journalists including James Foley and Steven Sotloff were being picked up and traded, until they eventually landed with a group that wouldn't sell them on – the group that later became known as the Islamic State of Iraq and Syria, or ISIS. After being held for years, Foley and Sotloff would be beheaded in 2014, within a month of each other. I remember filming with the rebel unit in the countryside when a pick-up truck pulled up. Two men who didn't look or sound Syrian started asking who I was. I knew something was wrong when half a dozen or so of the rebels I was with closed ranks around me, shielding me from the men's view. Al Khabir greeted the men, said, 'She's with us,' and told them to leave. When I asked who they were, the rebels said 'foreigners' with a degree of finality, indicating I should leave it at that. They were nervous. I quickly wrapped up filming so we could move on.

Now, Al Khabir, having been a gracious guide, felt comfortable enough to start asking me questions as his men fired off the rockets. Lying back against the grass, with a cigarette in one hand, he looked back at me. 'Ya, Yaara,' he said, in an almost defeated voice and using a term that is reserved for the familiar, 'When the world sees this, will they come and help us? Will your film help us?'

I had been asked questions like this many times before by people who were revealing their traumas, reliving their horror stories, putting themselves at risk and wanting to know whether it would be worth it. I always had the same tried and true response. All I could do was document what was happening, I would say, I don't know if my film will change anything. Promising otherwise would be disingenuous. But this time my answer rang more hollow than usual. The stakes seemed so high.

Syria is an incredible country that I could never tire of visiting. Steeped in history, its people are some of the warmest I have come across in the Middle East. But the ruling Assad regime had a history of brutality, the full horrors of which hadn't yet been revealed. It would get much worse as the war dragged on, with whole cities levelled, the use of chemical weapons and barrel bombs. A year or two earlier, I had filmed with democracy activists and documented the cases of political prisoners who ranged from human rights lawyers to eighteen-year-old bloggers. So I had a sense of what was coming.

But Western nations and their populations seemed accustomed to the idea of a violent Middle East (an image that academic Edward Said argued in his landmark book *Orientalism* was created by Western writers and artists in the nineteenth century as part of a strategy to justify European imperialism in the region) and were especially desensitised after the US-led wars in Iraq and Afghanistan. There would be tut-tuts and rhetoric about not crossing red lines that kept shifting further and further away. Fatigue would eventually set in, and the Syrian war would slide from prominence on the nightly news and then disappear altogether, as it has as I write this now, even though the war rages on.

I knew nobody was coming to help Bilal Al Khabir and his friends. And so it was there, on that hillside, that disillusionment about the impact of my reporting in Syria, or lack thereof, took hold and couldn't be shaken off. I wouldn't return to Syria for the better part of a decade.

IT WAS A radical democratic experiment in the former badlands of Islamic State territory that brought me back.

Of course, there was the obligatory trip to the frontline. The Syrian Democratic Forces, or SDF, backed by a US-led coalition, was nearing the end of its territorial campaign against ISIS. The militant group had once ruled over an area in Iraq and Syria the size of Britain and enforced strict Islamic rule that was so brutal it was even disowned by al-Qaeda. In early 2019, just a sliver of land remained under the group's control in the village of Baghuz in the Deir ez-Zor region. But there was so much more to document.

A little-known authority had formed, the Autonomous Administration of North and East Syria, and it ruled roughly one-quarter of the country. The dull name belied a set of principles that could challenge those of many Western countries. This Kurdish-led initiative in northern Syria was a secular, ethnically inclusive yet fragile state where women and men enjoyed equal representation in all levels of governance. It wasn't recognised internationally but on the ground it functioned as would any other state, from leading large-scale reconstruction efforts including the opening of schools and hospitals, to the bureaucratic work of registering births, deaths and marriages.

Rising in now-liberated ISIS territory, once one of the most brutalised places on earth, it had even introduced civil marriage, allowing people from different religious groups to legally marry. It may seem like a small detail, but it was radical in a region where sectarianism and tribalism dominate.

The idea of filming a wedding during conflict and showing female leaders emerging from a region where women were sold as sex slaves, subjugated or just plain invisible only a couple of years ago was too tempting. I wanted to capture it in a half-hour report for *Foreign Correspondent* on ABC TV. So when I made my way back there in 2019, I hoped tracking these contradictions would introduce a bit more humanity in my reporting of what seemed like an intractable conflict.

The person I thought represented the contradictions in the region more than any other was a young woman named Leila Mustapha. I sought her out in Raqqa, the notorious former capital of ISIS. It was here, in 2014, that the group raised its black flag and soon declared its caliphate.

When Leila ushered me into her office, I couldn't help doing a double take. Almost anywhere else the skinny-jeaned, leather bomber jacket-wearing thirty-year-old wouldn't have drawn a second look. But just a couple of years ago, women here were confined to the house, had all but disappeared from public life, and when they did emerge, it was in full covering, with a male guardian. And yet Leila was the city's new mayor.

She stood by the window and occasionally tipped the ash from a cigarette into a glass dish on the windowsill. 'Give me a minute to finish my cigarette; just don't film me smoking,' she said as she flipped back loose hair that had come out of a slicked-back messy bun.

While I wouldn't ordinarily film someone smoking, Raqqa's female Civil Council leader puffing away in her office would've been a simple way to show how far the city had come since it pushed ISIS out two years earlier. Smoking had been banned under ISIS, its treatment of women was atrocious, and you rarely saw female faces, let alone hair. For a moment, I questioned whether the scarf I had loosely wrapped around my head was necessary, but thought it best to keep it on. Raqqa was the only city in Syria I thought still called for it.

Someone brought in an Arabic coffee pot and poured thick coffee into a fenjan, a small cup with no handle. In between sips of coffee and some sweets, Leila told me she was born and raised in Raqqa but had fled during ISIS's reign. A Syrian Kurd, she had returned to the largely levelled city to guide it back to what it once was and more. At the forefront of that was the reconstruction effort and I was keen to start touring the city with the former civil engineer. We only had a few hours of winter sunlight left for filming and, for security reasons, had to leave Raqqa before it got dark.

Our Kurdish security team was more skittish here than on the frontline. There, they knew what the threat was and where it was coming from. Here, in Raqqa, as we mingled with a civilian population, we were exposed and it was hard to discern friend from foe. The city may have pushed ISIS out, but the extremist group had morphed into an underground network and still posed threats – especially to people like Leila.

'A number of colleagues, a number of people who were close to me, members of the Raqqa Civil Council, have been subject to attacks, assassinations,' she said. 'We're expected to take precautions, but these precautions don't prevent us from our work.'

We decided to take our own vehicles rather than the municipality vehicles on our tour of the city's reconstruction efforts. Leila directed us first to Al-Naim Square. The centre of a roundabout in the heart of the city, it had been the site of ISIS's grisly public beheadings and crucifixions. The spikes of its metal fences were used by executioners to impale heads. It was the stuff of nightmares, and many locals tried to avoid the area and kept their children at home. It was no wonder, she told me, that people here called it the 'roundabout of hell'.

Construction works were beginning, with arched columns built around a new central fountain. There were also plans to install multicoloured laser lights to turn the square into a central meeting point for families and couples alike and provide a refuge from the dull and lacklustre concrete sprawl of the city. 'We have construction work to decorate the Naim roundabout to remove the psychological effect it had on people,' Leila said, adding she hoped the cosmetic renovations to the roundabout would help erase its grim past.

Other reconstruction projects underway across the city saw her put her civil engineering skills to good use. One of the biggest involved rebuilding the main bridge over the Euphrates River, which linked the city to the countryside. Construction workers were on a break when we arrived, and boats were ferrying goods and people from one side to the other. Leila jumped out of the car and made a beeline for the male workers. We raced behind her to film as she began to greet them. Unbelievably, at least to me, she shook their hands.

I asked her how big a cultural shift must have taken place if these men were willing to shake hands with a woman and recognise a woman occupying the highest public office in the city. She smiled and waved her hand dismissively. But she understood the significance of such small, incremental acts.

'After the liberation, people were a bit afraid; should we shake hands or not? Is it okay or not okay?' she said. 'There was some hesitation. But now it is more relaxed. People greet each other normally.'

Leila has since been awarded the 2021 World Mayor Jury Prize for her work in Raqqa. Presenting her with the accolade, judges said she was 'the one consistent and significant figure in Raqqa's rebuilding and revival since 2017', which included the reclamation of Al-Naim Square, the restoration of electricity and water supplies, the rebuilding of hospitals, schools, homes and street markets. They were also impressed by her ability to transcend and work across 'complex traditional, tribal, cultural and religious boundaries' to achieve what they called the 'city's rebirth'.

It was a fitting tribute. Before I left Syria, Leila invited me for tea at her house.

'This area was occupied by too many armed groups, the Free Syrian Army, Jabhat al Nusra, ISIS. There was a lot of suffering. People were tired,' she told me. 'As much as they suffered, the people of Raqqa had a chance to remove this terrible situation. The administration that we created in the north-east came from the grassroots and we need to respect what the people need and want.'

In Leila's home I had a sense of how, in a place tested by disillusion-ment, she was determined to restore a sense of community – and humanity – that had been thought lost.

Yaara Bou Melhem is a Walkley-award winning journalist and documen-tary filmmaker. Yaara's recent documentary feature *Unseen Skies* (2020) interrogates the dangers of unfettered artificial intelligence use and mass surveillance. Previously, Yaara was one of the few Australian journalists based in the Middle East covering the Arab uprisings. She was an inaugural journalist-in-residence at the Judith Neilson Institute for Journalism and Ideas in 2021.

14
RANIA ABOUZEID: THE TASTE OF FIRE AND SMOKE

Beirut 1999–present
Freelance
by Trevor Watson

On the troubled streets of Beirut 2008.

'HOW DO I write about what they did to you, Beirut? About what they did to us? I'm supposed to have the words. I'm a writer and an international journalist, familiar with telling stories that are difficult, complicated and often about violence, but my fingers are frozen by the fear of failing you. You, the Lebanese capital, my beautiful, chaotically vibrant city by the Mediterranean Sea.'

Rania Abouzeid may have been lost for words, but the opening paragraph of her August 2020 *National Geographic* article speaks volumes about her passion for Beirut, the heartbreak she felt at its destruction and her love for its people.

'Why must every Lebanese generation endure violent chaos – and its aftermath?' chronicles Lebanon's suffering inflicted by decades of religious and political conflict, foreign intervention, political corruption and incompetence, economic collapse, 'cruel poverty', COVID and the 'horror' of the 2020 explosion which ripped Beirut apart. 'People are still unaccounted for under the rubble. Their families are waiting for them. Body parts gathered from various locations are still being identified,' she wrote. 'At a time when we can't even console each other with hugs and physical connection. How many disasters can Lebanese endure simultaneously, and why must we?'

The *National Geographic* piece ultimately becomes very personal. In it Abouzeid writes of her Lebanese heritage, family members who migrated to Australia via New Zealand (where she was born) and of those who remained in Beirut. During the civil war in the 1980s, she says, they 'cowered in basement shelters to avoid the shelling above'.

Rania Abouzeid is today a world-renowned journalist, author and filmmaker. Over the past twenty years, she has covered the Middle East for a veritable who's who of news media – *Time*, *The New Yorker*, *Foreign Affairs*, *The Atlantic*, *The New York Times Magazine*, *National Geographic*, *Foreign Policy*, *Politico*, *The Guardian*, the *Los Angeles Times*, *The Australian*, *The Christian Science Monitor* and the list goes on. She has also made regular appearances as an analyst and commentator on the world's leading radio and television outlets. In the vernacular of Australian journalism, she is a heavy hitter.

'I know the history of the Middle East region,' Abouzeid says. 'I know how it impacts current events and how social and cultural conditions shape today's news.' Nowhere was her insight into the forces and people shaping the Middle East more apparent than in her coverage of the recent conflicts in Syria and Iraq. 'Syria was the most dangerous place in the world to operate as a journalist,' she says. 'I was smuggled across borders so many times that I lost count, moving with families and fighters including Al-Qaeda. Being the only woman on the frontlines, there were challenges and dangers.'

In 2012, Abouzeid became the first journalist to interview a fighter as well as a well-placed leader of the shadowy Al-Qaeda–linked group Jabhat al-Nusra just weeks after it was designated a terrorist organisation by the United States. In a multi-award-winning 2014 article for the US magazine *Politico*, she explained how Al-Qaeda managed to gain a foothold in the Syrian conflict, and the inter-Jihadi dispute that gave rise to ISIS.

'The eight men, beards trimmed, explosive belts fastened, pistols and grenades concealed in their clothing, waited until nightfall before stealing across the flat, porous Iraqi border,' her article began. 'They navigated the berms and trenches along the frontier, traversing two-way smuggling routes used to ferry cigarettes, livestock, weapons – and jihadis – to enter the north-eastern Syrian province of Hasaka. It was August 2011, the Muslim holy month of Ramadan, and Syria was five months into a still largely peaceful uprising against President Bashar al-Assad.

'Their leader was a Syrian emissary from the al-Qaeda affiliate forged in the bloody conflict next door. He called himself Abu Mohammad al-Golani … His mission was nothing less than to bring down the Assad regime and establish an Islamic state in its place. No-one knew it at the time, but that trip across the border would turn out to be a crucial turning point in the Syrian civil war.' The US State Department would name him a Specially Designated Global Terrorist and place a US$10 million bounty on his head.

Abouzeid's two books focus on Syria. *No Turning Back: Life, Loss, and Hope in Wartime Syria* is the story of four young people seeking safety and freedom in a shattered country, while untangling and exposing the backroom dealings that fuelled the conflict. The young adult novel *Sisters of the War* tells of four young girls growing up in a world of 'arrests, killings, demolished homes, and further atrocities most adults could not even imagine'.

Rania Abouzeid maintains a strong connection to Australia, returning regularly to visit family. Her work has taken her from North Africa to South Asia and beyond. She says that her dual identity is core to her journalism. 'I am Eastern (by blood) and Western (by upbringing) and move seamlessly within and between both worlds, translating one for the other,' she says. Her childhood trips to war-torn Lebanon also taught her 'that a story is often more nuanced, more colourful, more complicated, and more personal than some reports suggest, and that you have to be on the ground to know that. It was a childhood lesson that guides my work.'

There's a song she remembers from those trips, 'For Beirut', by Fairouz, the 'soul of Lebanon' and one of the Arab world's most famous singers. It was also replayed in the days following the devastating Beirut explosion in August 2020. 'From my heart a greeting of peace to Beirut,' go the lyrics. 'She is wine from the spirit of the people, she is bread and jasmine from their sweat, so how did she come to taste of fire and smoke?'

15
THE HAMAS LONELY HEARTS CLUB OF GAZA

Diaa Hadid
Gaza 2009
AP

Gaza under Israel's blockade.

I T WAS A blue-sky morning on the balcony of the Associated Press bureau in Gaza, where I lived for most of 2009, my commute being a walk down a marble staircase from the penthouse apartment assigned to reporters, to the office below. We lived behind a bulletproof metal door that had a 'no guns' sign slapped on it.

We looked over most of the Gaza Strip, which isn't that much to begin with, an area just a little over 50 kilometres long and 11 kilometres wide. To the west of us was the main shopping drag, and the clump of pines in the Unknown Soldier Park, where students snacked under trees, lovers locked eyes and the lonely watched on. Beyond was the shining blue Mediterranean with its cooling, salty waves. It was the only outlet for most Palestinian men in the crowded, largely hemmed-in territory.

Gaza was then blockaded to varying degrees by neighbouring Israel and Egypt, and had been since the militant group Hamas seized power in mid-2007. That was after their Fatah rivals refused to hand over power after losing an election. Day by day, the blockade was deepening poverty and unravelling the lives of Palestinians, most denied the chance to work or study abroad, to trade or travel.

It was different for women though, harder. When they bathed in the sea, and they so rarely bathed, they submerged fully clothed, hijab, long robe and all. It always felt like a slap to see the odd female form in the water, trying to embrace a quick pleasure while constrained by the culture around her. A Palestinian woman's access to the sea was shorthand to me for her life in Gaza: not only did she bear the same burdens as men but she lived in a conservative tradition that repressed her even further.

And so it was for love, marriage and finding a match, over which Palestinian women had little control, even though they often faced social exclusion and derision if they stayed single.

That was what my colleague Ibrahim Barzak and I were contemplating that day on the balcony of the AP bureau. The chief Gaza reporter, Ibrahim was pointing out a neighbouring high rise. There, he said with a rare grin, was a great story: 'Hamas is running a matchmaking bureau. Why don't you do the story?'

Ibrahim was a stern and largely unsmiling man, which was unusual in Gaza, where Palestinians pride themselves on the black humour that gets them through the dark days. He was also deeply principled: his home had been smashed several times by Israeli rockets over the years, and yet his commitment to journalistic objectivity was unfailing.

He was keen on Palestinian politics and had great security sources. That made us a pretty good team, because I had little interest in those kinds of stories. He generously batted the weird stuff my way. I wanted to cover Palestinian life: the wonderful and sad ways that people found meaning, or just survived, in Gaza. While that might make sense to a civilian, within the circles I moved about in, it ensured that I was seen as a bit fluffy, a bit stupid. A typical female journo interested in typical female things.

It did not help that I was a single woman with what most Palestinians thought was an attractive accent in Arabic: a Lebanese-Australian drawl peppered with the salty takedowns of a Beiruti taxi driver stuck behind a slow-moving tourist's SUV. It did not help that I smoked, nor that I had a reputation for liking a party. I worried what my desire to do the Hamas matchmakers story would say about me, but I was going to do it anyway.

The story jarred with Hamas's well-deserved reputation as a militant group dominated by stern, bearded men. But it reflected the way that Palestinians also knew Hamas: a group that was in lock step with them from the cradle to the grave. They ran summer camps for boys where the graduation ceremony included jumping through flaming hoops of fire. They undertook medical clinics that diagnosed ear infections in children. They covered the cost of funerals for Hamas-loyal families, paying for the traditional mourning tent set up in alleyways and providing the dates proffered as a snack for guests. They found jobs for young men in the movement's police force, bureaucracy and ever-growing media wing. It was all laced with the group's staid conservatism, violent propaganda and actual violence. But in a place with little outlet for hope or prosperity, Hamas paid attention to people.

But a matchmakers' bureau? A lonely hearts club? It even made me laugh, and I had been living in Gaza long enough by then: some three years, on and off.

I wriggled my way into Gaza through the weirdest of luck. I had blagged my way into a job with the AP in Jerusalem after the bureau chief offered a Jerusalem correspondent position to my dear friend, Zainab Fattah, a Lebanese-Panamanian-American. We were both living in Dubai, where we worked for rival newspapers during the day and hung out together most evenings. When she declined the job ('My mother doesn't want me to go to Jerusalem, sorry'), I called the bureau chief, Steve Gutkin, and told him I'd be a better fit. After a 'test' to see how well I spoke Arabic – a quick chat on the phone with an uninterested producer – I was hired, and made my way to Jerusalem weeks later.

The day before I started on 25 June 2006, Hamas-backed militants captured a young Israeli soldier, Gilad Shalit, in a cross-border raid. As I walked into the Jerusalem office for my first day on the job, barely a reporter looked up to say hello as they furiously clacked on keyboards and chatted on phones wedged between their ears and their shoulders.

'Why don't you go to Gaza for a few days?' was nearly the opening sentence from an editor. Well, I did, and days turned into weeks.

My first job as a foreign correspondent was covering an Israeli operation against Palestinian militants in Gaza in a failed effort to rescue Shalit. I was handed a flak jacket so large that the weight of it pinned me to the ground when I fell over. I learned how to count bodies in morgues. I discovered through countless interviews with grieving families how Palestinians often described teenage boys as slain fighters and martyrs, even if they were just civilian onlookers, because they wanted the mothers to find some meaning in their sons' deaths.

I ended up more or less living in Gaza for the next few years. While I was ostensibly meant to 'swap out' with other reporters who wanted to work on their own stories, my stay there coincided with a spate of kidnappings of foreigners. The kidnappers were goons connected to a family of Gazan toughs, who demanded ransoms of tens of thousands of dollars and threatened their captives with death. Chief among those kidnapped was the BBC's Alan Johnston, taken in March 2007, who was the only foreign correspondent living in Gaza full-time.

For a while, the kidnappings emptied Gaza of foreigners. I was technically a foreigner, an Australian with a distinct bogan inflection. But I wasn't white and nobody around me saw me as foreign. For Palestinians, I was a Lebanese woman. I was part of the Levantine family.

Most white people I met in Gaza also presumed I was Palestinian, perhaps a fixer or a translator for a Western office. That's how unusual it was, just over a decade ago, for a person of Arab origin to work as a foreign correspondent, even in the Middle East – perhaps especially in the Middle East. The narrative I was offered by several well-meaning editors and reporters was that an Arab couldn't be objective about their own conflict, as if Westerners did not also walk the world with their own subjective experiences and cultural biases that they had to confront and challenge.

But there we were, and the unironic consensus in the bureau was that the kidnappers wouldn't see me as a high-value target. That explains why I passed kidnappers on the stairs to the old AP bureau one day, without them even noticing me.

All this is to say I was pretty familiar with Gaza's quirks after three years of living for large chunks of time in the territory. There was the trade in the synthetic opioid tramadol, for instance, which was roaring in 2009. The drug's haziness tuned out the nightmare of being young and stuck in Gaza. But young men told me it was more valued because it delayed ejaculation, in a society where so many of them feared sexual inadequacy and impotency.

Then there was the way men dominated the lady's underwear trade. In the bazaar in east Gaza, they'd hang up their wares of lurid, frilly nylon bras, sometimes with holes cut out for the nipples, with matching undies of netting and string. One young man explained to me that they hung up these fantastical outfits so women could demurely point at the one they wanted. 'How do you figure out their size?' I asked him. 'Oh, we know,' he said, giving me the once over.

So a quick phone call to check on the matchmakers' bureau: no, this was not a mass-wedding charity, of which there were a few in Gaza, established to help the poor marry without taking on enormous debt. Most of those mass weddings were a sight: tens of women in near-identical fluffy white gowns and matching hijabs, alongside a row of suited men, with cakes and endless photo-ops.

Hamas had its own mass-wedding charities, including one that specialised in helping disabled Gazans. I had recently seen a mass engagement party for blind Palestinian men, where the entertainment included a guy dancing in a monkey suit. Little girls in wedding dresses sang for the crowd from a stage alongside the grooms, leading to some confusion about whether Hamas was marrying off the children. But no, the real brides were in the crowd, many of them wearing face veils and swathed in long black cloaks, because the Hamas organisers did not approve of the genders mixing, even at their own engagement party.

So here in Gaza, on that sunny day, I wanted to understand why the militant group saw fit to open a matchmaking office. What need were they responding to? Was it how they perceived their responsibility as the territory's rulers, because young men and women had long been cut off from traditional marriage avenues in neighbouring Egypt and Israel? Was it a response to the growing numbers of young men being killed in clashes with Israeli forces? Who even did the matchmaking?

Traditionally, matchmaking in Gaza is a blood sport dominated by Palestinian mothers and older sisters. They coolly rake segregated weddings for potential brides for their sons and brothers. They check in with their neighbours over gossipy rounds of tea. The mothers muscle in to have first pick of the pretty female cousins – yes, cousin marriages are not only accepted in Gaza but are fairly common. It was a way of locking in marriage deals from a fairly young age, like, 'Sister, let's keep your Fatima for my Ahmed; and how about your Hafsa for my Mohammad?' and so on. These women had fabulously sharp elbows and, in my experience, far more personality than their dull, entitled sons, who entirely leaned on their mothers to lock in a lady for them.

The AP driver, Ismail, and I headed to the matchmakers' bureau – officially called the Tayseer Association for Marriage and Development. There we found young men with short, scruffy beards, open-neck shirts and sandals – almost a uniform for Hamas bureaucrats – gathered in one room, flipping through a binder of male applicants.

In another room, two young women in neat headscarves and long robes sat gossiping. One of them seemed pretty keen to chat about her own fiancé, who seemed to be a well-off, older academic. The other young woman appeared to be a natural matchmaker: twenty-one-year-old Nisrine Khalil. She said most women were shy when they first came in, because of the stigma associated with using a matchmaker to find a partner.

'I tell the girls, be like Khadija!' Nisrine told me energetically, referring to the Prophet Muhammad's first wife. Muslim tradition says Khadija proposed to the Prophet Muhammad and was years his senior. It was a powerful message to Palestinian women: if Islam's first lady bucked conservative Arab tradition more than 1400 years ago, then they could defy Gazan stigma now.

And there, defying Gazan stigma somewhat unhappily, was Tahani.

She sat slightly apart, her honey-coloured eyes set off by a maroon headscarf. At twenty-nine years old, she was already considered a spinster, and her prospects were slim: she had dark skin in a society that prized whiteness. She didn't have a job, nor did she come from money, in a desperately poor society where marriage was one of the few ways to social mobility. She did not possess a lucrative foreign passport. But it was hard to kill hope.

'I gaze at all the men on the street and think, Oh God, isn't there just one for me?' she told me as we sat down for a chat over a cup of bright, sweet tea. Tahani asked me to use only her first name, because her family didn't know she was using a marriage service.

Tahani's mother died when she was young, and none of her relatives were helping her find a groom. She wasn't even a good enough catch to be lined up for a marriage to one of her cousins. So here she was. She told me she became more determined to find a husband after

Israel's three-week war on Hamas, which ended in January 2009. Israel's assault killed hundreds of Palestinians. Gaza's residents hunkered down in homes and shelters during the shelling, not knowing where bombs would fall next. She watched her brothers hold their wives when they were scared. 'I felt lonely,' Tahani said.

Tahani was one of 287 women who had applied to find a husband – I knew because I counted the applications that the young women laid out for me on a desk in their office. The photographs stapled to the files showed women in Muslim hijabs, or headscarves. Some wore make-up and smiled fetchingly. Others looked startled.

In their application, women were asked to describe their ideal man: most shied away from physical attributes. They asked for a devout Muslim with a job and his own flat, a top find in crowded Gaza, where living with one's mother-in-law is considered a hellish fate. Women also had to describe their appearance and answer a killer question: 'Do you consider yourself pretty according to Gaza standards?'

If the women were to respond frankly, looking at their images, the answer would be no. That wasn't because they were unattractive with their shades of olive skin and thickly lashed eyes, it was because the Gazan standard of beauty was a skinny white woman in a headscarf.

I knew that, because I was also allowed to flip through the men's application folders. Most men, when asked to describe their ideal woman, really did focus on a physical description. Nearly all applications asked for a woman who was tall, slender, fair-skinned, with green or blue eyes, and light-coloured hair. Oh, and she should wear a hijab. 'Converted Russians,' joked one of the men in the office.

Nisrine, the twenty-one-year-old matchmaker, said she encouraged men 'to be a bit more realistic'. She said if she saw a girl that appeared to match up, she'd call and say, 'Well, she's pretty, but she's dark.' Or 'She's short, but she's white.'

While the Hamas matchmaking bureau served both men and women, it was particularly important for women, because remaining single could be a cruel fate in Palestinian society. Some are treated with derision; others end up as unpaid maids serving their extended families. Gaza's deep poverty also skewed the market at both ends for women: the dwindling number of middle-class men with steady incomes could have their pick of women, while it appeared that some poor families were reluctant to marry off working daughters, hoping to keep their salaries.

The Hamas matchmakers' bureau had arranged about forty marriages since it had opened two years earlier. The applicants, who paid a fee of between US$10 and $70, were divided into categories according to their eligibility. Women under twenty-five were easiest to marry off. In the challenging categories: women over thirty and divorcees.

But in a nod to Gaza's escalating poverty triumphing over its conservative culture, there was a special section for women with jobs. The best of the best catches were those who worked with the United Nations Relief Works Agency, which ran schools and clinics. Those women had reliable, good salaries and pensions. They, Nisrine said, could be fat, divorced, old, widowed, it didn't matter; bringing home a good pay packet trumped all other categories.

A few dozen men every month turned to the bureau to find a wife. If the employees believed there was a match, they quietly organised a meeting, with employees acting as chaperones in compliance with Islamic law: unmarried men and women cannot spend time alone in each other's company. Nisrine told me if it was a match, Gaza's traditional courtship kicked in.

The man's relatives would visit the woman's family, saying that a well-meaning stranger told them of a girl wanting to marry – a polite fib that kept the girl's honour intact. She wasn't seen, for instance, on the street. The potential groom had not already sat in a cafe with the young woman. The matchmakers were not mentioned, because their role was taboo, Nisrine said. If the woman's family accepted, and celebratory Turkish coffee was passed around, a wedding was planned.

One of the bureau's success stories was twenty-nine-year-old Rania Hijazi, who, two months after completing an application form, was married to Ashraf Farahat, a thirty-six-year-old divorcee. She said her family's matchmaking efforts were going nowhere. 'I felt embarrassed when I applied,' said Hijazi. 'But then I said, "I won't find a man any other way," and I tried to be strong.'

I later met another young woman who found her match through the Hamas matchmakers' bureau. She didn't want to be named, and all that could be seen of her were her eyes, a serene brown. She wore a long black robe, headscarf and face veil. She was quiet, tiny and thin, nearly the opposite of her matched-up husband, a big, rotund blind man with a melodious voice. He made a living reading the Muslim holy book, the Qur'an, for a mobile phone company, which used his voice as a ringtone option.

I sat with her in their tiny living room, on a thin mattress, the kind that many Palestinians in Gaza placed on the floor to sit on, rather than furniture. 'Why,' I asked, 'did you marry a blind man? I don't mean to be rude.' And I really didn't mean to be rude. He seemed like a nice enough fellow. What I wanted was to get a sense of the priorities of a young Gazan woman, and where being able-bodied sat in that list. It was particularly important, I thought, in Gaza, where so many men were amputees.

I could see her smile under her face veil. 'He has his own apartment,' the young woman said. 'I don't have to endure a mother-in-law.'

These were the match-ups that the matchmakers' bureau wanted to showcase, and they were lovely.

But friends whispered there was a darker side: Hamas officials and loyalists used the bureau to find themselves second and third wives. To be fair, the Islamists weren't the only ones with a leery reputation in Gaza. But they pretended to be better.

The AP driver, Ismail, managed to find one of these men. He was a prosperous businessman, and he met us in his apartment. He was clear that this was not his main home: that was for his first wife and children. 'This apartment will be for my second wife,' he boasted, gesturing to the new furniture. 'She has a university degree.'

'How did you meet her?' I asked, sipping bitter Turkish coffee from a tiny cup.

'Through Tayseer. I asked my mother to help me pick a new wife, I asked my sisters,' he said. His eyes widened. 'They all refused to help me! My sisters said, "By God, if we help you find a second wife, we will end up as co-wives as well!"' He chuckled and shook his head, as if to say, women, am I right?

This was a trope of humour I had little patience for. I was raised by conservative parents, but like most decent Muslim men, my father could not hide his distaste for men who enjoyed polygamy. For him, it was a way of sheltering women in extreme situations, like war widows who would be vulnerable to poverty or rape if they remained single. It wasn't meant to be something you actively sought out. But my father certainly had friends who thought it was hilarious to trigger women by joking about marrying a second, third and fourth wife.

If as a young woman I was offended because polygamy jarred with my Muslim ideals and my feminism, as a reporter it made me deeply angry. That's because I came to see up close how ruinous it was for women and children, particularly when I interviewed Palestinian Bedouins in southern Israel who seemed to take multiple wives as a badge of prestige. I met women tossed away by feckless husbands because they had grown too old, too unattractive, or because they had not birthed sons. The jealousy, insecurity and competition between women and children for a father's attention was corrosive. In my father's northern Lebanese village, they even had a saying about two people who squabble endlessly: 'They act like co-wives.'

The businessman continued, complaining, 'But it's my right to marry another! The Hajjeh,' he said, referring to his first wife as a pilgrim to Mecca, but which was also slang for an old lady, '*mashallah*, praise God, she's a good lady, but you know, she's old now, she's busy with the children.'

We thanked him for his time and walked out the door.

After the matchmaking story ran on the Associated Press service, my phone ran hot for a day with reporters for major television networks wanting the phone number of the matchmakers' bureau. I remember male reporters laughing down the line, telling me what a cool story I had found. 'Of course, you would do a story like that,' said one of them.

It felt like a backhanded compliment, and it was: for years onwards, I did stories that were incredibly popular with readers and other reporters. A profile of a Gazan tunnel smuggler who had fallen on hard times and become a tea seller in the Unknown Soldier Park. The Iraqi women who defied death threats from militants in Baghdad to keep their hair salons operating. The murder mystery of a Hamas commander, who, we discovered, was killed because he was gay. They were stories that cast a spotlight on the Middle East in three-dimensional glory, whose heroes were flawed humans. I was proud of them. I also knew they made me a little bit fluffy.

As for the Hamas matchmakers' bureau: in a follow-up call, I was told that they were declining more media interviews. They were surprised by the whirlwind of attention and I think they felt misrepresented. I explained, as I would come to do many times over the next few years, that I had been fair and honest in my portrayal of their work. But they had read an Arabic summary of the article, which was often done by partisan Arab outlets, and I could not control how Arabic newspapers translated or mis-translated and skewed the story.

Like most people I spoke to in those days, I quickly lost touch with Tahani and Nisrine as life, and the news cycle, moved on. In early 2022, I tried to find evidence of the matchmakers' bureau online but found nothing. But to be fair, so much had changed in Gaza since I lived there over a decade ago, when I had been covering the territory battered by one three-week long war. By 2022, there had been three more major conflicts.

That building where the AP once rented a penthouse studio, and where we stood on the balcony and smoked and watched Gaza go by, was flattened in an Israeli strike in 2021. After the strike, an old friend who works as a television producer sent me an image. It was a dusty AP banner retrieved from the rubble of the building along with pictures of us Gaza hands reporting over the years. There was my colleague Hatem Moussa. In the image, he was young. It was taken before left-over ordnance being dismantled by Hamas workers in 2014 exploded as he filmed. It blew his legs off and killed our colleague, Simone Camille.

And there I was, in glasses and a knitted jumper that I wore over a knee-length dress and jeans, my reporting outfit to this day, look-ing out over the Gaza port. I'm sure I was reporting on a wave of foreign activists who were arriving in Gaza by boat to protest the Israeli blockade. But what I recall most of all is how I felt in that image. I remember the deep love I felt for Gaza, battered, quirky and heartfelt, an unlikely match wrought by the gods of journalism and the bureau of the Associated Press.

Diaa Hadid is an international correspondent for National Public Radio, covering Pakistan and Afghanistan. Previously she covered the Palestinian Territories as a correspondent for *The New York Times*, and was a Middle East correspondent for Associated Press, where she covered the fallout of the Arab Spring, the Israeli military occupation of Palestinian Territories, the Syrian war, and the rise of ISIS. She lives in Islamabad with her partner and two children.

16
KATE WEBB: A LIFE FROM
A GRAHAM GREENE NOVEL

Cambodia 1971
UPI, AFP
by Trevor Watson

'D O YOU REALISE you are a prisoner of war? One shot through the head could finish you, just like that.' The old man's young hostage was Kate Webb, an Australian-born Phnom Penh correspondent for the US newsagency United Press International (UPI). 'That's up to you now. I can do nothing about it. Besides, I don't consider myself a prisoner of war, I'm not a soldier,' Webb replied. 'Then consider yourself an invited guest,' responded the old man and everyone laughed.

It was April 1971. Cambodia had lost its neutrality; US bombers pounded Vietcong sanctuaries inside the country's eastern border; North Vietnamese regulars backed Pol Pot's infamous Khmer Rouge; and the area controlled by the Lon Nol regime contracted daily. Webb was travelling with Cambodian government forces on Kirirom Mountain when she and five other civilians were captured during a North Vietnamese army ambush. 'This turned out to be a lucky break, because the usual enemy were the brutal Cambodian Khmer Rouge, who invariably killed their prisoners,' her friend, veteran *Newsweek* correspondent Tony Clifton, later wrote in a 2007 obituary.

But her colleagues had assumed it was the Khmer Rouge, and that she was dead. 'Missing U.P.I. correspondent is reported dead in Cambodia,' one US headline announced to the world. *TIME* magazine reported that a white woman's body had been found in a shallow grave with a bullet in the head, and another in the chest. Webb's family held a memorial service for her not long before the missing journalist was released by Vietnamese forces and emerged from the jungle, twenty-three days after her capture. 'Miss Webb, you're supposed to be dead!' said the army officer who found her on the highway to Phnom Penh. 'It is Miss Webb, isn't it?'

Webb recalled the moment in her book *On the Other Side: 23 Days with the Viet Cong.* 'Everyone started talking at once, shaking hands, exclaiming, shouting. There was a lump in my throat as big as a foot-ball. I pulled out my last cigarette. It was crumpled. I couldn't talk, afraid I'd cry. My hand was shaking badly; a soldier, staring solemnly at me, gave me a light.'

Back in Phnom Penh, Webb wrote, 'I looked at the Royal Hotel and the big tree in the yard and told myself I wasn't dreaming. With all the noise and people dashing around, there was a stillness inside me I had never felt before or since. It was over.'

Asked at a Sydney media conference about her capture, Webb said, 'We were trying to run away, and it was a fight – it was a hell of a fight. We're trying to get through Cong lines and back to a government position and a combination of getting tired and just taking the wrong turn on a trail and we ran into two chaps who seemed pretty surprised to see us.'

Of course, this was the early 1970s and a Webb profile written by Nan Musgrove of *The Australian Women's Weekly* carried almost no reference to her work, reflecting the interests (or perceived interests) of the magazine's readers. '[Webb's] thick dark brown hair is cut short, her olive skin is smooth, unlined, her eyes a hard dark brown. She looks more 18 than 28,' Musgrove wrote. 'She wears no make-up, says it just drips off in the tropics, disdains lipstick. She has a good mouth, nice teeth, a nose too long for beauty. A second look reveals femininity in her gestures, the hint of a bosom under the enveloping sweater. [Before the kidnapping, she had been] the envy of the bar girls in Saigon.'

During her stellar career, the New Zealand-born and Australian-raised Webb covered wars and politics from Indochina to Afghanistan and Iraq, and points in between. 'Like the French photographer Catherine Leroy,' Clifton said, 'she opened the way for the legions of young women who now routinely report wars.'

Webb 'trained on Australian newspapers, working on Rupert Murdoch's *Daily Mirror* in Sydney, then, seeking adventure, arrived in the South Vietnamese capital, Saigon,' Clifton wrote. 'She began working for UPI in 1967, mainly to cover Vietnamese politics, because there were then hardly any women out on the battlefield. But she found herself filling in when male reporters came back for rest from tough assignments.

> Webb had hardly settled in as a junior reporter with UPI when the combined Viet Cong and North Vietnamese forces launched the 1968 Tet offensive, the country-wide attempt to overthrow the South Vietnam government. Because it was a huge New Year holiday, Saigon was very quiet and Webb was one of very few correspondents in the city. When the heavy firing and mortaring began, Webb headed to the American embassy. Under fire, she reached the walled compound to find it was under attack, with dead soldiers from both sides littering the grounds and the buildings. As she memorably wrote at the time: 'It looked like a butcher's shop in Eden, beautiful but ghastly.'

Webb spent six years in Vietnam at a time when 'reporters in Indochina lived lives straight out of a Graham Greene novel'. She became UPI's bureau chief in Cambodia in 1971. British correspondent Jon Swain reportedly claimed that the only time he had ever seen Kate out of her usual baggy pants was in Chantal's, the famous Phnom Penh opium den, where clients always changed into sarongs, and where a group photograph of him with Webb was the parlour's only decoration.

Associated Press correspondent Carl Robinson recalled a 1971 dinner with Webb in Phnom Penh: 'It was a cous-cous dinner in a restaurant in Monorom Boulevard, notorious among the tight-knit press corps for the inclusion of a heavy dose of marijuana in one of the dishes, but you would never know which one. But the effects didn't take long to get things rocking and voices rising. I was sitting next to Kate, and we talked, or tried to above all the noise; the usual talk about the "situation", as we called it. What was happening out there in the field. The war. So quiet-spoken that I had to lean right in to hear her. She was quiet and calm. Very unlike the rest of the raucous crowd. Truly reserved.'

According to Clifton, soldiers were curious about Webb but accepted her immediately. 'If you don't make a thing out of being a female,' she once said, 'if you don't demand special privileges and don't ask where you plug in your hairdryer, you have no problems.'

Webb left Vietnam for Hong Kong in April 1975 but returned as Saigon fell to North Vietnamese forces. She continued to work across Asia for UPI until 1977, when she joined Agence France-Presse. In her seventeen years with the French agency, Webb covered the Tamil Tiger uprising in Sri Lanka and events in Pakistan, the Philippines, East Timor, Nepal and Afghanistan.

'In 1990–91, her work included the first Iraq war, the fall of Bangladesh's President Ershad and the assassination in India of Rajiv Gandhi. In 1994 she had an exclusive on the death of North Korea's dictator Kim Il-Sung. In 1997 she was there for the end of British rule in Hong Kong. Her last big story came in 1998 – reporting on the collapse of President Suharto's regime in Indonesia,' Clifton said.

Webb's book on her Cambodia hostage ordeal opens with the words, 'A hell of a lot of things are damn fool when you look back on them. When you're sitting in a ditch with bullets whizzing around your head, everything including yourself is damn fool. Everything, especially the steps you took to get there.'

And yet, according to Tony Clifton, Webb's determination to 'get there' was her great strength and will be her enduring legacy.

'Kate was a good writer, but her value for future historians will be that all her best stories were written from the heart of the struggle, in the heat of the battle, in conversation with the major players – whether generals, grunts in foxholes, peasants in their fields, rulers in their palaces or guerrillas in their caves. Those historians will pass over the prognostications and predictions of desk-bound pundits to read Kate, knowing she was really there when it all happened.'

Kate Webb died in 2007 at the age of sixty-four.

17
A REPORTER'S NOTEBOOK:
'FORTUNE FAVOURS THE FOOLISH'

Ginny Stein
Correspondent at large 1997 – present
ABC, SBS, freelance

Setting up in Jakarta.

Dateline: Cambodia – Phnom Penh, July 1998*

R UNNING BATTLES ERUPTED sporadically on the streets of the
Cambodian capital, Phnom Penh. Pol Pot, a genocidaire of epic
proportions, was still alive, but the Khmer Rouge, his savage movement which had caused so much suffering, was on the wane.

This battle was a power struggle of a different kind between
Hun Sen, the man who helped bring down the murderous regime, and
those who would challenge him.

Watching the young men shoot at each other, I felt invisible, perhaps
because I was both a woman and a foreigner. I knew I was not immune
to stray bullets, but none of the fighters in these skirmishes seemed

---

* (Some names have been changed to protect people's identities.)

remotely interested in or fazed by my presence. One man shooting with a pistol flicked his eyes briefly to me from his distant target to wordlessly ask permission to step in front of me.

Adrenaline fuelled me that day, but it was luck, not skill, that ensured my survival. It was my first frontline reporting experience and one for which I was woefully unprepared. But it catapulted me into three decades of work as a female correspondent and video journalist covering Asia and Africa, with a dash of Afghanistan in between. It's been a journey through great changes in the media, in the technology we use, and for women in the news industry.

As the afternoon news deadline drew near on that Phnom Penh day, I rushed back to the Regent, my small, three star hotel close to the Royal Palace. It was usually an oasis of calm, but as I arrived with camera operator David Leland, I could hear gunfire nearby. A firefight had broken out up the street.

The hotel was filled with cameramen and correspondents who had flown in from neighbouring Bangkok to cover an election that was rapidly spiralling into chaos. While covering the fighting, I had just missed a media conference with the country's wily authoritarian leader. My search for a soundbite from the news event led me to a newsagency cameraman known as Shagger.

When I applied for the position as the ABC's South-East Asia correspondent in 1997, I was the only woman among nine candidates. The mutterings in the newsroom suggested I had little chance of success. But then, with the twenty-first century approaching, there I was, the first female formally appointed by the national broadcaster as South-East Asia correspondent.

My career with the ABC also began with another breakthrough; I became the only woman in its radio newsroom in Darwin. I was poached from the local newspaper, *Northern Territory News*, over drinks in a hotel beer garden. 'We had one woman, but she left,' explained my ABC contact. 'Would you be interested? We think we could get along with you.'

Sexism wafted like bad cologne throughout my early career. As a Sydney police reporter in the late 1980s, I can recall the pressroom wall at the Central Police Headquarters being covered in images of bikini-clad Page 3 girls. The male police reporters had large moustaches, bad hair, polyester shirts, and body odour.

In South-East Asia, the ratpack of roving male correspondents was more of the same. That's not to say I was operating on my own. There were women in the field, too. Most were freelancers.

I knocked on Shagger's door at the Regent Hotel. The cameraman answered, a towel draped around his waist. Behind him, two women lay on the bed, covered by a sheet. He was suddenly all business. He grabbed the tape from the editing deck and passed it to me. 'No rush, I'll get it back from you later,' he said and closed the door. Living in Bangkok, I was used to seeing middle-aged white men parading the streets with Asian women half their age. Like the men waging war on the streets in Phnom Penh, I was happily invisible to them too. As Phnom Penh was being torn apart by violence, and as international television networks made satellite bookings at a cost of more than a thousand dollars a minute to beam images of the chaos to the world, Shagger had found time for a midday booty call with two young Cambodian women.

Back in my room, I proceeded to piece my report together. I'd earlier pulled the room apart to find the telephone socket hidden behind the bed. A quick call to the Sydney lines room, then I tapped the line with alligator clips and filed my package for the evening current affairs program.

While I filed for radio, David Leland put the finishing touches to our TV news story. We had rented editing decks from a production company based in an old French colonial house nearby, carrying them across the park between gun battles. Now we braved the streets again, crossing town to the 'feed point' at the government telecommunications building from where our TV piece would be relayed to Sydney via satellite.

It was quiet as we left the hotel, but on the main boulevard, our driver slammed on the brakes. An armoured car was rushing in from a side street, blocking our way. Another vehicle headed towards it. Both vehicles stopped, and the shooting began. David jumped out of the front passenger seat and crouched down low to film. I followed him, scrambling out over the equipment on the back seat to hide behind our car. Our driver ducked down low inside the vehicle. As quickly as it began, the shooting ended and the gunmen retreated. We piled back in. David had successfully filmed a perfectly timed street battle.

As gunfire raged across a city yet to recover from the horror inflicted upon it by the ruthless Khmer Rouge, I was a frontline newbie in this conflict, but I was with a seasoned colleague, and the guns were never aimed at us. We were observers. In the years that followed, I would travel to conflict zones around the world, learning each time that timing, and luck, is everything.

Dateline: Kabul, Afghanistan 2003

A year after allied forces claimed to have successfully overthrown the fundamentalist Taliban regime, Afghanistan was a volatile and dangerous place. The Taliban was recovering and would soon have the strength to again threaten every corner of the country. I was on my way to meet a warlord who had changed sides many times. Pacha Khan Zadran was above all else a survivor, and right now, a very angry one.

He was the very poster child of a warlord, with the most amazing handlebar moustache, full eyebrows, and a turban which stood tall on his head. Pacha Khan was deep in a dispute with Afghanistan's president, Hamid Karzai. He was demanding to be reinstated as governor of the region. He had been stripped of the post the previous year, and in retaliation, had bombed the nearby city of Gardez. A former US ally, he was now out of favour; his army's rockets had killed twenty-five people, many of them children.

We were four in the car: Omar, the driver; Nas, my regular translator and explainer of Afghanistan to the uninitiated; plus an Afghan journalist I will call Ahmed, who was freelancing to pay for his medical degree. Ahmed knew Pacha Khan and he assured me we were welcome. The warlord had a message for the US, and we were meant to deliver it.

Pacha Khan had fought with the US-backed Mujahedin against the Soviet invasion in the 1980s and had supported the 2001 US invasion, lending his men for battle. Now he was calling in the favour. Through us, he wanted to remind the Americans of his importance and was ready with threats to withdraw support if they did not back him against Karzai.

Making our visit even more tense was the death just a week earlier of Pacha Khan's son. He had died in a US air strike.

As we left Kabul to head south, Nas was visibly nervous. He knew how dangerous his nation could be and how quickly things could change. We had a very small window to meet with Pacha Khan.

The US was poised to invade Iraq – what we didn't know was when. We needed to get to Pacha Khan and back to Kabul before the US struck at Saddam Hussein and enraged the Muslim world. Failure would leave us totally exposed in a very dangerous part of the country.

It was on a lonely road like this that my friend Australian Reuters journalist and cameraman Harry Burton had been shot dead along with three other journalists, one a woman, in the first weeks following the fall of the Taliban. It was only when we picked up one of Pacha Khan's men, to ensure safe passage through the snowmelt and the winding mountain pass to his base in Paktia Province, that Nas relaxed a little. Sitting in a now very cramped Toyota Corolla station wagon next to the fighter with a small machine gun, I was not relaxed.

Pacha Khan strode out to welcome us, his fighters gathered around him, some stepping down from the converted machine-gun vehicles where they had been resting. One of his men approached carrying a dainty teapot with warm water to wash our hands, before we were ushered inside his command post to talk.

He offered me the same respect and access as my male colleagues. After sharing a meal, we were taken to another battle-scarred building high on a hill and shown into the mehman khana, the meeting room, a sanctum usually reserved for men. Pacha Khan turned on his charm. He told me that with my head covered in a scarf, and sitting under layers of blankets to keep warm, I looked like a good Muslim woman.

We had a wide-ranging conversation about philosophical differences between the Muslim world and the West. Pacha Khan had taken off his shoes, and a young boy, who had earlier brought in sweet tea, was now massaging the warlord's feet. He was curious and wanted to know what drove Western thought, how the West saw the world. I wanted to ask him why I could sit with him, to talk to him, but an Afghan woman could not. I wanted to know how he processed the difference. But for the sake of peace, I kept those questions to myself, much like I sometimes had to do in the West, not wanting to upset the men in the room.

That evening, Ahmed, Nas, our driver and I shared a room, for my protection. After a young soldier turned down our beds on the floor, we pulled a metal barrel across the door to warn us of any attempt to break in during the night. Despite all the hospitality, we were under no illusions about where we were.

The next morning, the sense that something had changed was palpable. Pacha Khan and some of his fighters were listening intently to a small radio. Ahmed bravely strolled over to find out what was going on. We had to leave, Ahmed reported back. Now. The US had invaded Iraq. And Pacha Khan had ordered us out.

In any conflict, the start and beginning, the getting in and getting out, are the most dangerous and unpredictable moments. There would be no escort, no armed guard on our return trip to Kabul. We drove at speed, back through the winding mountain passes on unpaved roads. It was extremely frightening. We expected an attack from Afghans angered by the assault on Iraq by the 'godless' Americans, but thankfully it never came. I filed for *Dateline*. 'Unfinished Business' was about the new threat to Afghanistan's security from the very warlords who had helped America overthrow the Taliban. The US had won the war, but not the peace.

Dateline: Zimbabwe, 2009

It was a diamond rush. When one of the world's richest diamond deposits was discovered in Zimbabwe, thousands of prospectors swarmed to the tiny town of Chiadzwa in the country's north-eastern Mutare District to try their luck. They lived in squalor and clawed vast numbers of low-quality stones from the dirt to sell to corrupt government officials or to smugglers.

Rights to what became known as the Marange fields, not far from the Mozambique border, had been held by foreign-based multinational interests, but in 2006, the government of Prime Minister Robert Mugabe informed the nation of the riches, triggering a mad scramble by artisanal miners from across the country.

The legal owners were driven off the field, and in November 2008, the government turned the military on the artisanal miners, who were in turn chased off, this time with air attacks, dogs, beatings and rape. Now, in the run-up to a national election, the politically teetering and financially desperate government was in full control. It could exploit the remote site and enrich Mugabe's cronies.

Securing a commission for a story was straightforward. *Blood Diamond*, the movie starring Leonardo DiCaprio, an epic tale of greed, treachery and diamonds elsewhere in Africa, had just been released, and international efforts to clean up the industry were underway.

My good friend and colleague Dee and I had worked together across Zimbabwe for many years. On countless occasions we had witnessed the brutality of the state towards its own people, and we had lived through some scary adventures covering Zimbabwe's economic collapse and its political bloodletting.

But filming in the diamond fields of Zimbabwe was shaping up to be the most dangerous assignment of them all. As I had done in the past, I carried a hidden camera. It was low-tech, just a lens mounted in the strap of a small daypack and connected to a camera inside the bag. Broken down, and carried in separate bags, it would hopefully not attract attention if I was searched.

In Zimbabwe, there is a proverb for every occasion. And this one in Ndebele, Dee's mother tongue, 'Amajodo awela abangelambiza', fortune favours the foolish, seemed well suited to our assignment.

I was heading there to cover a story, but for Dee, the bloodletting was much more personal. His family had suffered greatly at the hands of the Zimbabwean army. He believed the diamonds could create a new future for his country; in neighbouring Botswana, a boy who once herded cattle had become president and the nation had been transformed by diamond wealth. Why could the same not happen in his country?

But the diamond find in Zimbabwe couldn't have come at a worse time. After losing the previous election, President Mugabe had unleashed a campaign of violence, and pushed his political foe into accepting a power-sharing agreement. As his grip on power weakened, control of the fields was transferred to the police, then the military, to buy their loyalty. With each handover, the death toll climbed. We told ourselves that the worst of the killings was over now Zimbabwe's security forces controlled the diamond fields, although we had no way of knowing that for sure.

If ever we had any doubt about the government's ruthlessness, mining minister Obert Mpofu, a former policeman, put it to rest. I had asked a local journalist to question him at a media conference about the November 2008 killings by government forces at the Marange fields. I had slipped across the border and couldn't attend the media event without blowing my cover.

'We moved in, and we don't regret having done that,' Mpofu said. 'We moved in through our police who were supported by our military because of the magnitude of the invasion by the diamond panners, and that has been achieved. The panners have been cleared.'

But despite government efforts, blood diamonds were still flowing out of the Marange fields, and out of the country, illegally, in the shoes and tyres of smugglers. We were going to have to smuggle ourselves into the now military-controlled diamond fields. Our plan was to drive towards the fields, find a diamond buyer and follow him in. As for Plan B? Well, there wasn't one. As a freelancer, getting paid depended on coming back with a story.

Through my contacts in Zimbabwe's main opposition party, the Movement for Democratic Change, I met retired lawyer Lyn Rogers, who lived near the fields. In a time of optimism, he and his wife Rosalind had established a popular backpackers' lodge for overland adventurers looking for a taste of Africa. Now, they were clinging on by a thread. 'The diamond dealers and smugglers,' Rogers said from his verandah overlooking the resort they no longer ran, 'are down there in the bar.'

We headed down to the bar in search of a dealer. At first glance, it looked empty, but as our eyes adjusted to the dim light, we spotted the bartender at the far end of the counter, and elsewhere a few other groups of twos and threes. I hoped none of them were undercover government agents.

'*Kanjani*,' Dee greeted the bartender in Shona, the main language of northern Zimbabwe. We ordered beers and Dee chatted with the bartender, working his magic. A natural leader, he could put people at ease, find a connection and get them to talk. Back in his home village, he is a chief. The bartender relaxed, even when I heard Dee mention *ngoda*, the slang word for diamond or diamond dealer. 'Those two, they are buyers,' the bartender said, nodding at the men at a table in the corner.

'The women over there are *mahure*,' he said, sex workers. I had seen them sizing us up as we entered. The two men on the verandah had come to sell their gems. The bartender introduced Dee, I slipped outside to let them talk more freely, and before long, they were all laughing. Dee looked up at me and smiled. He was onto something.

The next morning, we headed towards Mutare, the capital of diamond rich Manicaland Province. 'One of the dealers knows my nephew,' he said. 'They gave me the name of someone who might be able to help, an ex-policeman.'

Outside Mutare, and out of sight of strangers, Mishek walked towards us with a confident, loping gait. He had quit the police force, unable to feed his family on a salary reduced to nothing by hyperinflation. Getting to work cost more money than he earned. Hundreds of thousands of people starved to death or died of disease during Mugabe's reign (that millions also survived is truly remarkable). When news of the diamond find hit the streets, Mishek had become a diamond dealer overnight.

We crouched down in the dirt as he pulled a tiny pebble from his pocket. The small steely grey metallic stone he rolled between his fingers looked nothing like the diamonds displayed in jewellery shop windows. It was raw and uncut. From his bag he pulled out a scale to weigh the gem. For the past year Mishek had headed into the diamond fields almost every day to buy gems, bribing his way through checkpoints to meet up with illegal panners known locally as *gwejas*. Then he'd race back to Mutare to sell the gems for a decent mark up, to foreign buyers hiding out in small hotels and boarding houses throughout the city.

'How much for that,' I asked, pointing to the gem between his fingers.

'I was offered US$5000, but I think it is worth more,' Mishek said. 'It has few flaws and its clarity is good.' He would not tell me how much he paid for it.

With the army now in control of the routes in and out of the diamond fields, and undercover police patrolling the city on the look-out for diamond dealers, most foreign buyers had fled Mutare, slipping over the border to Mozambique for their own safety. But despite the dangers and often fatal consequences, the supply chain was flourishing. Mishek planned to acquire a few more stones and smuggle them across the border in his shoes. He offered to take Dee with him into the diamond fields that night.

The Marange fields, stretching over 10 hectares, were fenced off, but were not so closely watched at night. *Gwejas* slipped under the fence at dusk, panned in the dark, and disappeared back into the Chiadzwa community before sun-up.

Calmly and almost apologetically, Mishek refused to take me. As a white woman, I was too conspicuous. 'If they catch you, they beat you till you can't walk. If they don't kill you, you will end up crippled,' he said, rolling his valuable pebble between his fingers.

I wasn't surprised. I had my own plan. I had arranged with the Mayor of Mutare, an opposition party member, to help deliver boxes of health and hygiene kits for needy rural clinics around the diamond fields. We would have to navigate our way through at least two checkpoints, but we would be in, and I would film whatever I could with my hidden camera.

Dee and Mishek left as soon as the sun went down, catching a local bus to take them as close as possible to the first checkpoint, and then walking. Mishek said it should only take a couple of hours. They left their phones with me in case they were caught. With no way of contacting Dee, I just had to trust Mishek. The two-hour journey became a seven-hour one, as they were forced to navigate around new checkpoints. It was dawn when they reached the fenced-off fields. Dee found children sifting through tailings that the *gwejas* had smuggled out under the wire, and filmed buyers and sellers trading stones.

The next morning I headed off in a truck to deliver the aid, my hidden camera in a large pink handbag at my feet. We sailed through the checkpoints: smuggling diamonds is a one-way affair. Supplies successfully delivered, I set up my hidden camera. We had scurried around Harare buying backup batteries, but as I connected the 9-volt batteries, the camera was dead. The rest of the day passed in a blur of failed film-making misery.

But Dee filmed proof of the ongoing illicit trade and soon we would follow the gems over the border. However, first we had an appointment to keep at the town's main cemetery.

Before I left for Zimbabwe, I had talked to diamond traders, human rights investigators and industry regulators, including Ian Smillie, a founding member of the Kimberley Process, an international certification scheme operating under a UN General Assembly resolution aimed at stopping the trade in conflict diamonds. 'The whole point of the Kimberley Process is to stop blood diamonds,' he'd said.

Local human rights investigators had gathered evidence to present to a Kimberley Process delegation travelling to Marange to assess whether Zimbabwe was producing blood diamonds. The investigators had tracked the bodies of people killed by the government in the nearby town of Chiadzwa months before to morgues and hospitals, and finally to this cemetery. I saw papers revealing that scores of unnamed bodies had been dumped there.

A morgue official told us prisoners from Mutare Farm Prison had been trucked in to bury the dead; I met local people abused by authorities including a sixty-seven-year-old former farmer who had been held in a cage for two days, only let out to be flogged, and a woman selling second-hand clothes to the miners, who had been set on by dogs at the direction of police.

I wanted to go back to Chiadzwa one more time to speak to people who had seen so much, this time on camera. But, as we approached a checkpoint, a soldier brandished his weapon and fired questions at me.

'Do you have a camera? A phone?' he demanded. 'No, I do not,' I replied. Now was not the time for honesty. I kept looking at him. I did not want my eyes to betray me. I feared looking down at my handbag with the cameras and my phone inside.

Behind him, another soldier emerged from a small building, doing up his pants as he approached. A woman appeared behind him. She too was rearranging her clothes. He didn't look happy to be disturbed. She was indifferent.

He shouted, threatening to arrest us and seize our vehicle. He demanded Dee's driver's licence and my passport and ordered us to report to the police in Mutare the next day. I was relieved to escape, but my heart still sank. I couldn't leave Zimbabwe without my passport, and Dee would be hunted down as a suspected diamond dealer if we didn't turn up. We were both sure it was not the local police we would be meeting, but officers from Harare's feared Central Intelligence Office, the CIO.

We arranged for a contact to smuggle our tapes and notebooks over the border, and the next day we presented ourselves to the police. We had our story straight and promised each other we would not waver from it. I could only hope I would be able to stick to the story if the worst came to the worst. We would keep it simple and close to the truth. I had come from New York to visit Dee and our mutual friend, the mayor of Mutare, who offered to let us help deliver aid supplies so I could see more of Zimbabwe.

Neither of us knew how difficult the interrogation would be, or how long it would last. At the station, Dee and I were immediately separated. I was taken to a room where a man in plain clothes, who I assumed was a security officer, sat behind a desk.

'Why are you here?' he asked. I stuck to my story, trying desperately to stay calm. 'Didn't the mayor tell you it was dangerous?' The officer stared straight at me.

'Yes, you can check with him,' I said, sending him a deliberate message. 'He knows we are here.' But the questions kept coming. Whose car were we in? Who was Dee? Why was I in Zimbabwe? The officer was polite but insistent. I feared any slip would endanger both of us. And then, suddenly, it was over.

'You can collect your passport on your way out,' he said.

I got up and walked out, stunned. Dee was already in the waiting room. His face was expressionless. Neither of us could quite believe we had managed to walk out of that police station unscathed. We both knew what could have happened. The sense of relief was immense. I'd like to think it was because we both held true to our stories. But the truth emerged some weeks later. It was luck. There had been a shift change. The CIO team that had brutalised so many over the past few months had been recalled to Harare.

The next day, we followed the diamonds across the border, stashed in Mishek's shoes. Once out of Zimbabwe, we set him up with the backpack camera and he filmed as the buyer viewed the diamonds and they quickly settled on a price. The deal was done. And so too was our story.

Ginny Stein was posted to Bangkok as South-East Asia correspondent for the ABC in 1997, a position she later held in Jakarta and East Timor. In 2002, she joined SBS's *Dateline* as one of its first video journalists. For almost a decade, she filmed stories across Asia, the Middle East and throughout Africa, winning three Walkley Awards. She returned to the ABC in 2010 and was appointed Africa correspondent. She now lives in Vanuatu, where she continues to film and file stories for a range of broadcasters, including SBS, ITV (Independent Television), Al Jazeera and VOA (Voice of America).

18
MORNING IN AMERICA AND A NIGHT OUT WITH MALCOLM

Janine Perrett
New York 1985–1989
The Australian

Covering the turbulent world of business.

MAY 1986 AND Manhattan's then new South Street Seaport promenade on a Friday night is a sea of dark blue. It's not the nearby financial district suits that you see: it's what they are drinking. Giant tinnies of Foster's beer in what the yuppies (young urban professionals) dubbed oil cans.

There are three colours that summed up New York at that time in my mind's eye – blue, yellow and white. Blue for the oil cans, yellow for the so-called power ties that were ubiquitous on Wall Street, and white for the cocaine that fuelled these Masters of the Universe, even more so than the new Aussie beer.

It was 'Morning in America', in the words of the famous Ronald Reagan slogan that won him a second term in 1984: the Roaring

Eighties. The stockmarket was booming, greed was good and New York was the centre of the world. It was bouncing back from near bankruptcy in the late 1970s, to be a heady mixture of glamour and grime. Expensive, outrageous nightclubs were emerging downtown, where the newly rich were required to step over the still prevalent homeless. You still ran the constant risk of being mugged and the first advice I was given if daring to take the graffiti-ridden subway was: 'You have to look like *you* are the one carrying the knife.'

Thanks to a recent pre–*Crocodile Dundee* Paul Hogan commercial on American television urging them to 'put another shrimp on the barbie' and head Down Under, and with our new breed of swashbuckling entrepreneurs selling beer and buying up US companies, Australia was flavour of the moment.

Talk about right person, right time.

For a seasoned financial correspondent – but fledging foreign one – in her mid-twenties, they were heady days. My story is a snapshot of those times and is as much about the lessons I learned as the knowledge I managed to impart through my stories as *The Australian's* US correspondent.

I started covering business as a cadet reporter for *The Australian* in 1981, basically because few others wanted the job. Finance was considered dull and tedious compared with the excitement of, say, politics or crime. But the boring business beat was about to be transformed and my career trajectory elevated along with the new breed of colourful entrepreneurs; Alan Bond, Robert Holmes à Court, Christopher Skase, John Elliott were among the most infamous of the decade.

Incredibly, *The Australian* still had a specialised financial correspondent based in London, officially titled the European business correspondent, so when Phil Beard defected to the rival *Australian Financial Review*, I went for the job – or, as Phil joked, 'She moved in while the corpse was still twitching.'

It was there that I had my first taste of the joy of being a foreign correspondent, doing stories that showed how business intersected with politics and every other big story of the time, from Maggie Thatcher's economic, and thus social, transformation of Britain, to the coal miners' strike and the G7 summit.

But I had always really wanted the New York correspondent's position. I had done a good job in London, so when the US bureau suddenly lost a journo temporarily, it was thought easiest to transfer me across the Atlantic for a few months, which ended up being four incredible years.

Trying to sum up everything brings to mind the Billy Joel song 'We didn't start the fire', although in my case, the lyrics would be:

Ronald Reagan, Maggie T, Gorbachev, Baby Doc, Noriega, Pinochet – what more can I say? Iran-Contra, Ollie North, Crocodile Dundee. Hijackings, terror plots, Evil Empire, Perestroika … you get the idea.

I watched a space shuttle go up; I covered one going down. There were uprisings, elections, coups, revolutions, from the US to Haiti to Panama to Chile.

There were even a couple of interviews with a brash young New York bizoid called Donald Trump who had designs on a casino in Australia. When he failed at that, I thought we, at least, had heard the end of him.

I've learned that if you live long enough, the stories you covered will eventually become a movie or Netflix series. Then you just have to convince a new generation that the stories were actually factual, because you covered them. We called it news. (Though it can make you seem a bit Forrest Gumpish, popping up at every historical event of the eighties.)

Take *Bohemian Rhapsody*, the movie: I was at the 1985 Philadelphia Live Aid concert, held simultaneously with the London concert. While we didn't have Freddie Mercury, we made do with the likes of Bruce Springsteen, Mick Jagger, Madonna and Phil Collins, the only one to play both concerts, thanks to the supersonic Concorde jet.

And then there's *The Front Runner*, a film starring our own Hugh Jackman as failed presidential candidate Gary Hart. I was at Hart's infamous press conference when he was brought undone by a blonde called Donna Rice and a boat called *Monkey Business*.

The Eyes of Tammy Faye is an Oscar-nominated movie based on the bizarre sex and money story of the tragic televangelists Tammy Faye and Jim Bakker – been there, done that, and I even managed to visit their ludicrous religious theme park in South Carolina.

Then there was the six-part Netflix series *Wild Wild Country*, which even I found hard to believe, except that I have the photo of me in socks interviewing the even more bizarre Bhagwan Shree Rajneesh surrounded by machine gun–wielding orange-clad disciples at his heavily fortified ranch in Oregon. My room at the ranch sported plenty of condoms as part of their free love philosophy, along with special soap with which to wash before the interview with the notoriously germophobe Bhagwan. I was only granted one of these rare audiences because the story had a distinctive Australian angle at the time, as the cult was trying to establish another base in Western Australia.

Perhaps one should say it wasn't all fun and games and as glamorous and exciting as it sounds, but often it was. I could not believe I was being paid to do this job. Every story was a learning experience, and perhaps because I was so young, I had less fear of failure – or even being killed.

The first time I covered the miner's picket line in North England, I stood in the dark among the angry coalminers facing a line of horses and police in terrifying riot gear. 'You're new to this, are ye?' asked the burly man next to me. When I nodded, he pointed out, 'Ye meant to be on that side,' as I belatedly noted the other journalists were standing *behind* the police lines.

My first uprising involved a week in Haiti chronicling the downfall of despised dictator Jean-Claude 'Baby Doc' Duvalier, who was still driving through the streets of the world's poorest nation tossing coins to the peasants from his luxury limousine. The day I arrived, tensions were high, with the streets full of his feared secret police, the Tontons Macoutes, intimidating the world's media who had descended on the beleaguered Caribbean island.

Yet the most worried I saw my veteran colleagues was on the first night, when we sat down to eat dinner at the Hotel Oloffson, made famous as the Hotel Trianon in Graham Greene's novel *The Comedians*. I blithely ordered a salad, at which their eyes widened as they exclaimed in horror, 'You cannot have a salad. It's washed in water – that's more dangerous than the bullets flying out there!'

First lesson learned, though I'm not sure about the bullets – the first story I filed was sent from under the bed, over the sound of nearby gunfire, as the copytaker asked incredulously, 'That popping sound isn't bullets, is it?'

Ah, copytakers. Another extinct media tradition from last century. Of course, there were no mobile phones in the eighties. We still used typewriters. The New York bureau was quite advanced, as we had a primitive form of computer, but most urgent communication was done by fax, the facsimile machine.

On the road, the quickest and most efficient way to file copy was to handwrite your notes or even just jot down a few points and then find a phone and ask for the copytakers. The reassuring voice at the other end would calmly transcribe the story you were dictating. Looking back, it probably helped in my later career as a television journalist, as I learned to write as I would talk. But even the copytakers couldn't help me when Baby Doc eventually fled – all the phone lines were down, making it virtually impossible to file for days afterwards.

In fact, I nearly missed the main event because, after days of false starts and rumours that the Duvaliers were fleeing, the night they were actually airlifted out by US military aircraft, I had dragged a group of colleagues to a real voodoo ceremony where we watched a man bite the head off a chook.

Lest business stories look a tad dull after all that, it was at a dry trade conference in Orange County California that I struggled to place the wife of one of the delegates as an almost unrecognisable Jane Fonda. Elizabeth Taylor's 1987 launch of the perfume Passion was the precursor to a multibillion-dollar business trend for celebrity fragrances. But for me, the biggest celebrity interview I did was in Boston with legendary economist John Kenneth Galbraith, and I still treasure the signed copy of his seminal book, *The Great Crash 1929*.

When the Aussie media assembled in Cape Canaveral in 1985 to watch the launch of the space shuttle *Discovery*, it was because it was carrying our first satellite, Aussat, into space. I was back there a few months later to cover the tragic *Challenger* explosion which briefly halted the NASA program. I later got to see *Discovery* return to space in 1988. It was always fun to stay at Cocoa Beach, of *I Dream of Jeannie* fame, and the earth-shaking feel of a rocket taking off is still one of the most thrilling experiences of my life.

Even sitting in on a mafia wiretap session with federal prosecutors had a business angle, when I heard just how much every New Yorker paid each day thanks to the organised crime infiltration of so many legitimate industries throughout the city.

There was an even closer encounter with the Mob when the crime boss Paul Castellano was gunned down outside Sparks Steak House in midtown Manhattan in December 1985. As I was writing the story,

I realised the assassination had taken place next door to my apartment building, so I rushed home to find a group of beefy men in ill-fitting suits standing on the sidewalk admiring the crime scene. 'Nice hit,' said one to his mate in a strong Brooklyn drawl. Nearby, a young gawker had set up his 'ghetto-blaster' cassette tape machine, which was playing the theme from *The Godfather*. The next morning, I opened my apartment door to find two federal agents asking me if I had seen anything, as my window overlooked the site. If only.

The Australian's bureau was based in the *New York Post* building, in the depths, then dregs, of Manhattan on South Street between the Brooklyn and Williamsburg bridges. It had been run for years by the dynamic Sally MacMillan, who worked all hours, drank through the rest and was as supportive a friend as she was a colleague. The bureau housed about a dozen journos, with a handful of Australians filing for the tabloids back home alongside the formal English correspondents from *The Times* and *The Sunday Times*.

Outside our little area was the bustling *Post*, which was also full of ex-Aussie journos, led by the legendary Steve Dunleavy. He always looked after young Aussie blow-ins, and if you could keep up with his drinking, then, like me, you became a firm friend and were even introduced to the seedy night-time bars full of colourful identities, which you could never locate again during daylight hours. Often we would start our adventures at midnight after I finished filing on Australian time and come back to work early next morning. Steve would take a nap in the sauna and once asked me to send someone to wake him in an hour. When I forgot, an angry, red-faced sweating man stood at the bureau door accusing me of trying to kill him, or at least turn him into a prune. It didn't stop us heading out again the next night.

It was after one of those all-nighters that a particularly jealous old male colleague thought he would try and get me sent back to Australia by taking a photo of me fast asleep in the 'sick bay' early in the morning. It backfired. Sydney was very happy with the huge amount of copy I was filing and thought the photo was proof of how hard I was working.

In 1986, the office next door was occupied by a small team working on a secret project for *The Australian*'s proprietor, Rupert Murdoch: the launch of the new Fox Television network. We in the bureau were less than impressed, as they seemed to spend all day annoying us by bouncing tennis balls against the wall as part of their planning sessions.

YOU CAN'T TALK about business in the US in the eighties without acknowledging the elephant in the room – Rupert Murdoch. No other Australian then or since has so dominated American business, notwithstanding the fact that he had just swapped his citizenship to meet regulatory requirements for owning a television network there. He would often drop into the bureau for a chat and catch up on what was happening at home.

Murdoch had started with the brash *New York Post* tabloid, which he bought in 1976, then ramped up his business footprint in the US, culminating in the purchase of the 20th Century-Fox movie studio and Metromedia television, which was to become Fox TV, the fifth free-to-air network in the US. But this was the 1980s, long before the pernicious influence of Fox News on US politics and democracy.

He was still reviled by many on the left for supporting the down-fall of the Whitlam government in 1975 in the pages of his flagship *The Australian*, and he was a staunch supporter of Ronald Reagan's free market policies during the 1980s. But during those years, he supported the Hawke–Keating economic reforms and was an advocate for Australia's push for global trade reform.

While the Australian invasion of American business was in full swing by the mid-eighties, most of the invaders did not survive the decade. They were wiped out when the 1987 stockmarket crash exposed a slew of them as debt-ridden frauds. Some were jailed, some fled, and some like Murdoch were nearly crippled by the huge debts they incurred to fund their rapid expansion. Though none bounced back to thrive quite the way he did.

Most of the worst names are dead now, but back then, they were having their moment. The late great Chicago economist David Hale was one of the first to focus on the rise of these Australians and wrote a paper about the phenomenon after our America's Cup win in September 1983. Alan Bond, who had bankrolled the winning boat, *Australia II*, was the most visible of the financial pirate class, with the patrician Robert Holmes à Court coming a close second through his audacious and ultimately unsuccessful attempts to take control of BHP (Broken Hill Proprietary), the company that was then known as The Big Australian. I was one of the first to confirm his moves. I had chanced on a story in *The Wall Street Journal* that described a small new firm, McCormick and Pryor, as 'shark watchers' and I was fascinated by this new idea of monitoring share registers for hostile bidders. When I visited their modest office, one of them happened to mention they had just been hired by BHP to unmask some recent share activity.

Along with Christopher Skase, who tried to outbid Murdoch for the MGM movie studio, and John Elliott, whose Carlton & United Breweries was Fosterising the world, were some long-forgotten names, including a fellow called George Herscu. He owned the Hooker property group in Australia, but through the eighties was on a retail buying binge of hyper stores across the US. In New York, he was the proud owner of two of the best known, now extinct, luxury brands, B. Altman and Bonwit Teller, the latter situated next to the then glitzy new Trump Tower. By the end of the decade, his empire had collapsed, owing the banks billions, and he was one of the few who actually spent time in prison, though it was for bribing a Queensland politician and not for any financial crimes.

It was impossible to keep up with the avalanche of Aussie spivs, shonks and general chancers and opportunists who made the pilgrimage to Wall Street during those years.

The locals provided plenty of colour for a business journo as well. In addition to the ambitious Trump, I interviewed notorious insider trader Ivan Boesky and went to Texas to meet greenmailer T. Boone Pickens, who lived up to his name. However, I never got to travel with the coked-up stockbrokers who would finish share trading then charter a chopper to nearby Atlantic City to continue their gambling all night before heading back next morning for another day on the other great casino, Wall Street.

But the party was coming to an end. First came the crackdown on coke in the financial district. In April 1987, fifteen employees of various Wall Street firms were charged with selling cocaine and trading drugs for information, stocks, and lists of preferred clients.

'To emphasise the amount of drugs flowing to Wall Street, the NYPD states that 114 people were arrested for buying and selling cocaine on the streets and in parks around the financial district so far in 1987,' said a report at the time. 'Two undercover agents, who were part of the federal bust, state that cocaine is either used or accepted by 90 per cent of the people on Wall Street.'

It was a race between drug dealers and insider traders for the most busts. Top firms from Goldman Sachs to Merrill Lynch and

Shearson Lehman were all implicated in the insider-trading crackdown by the ambitious young US attorney Rudolph Giuliani.

Then came the crash.

My overriding memory of the 1987 stockmarket crash was the ambulance parked discreetly outside the New York Stock Exchange for days afterwards, indicating how serious it was. The battered brokers, in their typical sardonic style, joked it was there in case any of them jumped out of the window. Unlike the Wall Street Crash in 1929, no one actually did jump, and the ambulance was probably there because of fear of heart attacks, given the number of palpitations and panic attacks occurring around the financial district that week. But the so-called Masters of the Universe did metaphorically plunge to earth as quickly as the Dow Jones in its biggest ever one-day fall on Black Monday, 19 October.

The previous record Dow fall came in the earlier crash, on a Black Tuesday in October, fifty-eight years before. But in percentage terms, the two don't really compare, with 1929 seeing a mere 13 per cent drop on the day, whereas 1987 saw a whopping 23 per cent, a fall that has never been bettered, or worsened. By the end of that day, the market had actually started to recover, although the shockwaves would be felt for weeks, months and years. Some would say decades.

One of the first victims that week was Holmes à Court, who saw a billion-dollar credit line from Merrill Lynch suddenly withdrawn. Others struggled on, punch drunk, like nothing had happened. It was just one month later, in November 1987, that Alan Bond bid a world record US$59 million for van Gogh's *Irises*. He only informed Sotheby's later that he didn't actually have the money to pay for it. They secretly lent him half the purchase price to maintain public confidence in the art market.

Wall Street was released later that year. In the cinema where I was watching, when the dastardly Gordon Gecko gave his 'greed is good' speech, the audience jumped up and cheered. Thus, the term became part of the lexicon – shorthand for the Go Go Eighties, the era of excess and conspicuous consumption.

IF THE 1987 crash was the most significant story for me as a finance journo, there was another story which was more memorable for others – my encounter with former prime minister Malcolm Fraser, which has been described as a harbinger of the #MeToo stories three decades later. I have deliberately avoided presenting my career at that time through a gender lens, because I never saw it as relevant. That is not in any way to downplay or disparage the incredibly brave new generation of younger female reporters still fighting for their place today.

Back then, being a woman was simply not an issue for me in the male-dominated worlds of journalism and finance. I never felt it held me back, I never felt it helped me get a job. I worked, and played, as hard as any of the blokes, so I never saw a distinction. My only reservation was my youth and relative lack of experience, which I made up for with drive, determination and dedication.

And when I talk to some of the other fantastic female correspondents who were my competitors in the US at that time, Jennifer Hewett and Marian Wilkinson, to name two who are still at the top of their field, the gender question seemed irrelevant to them then as well. In her memoir *Unfettered and Alive*, the great feminist writer Anne Summers talks candidly about her time in New York as correspondent for the *AFR* and her personal experience of covering finance stories.

'It wasn't simply that I was female, although the financial world was astonishingly masculine in makeup and ethos,' she wrote. 'Janine Perrett, who was in New York for *The Australian* newspaper, was totally at ease with business and finance stories. We'd often go for drinks together but we would mostly talk about politics, a subject I felt far more at home with, or gossip about expatriates. When it came to the capital markets, I simply felt out of place.'

And so to my 'Unforgettable night with Malcolm', as the story was headlined in *The Australian* in October 1986, one year before the crash. Australians had just been stunned by the story from the US that former prime minister and all-round stuffed shirt Malcolm Fraser had been found in a Memphis hotel room minus his trousers after an 'innocent' drink with a woman we later found was called Peaches.

But it came as no shock to me, given an encounter I'd had with him only a few weeks before. Fraser was in New York as part of the Commonwealth Eminent Persons Group inquiry into apartheid in South Africa. It was three years after he had lost the prime ministership to Bob Hawke and eleven years after he had sensationally replaced Gough Whitlam. Fraser was still reviled by many for his controversial role in what became known as The Dismissal, when the Governor-General dismissed the elected Labor government and called on Fraser, then opposition leader, to form government. It was many years later that he joined with Whitlam in turning on Murdoch, who had supported him in 1975, and later again that he moved further away from his former right-wing party in his strong advocacy for refugees.

He had always been a virulent opponent of apartheid, and it was after his Eminent Person's press conference that Fraser took a group of reporters to dinner. As we were leaving, he asked me if I wanted to go for a drink, and I saw no problem; it was staid old Malcolm Fraser, after all. Even when he asked the driver to take us to a 'dark smoky smoochy bar', I countered by directing him to the busy noisy Blue Note club in Greenwich Village.

'What drink gets you drunk?' was his classy line as soon as we arrived. As the night wore on, he became more and more handsy, at one stage pinning me against a wall in a banquette. I was only able to wriggle out when his attention was diverted by a drunk woman who bailed him up claiming she recognised him but could not put a name to that distinctive Easter Island face. 'No, don't tell me. It'll come to me,' she slurred in an Aussie accent as I tried to tell her it was Malcolm Fraser and he tried to shoo her away.

Eventually, I fled to a cab to escape him, but he jumped in after me. I tried to push him away with my feet on his chest until the New York cabbie said, 'I can see you are in trouble lady,' and dropped me off at the next corner, speeding away with the bewildered Fraser. When I recounted the story, my colleagues were sceptical the dour Fraser would misbehave like that.

Then came the Memphis story.

It was naturally huge news, and most Australians were incredulous that Fraser could have been in any way responsible for the unfortunate incident. I knew instantly that my experience with him was now part of the story, so promptly proceeded to detail exactly what had happened. I thought I should own my own story and sent it to the then foreign editor to use if he thought fit.

The next day 'Unforgettable night with Malcolm' was plastered over the front page of *The Weekend Australian* and I became the subject of vitriol from many politicians and some sections of the press gallery who felt I had broken some unwritten rule about reporting on private encounters.

'Bugger them,' I wrote many decades later in *The Australian,* in 2018, after an allegation that a senior NSW state politician had groped a female reporter. 'To this day I believe that what is said off the record should remain so. However even back then I knew when someone stepped over the line, and it became public, that you must write it yourself. As a journalist I had no choice. The story never defined me. If you do your job fairly and honestly it will simply be one of the stories you wrote rather than one you should have written.'

Looking back on it today, I can see it was probably one of the first times a young female reporter had written about the inappropriate behaviour of a senior politician in such a way. Only now do I see that it might be seen as brave or reckless. But credit to the team at *The Australian* who backed my version of events, ran the story prominently and supported me afterwards, which is more than can be said of many others at the time.

Meanwhile, in New York, my phone rang hot for weeks with women in America telling me of similar encounters. (Unfortunately, Peaches was not one of them.)

I chose not to keep focusing on it. I had better stories to write.

Janine Perrett was posted to London as business correspondent for *The Australian* in 1984 and then to New York as US correspondent from 1985 to 1989. At the Nine Network, she worked on *Sunday* and *Business Sunday*, and both founded and hosted *The Small Business Show*. At Sky News she hosted *The Perrett Report*. She was awarded a Knight Journalism Fellowship to Stanford University in 2007 and now writes columns for media outlets and appears on ABC TV, including as guest host of *Media Watch*.

PART THREE
BEING A CORRESPONDENT

'Our mission is to speak the truth to power. We send home that first rough draft of history. We can and do make a difference in exposing the horrors of war and especially the atrocities that befall civilians.'

– Marie Colvin, journalist

It is impossible to be a foreign correspondent and remain unchanged. Reporting from abroad can be physically arduous and dangerous. Above all, it can be emotionally challenging.

Border guards pose challenges. So do crooked (or amorous) politicians, artillery, soldiers and anti-government insurgents, even social media.

Perhaps most challenging and life changing is the human suffering that goes with the job – refugees, disaster victims, war casualties: the ordinary people swept up in the tsunami of what journalists call breaking news.

19
WHAT'S NEWS?

Emma Alberici
London 2008–2012
ABC

Covering Europe.

AFTER A VALIANT rescue at sea, Norwegian captain Arne Rinnan was headed for the closest dock. Onboard his freighter, the MV *Tampa*, were 434 people, mostly Afghans, picked up from their stricken fishing boat heading for Australian shores. It was August 2001, and the country was about to witness one of the most shameful periods in our political history.

Within days, cameraman Terry 'Trakka' Ross and I were heading for the tiny Pacific Island of Nauru for the Nine Network's *A Current Affair*. After refusing to allow the *Tampa* to deliver the Afghans to Christmas Island, and so Australian territory, the government loaded them onto the HMAS *Manoora* for transfer to Australia's first offshore detention facility. We were the first and only television crew to be granted official access. This was a genuine moment for Australia and, curiously, the country's most tabloid TV show had the story.

Prime Minister John Howard was showing none of the warmth and compassion of his conservative predecessors, Malcolm Fraser and Robert Menzies. Their approach to both the Vietnamese escaping communism and the economic migrants of postwar Europe had been generous and welcoming. The Howard government, behind in the polls, would go on to cynically exploit public anxiety towards people who were largely fleeing Islamic fundamentalism. Just weeks out from a federal election, Christmas Island was excised from Australia's migration zone and emergency legislation was passed to allow the processing of asylum claims by third countries in the Pacific. It was the genesis of Australia's offshore processing regime – a policy that was the product, not of evidence and argument, but of prejudice and fear.

The *Tampa*'s human cargo was denied entry to Australia and traded with Nauru for $20 million in foreign aid: now its only source of income after its phosphate deposits were depleted and its tax haven status removed.

My early career took shape in an era when people watched television news on a television, at an allocated time, or missed it altogether. There were no other platforms broadcasting pictures from around the world. Free-to-air TV was the only way millions of people could see global events as they happened.

None of us had any clue of just how ubiquitous digital platforms would become and how they would warp the definition of news and the model that once funded its distribution. In the year before the trip to Nauru, market speculation about the capacity of the internet to replace various business sectors led to what became known as the dotcom bubble. People lost a lot of money betting on the potential rather than the commercial reality of the digital world. Google was a word my Nine network colleague Kellie Sloane and I discovered while sitting in our shared office using phones with curly cords attached to the desk.

Two decades later, we communicate and exchange ideas with ease. Anyone with an internet connection can call themselves a blogger and sign up to be represented by the journalists' union. Podcasts, email newsletters and social media are the new tabloid press. With the average person spending three seconds on any piece of content, it has shortened our attention spans, entrenched biases and sullied public debate. Most critically, it's undermined the value proposition of mainstream news organisations. With so much information available for free, why pay for it? What is news anyway, and who decides? In a career spent asking questions, it's this one that confounds more than any other.

Facebook, YouTube, Twitter, Instagram and TikTok didn't exist when the Australian government ignored its responsibilities under the United Nations refugee charter and introduced its chillingly named Pacific Solution. There were no online mobs to goad the coalition government when the 25th prime minister treated strangers to our country like enemies of the state and banished them to a makeshift prison camp on a remote island, in violation of their basic human rights. Many of these refugees were subject to a slow death of spirit and mind. Their crime had been to board a boat rather than arrange themselves in an orderly queue at an airport gate. It's hard to imagine treating Ukrainians like that as they flee the Russians in 2022.

'We will decide who comes to this country and the circumstances in which they come,' cried Howard with the political hubris that became his signature. The minister for Foreign Affairs, Alexander Downer, assured the country he would have the arrivals frisked for weapons. A Senate committee later found that defence minister Peter Reith 'deceived the Australian people' by telling them the asylum seekers had thrown their own children overboard.

The vitriol continued until election day, with immigration minister Philip Ruddock claiming in parliament that those already in deten-tion had clogged the courts with their applications for refugee status. He bellowed about the A$15 million price tag Australian taxpayers would have to wear to fight the claims, neglecting to mention the A$20 million up-front payment it would cost to convince Nauruan administrators to take responsibility under the spurious guise of foreign aid.

I was only on Nauru because Nine had slipped a sweetener into my employment contract, agreeing to send me on one overseas assignment every year. In 2000, I'd been the network reporter at the Academy Awards. Twelve months later, my executive producer was not nearly as excited when I pleaded with him to let me tell the story of languishing refugees, but, to his credit, he agreed to it. Now, with a big story to ourselves, we were quick to seize the advantage. A Current Affair had one million people tuning in each night. We were influencers before influencers had a name. And now we had a chance, and arguably an obligation, to interrogate the alternatives to locking innocent people up.

There was a formula for keeping people hungry for tabloid television. At *A Current Affair*, we peddled outrage, disgust, anger and sadness. The audience wouldn't remember our words or pictures, only how we made them feel. It started with a pithy one-line promo identifying heroes and villains. Emotionally charged language promised tales 'no family can afford to miss'. Often, the story itself was not nearly as sensational as the promo suggested. But if we couldn't maintain their attention, we couldn't reel in the advertising revenue.

I had a problem: the Nauru story couldn't be neatly packaged into ACA's boxing ring. The inhumane treatment of asylum seekers, including forty-three children and three pregnant women, was bipartisan policy.

For all the talk of border security, the international conventions to which we were signatories obliged us to keep the people on that ship safe, not the other way around. Keeping these refugees out of sight was key to the government's strategy of maintaining public apathy.

My own parents arrived in Australia by boat in 1955 and were roundly welcomed by a public warmed to the idea of multiculturalism by the Chifley and Menzies governments. Now, John Howard's support came from people like my mother: migrant Italian, conservative, Catholic. Strangers were not to be trusted.

According to economist Philippe Legrain, a former advisor to the European Commission, any money a state invests in refugees will be returned in double through economic growth within five years. In a major international study on the effect of refugees on the EU economy after German chancellor Angela Merkel invited one million Syrian refugees to her country in 2015, Legrain found that refugees stimulate an economy by creating employment, encouraging innovation and taking lower-level jobs, leaving higher-paid and higher-skilled work to the native citizens.

Has anyone in Australia properly modelled the impact of an open border policy? Where is the evidence that Australia would be in worse shape by allowing several hundred thousand more people into the country each year? As author Glennon Doyle reminds us, unasked questions become prejudices.

It took about seventeen hours to get to Nauru, where Alexander Downer was already busy drafting the terms of the offshore processing and detention agreement with President René Harris. Trakka and I had thirty hours from the time we left Australia to gather the intelligence, film the setting, interview key characters, write the script and pray for a decent internet connection to deliver the film rushes to be stitched together back in Sydney. We'd been allocated eight minutes of airtime at 6.30 pm.

It was cripplingly hot on the largely barren island when we arrived. It isn't the kind of place where you can hail a taxi, so we stopped a motorist on the road to our hotel and offered him US$200 to borrow his car. Foreign correspondents often carry wads of cash for just that sort of contingency.

We were filming an interview with Alexander Downer when the camera malfunctioned in the heat. With the temperature gauge on the car reading 47 degrees Celsius, we raced back to the hotel to blow cold air from a hair dryer into the camera body for an hour. Mercifully, it worked, and I had my opportunity to interrogate Downer and Harris on tape. We also managed to blag our way into the detention centre, film the rooms and capture an unauthorised conversation with the supervisor.

We spoke to the locals about the new neighbourhood prison camp and to businesses about the impact it would have on their community. Logging vision, transcribing interviews, fact checking and writing a script took most of the night. One of my early lessons in television was to give the cameraman ample opportunity to film in early morning light. Arriving at the wharf in Nauru must have been quite something for the people about to disembark. Still and tranquil, the clear water and the empty stretches of sand gave the impression of paradise. It would be the furthest thing from it.

Proud of what we'd been able to achieve against the odds, we sent the vision to Sydney across an unreliable connection. It was 4 pm back home. They'd have two and a half hours to stitch it all together before broadcast. Our talented editors had worked to tighter schedules before.

But as we limped towards thirty-two hours without sleep, running on pure adrenaline, the voice of the production manager was barely audible as she broke the shocking news to me over the phone: the story was being dropped. Another reporter had managed to secure an exclusive interview with the inventor of a revolutionary sweat cure that would soon be marketed widely. A SWEAT CURE! Apparently it was time critical.

As I turned, ashen faced, to Trakka to tell him all that we'd produced had been for nought, his reaction was physical. He vomited.

No amount of pleading and protest would convince the office back home to run our story. At what point had Nine abandoned journalism in favour of advertising disguised as news? Who said Nine viewers didn't care about the plight of people who would put everything on the line to escape to the other side of the world, where they didn't speak the same language, had no prospects and would need to start life again? How was this not a story worth telling? Perhaps the problem is as simple as the observation of Oscar Wilde: the public have an insatiable curiosity to know everything except that which is worth knowing.

I organised us onto a plane back to Sydney and called the boss from the airport to let him know, in colourful language, how I felt. It had been more than a decade since I started my career as a cadet on Melbourne's *Herald Sun*, the country's biggest selling newspaper. *A Current Affair* was the most watched current affairs program on television. It was our job to publish and broadcast stories that passed the public interest test. We had failed in that duty.

Journalism may be the first draft of history, but, as scholar and author Sally Roesch Wagner says, 'History isn't what happened, it's who tells the story.' Stories that are ignored or nixed speak volumes about the opinions and motivations of the editors calling the shots. Journalists will tell you they keep their opinions to themselves, but this is patently untrue. Every frame we choose to broadcast, every line we write and every person's quote we elect to include or leave out of a story is shaped by our judgements and the experiences that form them. I no longer wanted to be part of a team who would ignore such a momentous story.

The Howard government returned many of those *Tampa* asylum seekers to Afghanistan, where up to twenty of them were killed. According to *The Guardian*, others died trying to run away again, like Mohammad Hussain Mirzaee, a *Tampa* returnee and a former anti-Taliban fighter. He was caught by insurgents in 2008 and dragged to his home village. In front of his family, he was beaten and thrown down a well. His tormentors threw a hand grenade down after him.

I got home from Nauru at 10 pm, sank into the lounge, sulking, and turned on the late news in time to see two passenger jets plough into the World Trade Center in New York. It was 11 September 2001.

The next morning, the chief of staff came blustering into the office I shared with reporter Kellie Sloane, barking, 'Find Osama bin Laden and get a satellite phone to him.' While we appreciated the vote of confidence, if the most senior ranks of the CIA couldn't find a terrorist leader, there was no chance we could. Given the head of al-Qaeda had been on the American government's list of ten most wanted fugitives since 1998 for his involvement in the US Embassy bombings in East Africa, this was an absurd directive from someone with one of the most senior news jobs at Nine.

I was entirely dissatisfied with the editorial input I was allowed to provide. Just shy of my thirty-second birthday, I had just become a finalist in the Walkley Awards for a second time and had written the third edition of my *Small Business Book*, which had sold a record 60,000 copies. I'd earned a voice at the decision-making table.

Serendipity put me on an early flight back to Sydney from Canberra on 11 November 2001, the morning after the federal election. Nine News director Peter Meakin had appointed me as the network's tally room reporter on the night, to dampen my lingering post-Nauru rage. The Howard government was returned promising stronger borders.

When ABC news director Max Uechtritz sat down next to me on the flight, I had no idea who he was. Hungover, and having not looked in a mirror before throwing on a pair of ripped jeans and a sleeveless jersey tank, I had not expected to face a job interview at 30,000 feet. We talked endlessly about the ABC's network of foreign bureaux. He told me Michael Brissenden would be the last of the Rome correspondents and I expressed my disappointment. Given my fluent Italian and a burning ambition to tell international stories for an Australian audience, Rome would have been the ultimate prize.

Four weeks later, while I was out on the road 'investigating' the causes of cellulite, Max called me to suggest I join the public broadcaster. In 2002, it was not considered de rigueur to take news roles at the ABC, which struggled in the ratings. But, lucky for me, popularity wasn't my drug of choice. I wanted greater authority over the content I was producing. The people who decide what is and what isn't news are among the most powerful in the country. Ex ABC director of news Kate Torney was the first woman to claim the title at the ABC. She left in 2016, to be replaced by two men. SBS appointed Mandi Wicks to head its news division in 2020. She is only the second woman to lead that team after Irene Buschtedt, who held the role between 1993 and 1995. Every other broadcast director of news in Australia has been a white man.

I got my kicks from chasing stories that basic morality demanded be told. Unfortunately, too many editorial chiefs confuse sensationalism for journalism. Nine's US correspondent was based in Los Angeles, not Washington, and the network's London correspondent spent more time at Buckingham Palace than at Westminster. It made the decision to leave commercial broadcasting an easy one.

Hoping the gig was overseas, I met with Max to discuss what turned out to be an offer to host a new morning TV show, *Business Breakfast*. It was the first turn on the circuitous route to the ABC's European bureau. The tied funding that powered *Business Breakfast* ran out after just eighteen months. Curiously, the money – specifically designated for business broadcasting – had come from the Department of Foreign Affairs and Trade and not Communications, which funded the ABC. Then managing director Russell Balding had seen a gap in programming and I can only posit that the ABC's chief critic and the country's longest serving Communications Minister, Richard Alston, was loath to give the corporation any more support. Too many like him contend that finance journalists should always champion the free market, even when it fails communities, entrenches disadvantage and widens the gap between rich and poor. Even with productivity and wages growth at record lows, they reject the slightest suggestion that the accepted economic orthodoxies might be flawed. This blind acceptance of tired, antwacky logic has long debased our public debate.

When *Business Breakfast* was axed, I accepted an offer to co-host a half hour of midday news with returned foreign correspondent Chris Clarke. This arrangement proved less than ideal after he successfully argued that, given his seniority, he should be the one to introduce all lead stories in the bulletin. I was very much relegated to second banana.

I needed to get out of the studio. To my mind, there was no substitute for the thrill of travelling around the country hearing and telling people's stories from their own homes and workplaces.

Two years after joining *7.30 Report*, and having broken several stories, I was appointed finance editor on my return from maternity leave. Host Kerry O'Brien was sceptical of the choice. The long and unrelenting hours of daily current affairs television meant no woman had come back to *7.30 Report* full-time after the birth of a child, and certainly not to one of the two biggest jobs in the stable. Kerry and I got on well, but he wasn't confident I could manage the roles of mother and editor concurrently. I was determined to make it look easy, even though they were the toughest years of my life. My then husband was travelling a lot as a location sound recordist in television, and we were leaning heavily on our family day carer, Denise Anderson.

Career and ambition did not blend well in the minds of my traditional Italian family. My father had died in 1991, leaving his wife and three daughters behind. When I left a family holiday to return to Sydney to host the coverage of Kerry Packer's death on Boxing Day 2005, my sister stopped talking to me for two years, such was her disgust. But one of the most consequential figures in corporate Australia was dead and it was my job as finance editor to write and deliver a thoughtful television obituary.

In 2008, I won a competitive process and was appointed the ABC's Europe correspondent. That was an even bigger job, and by then I had three children under three. With my then husband working full-time and the ABC putting me through endless rounds of hazardous environment and technology training, I wondered how the logistics would be organised. Despite posting Australian journalists overseas for seventy-six years, there was no department or consultant employed to help with things like finding a home or enrolling children in schools. Being only the second mother to win a foreign posting in the ABC's history (Catherine McGrath was the first), I was horrified when the head of international brushed off my queries with the quip 'normally the wives work it out'.

We arrived in London at the start of the Global Financial Crisis and I was hungry to examine the collision of power and profligacy and how it had broken Europe's financial systems architecture. At an investment banking lunch just before my departure, one cocky young executive used the analogy of a bomb to explain the subprime debt that had been pooled, parcelled up and sold to investors. He said the debt was being passed around so many times, it was bound to explode and take down one or more of the big banks. He wasn't wrong. Six months later, I was on London's Canary Wharf when the collapse of Lehman Brothers became the biggest bankruptcy in US history. Capturing the distress and confusion on the faces of the 5000 people spewing out of the bank's giant British tower brought the enormity of the crisis into sharp focus.

The Apple iPhone was barely a year old, YouTube was three years old, Twitter and Facebook were barely two, and it would be another two years until Instagram launched. In the four years I was Europe correspondent, advances in technology would dominate, disrupt and disarm every industry in the world. In her searing 2009 book *Fool's Gold*, exposing the corrosive nature of greed on the power of regulators and ratings agencies, former *Financial Times* editor Gillian Tett documents how advances in technology created sophisticated trading platforms that allowed debt-drunk bankers to fuel their addictions. In the chapter 'Leveraging lunacy', she says that from 1995 to 2005, innovation meant that credit default swap (CDS) contracts – derivatives that allowed investors to offset or swap their credit risk – ballooned to US$12 trillion, the equivalent of the entire US economy. Underpinning this debt binge were home and corporate loans that often made little sense. But the fees garnered from packaging up and selling that shaky (subprime) debt made rich bankers richer and ruined the lives of too many ordinary people who'd trusted the system.

With the world's gaze fixed on financial markets, not enough attention was paid to the criminal investigation that saw Rupert Murdoch's News International found guilty of phone hacking and paying bribes to police.

The longstanding funding model for legacy media was collapsing. Advertising dollars that had once funded journalism were flowing to the new digital platforms that provided higher-quality content or content that was user generated rather than prescribed by newsroom editors. Traditional news businesses were fighting for relevance any way they could.

In 2007, the veteran royal reporter Clive Goodman and private investigator Glenn Mulcaire were jailed for hacking the phones of Prince William and Prince Harry's advisors. Rupert Murdoch's UK-based empire, which even had the temerity to call itself News, denied that phone hacking was widespread in the organisation and put it down to the off-piste work of one 'rogue reporter'. But there was a smoking gun that would prove otherwise and the story would dominate my final year as Europe correspondent.

Goodman had accessed and listened to hundreds of private voicemail messages from the British royal family, their staff and medical professionals. It was this praxis of evil rather than any leaky source at Buckingham Palace that, in 2005, had led to his series of front-page scoops. He'd published stories about Prince Harry's knee and shoulder ailments and questioned his fitness ahead of an intended British army deployment.

Not since Nauru had I fixed as hard on the question of what is news, who decides and what are the consequences of getting it wrong? The answer, too often, had no regard at all for the public interest.

In his sixteen-month inquiry into the culture, practices and ethics of the press, Britain's Lord Justice Leveson concluded that 'too many stories in too many newspapers were the subject of complaints from too many people, with too little in the way of (newspaper) titles taking responsibility, or considering the consequences for the individuals involved'.

Eighteen years before the royal reporter's nefarious activities were revealed, one of the Murdochs' then Australian publications, *New Idea*, had broken a story by publishing illegally obtained phone banter between Prince Charles and his then lover, Camilla Parker Bowles. Their respective marriages crumbled over the Prince's lust-filled musings on being Camilla's tampon.

Rupert Murdoch, the left-wing Oxford undergraduate, who became the print and pilot union-busting strongman, would, over the ensuing decades, commit himself to nothing more than opportunity.

Among documents filed with the court in the case against the private investigator Glenn Mulcaire was a trove of meticulously curated notes with the names of the people whose calls had been intercepted. Among them was the Professional Football Association's chairman, Gordon Taylor. If hacking was the misconduct of only one rogue palace reporter, how would News explain away the pursuit of a high-profile footballer? In 2008, lawyer Mark Lewis, representing Taylor, would reach an agreement with James Murdoch to settle the matter in return for a payment of £750,000. The money was paid with no admission made of the widespread use of illegal phone taps. *News of the World* had published a story claiming Taylor was having an affair. It was later conceded the story was the result of a misinterpreted voicemail.

Australian supermodel Elle Macpherson became embroiled in the affair when, in 2005, the *News of the World* published stories that repeated, verbatim, words her business manager, Mary-Ellen Field, had left in a voicemail message. Macpherson assumed that Field had leaked the private information to the tabloid press. Field was sacked and her reputation irreparably damaged. Justice Leveson described her as an 'innocent bystander who was not even targeted or explicitly written about but became "collateral damage" because of the suspicions generated by subterfuge'. She would eventually learn that hers was among more than 4000 phone numbers whose voicemails had been unlawfully accessed.

More celebrity names began to emerge after the actress Sienna Miller launched a civil action and *The Guardian* newspaper's investigative reporter Nick Davies took up the cause. As Leveson noted in his final report, 'had Mulcaire been less assiduous with record keeping, what has now been uncovered would have remained unknown'.

Sienna Miller claimed *The Sun* obtained medical records of her 2005 pregnancy through illegal means and that the paper's then editor, Rebekah Brookes, knew that she was a mother-to-be before her friends did.

She brought legal action against the newspaper's publisher, now known as News Group Newspapers (NGN), which denied that any illegal information-gathering took place at *The Sun* and agreed to settle her case for damages without any admission of liability.

'I wanted to expose the criminality that runs through the heart of this corporation,' she said, 'a criminality demonstrated clearly and irrevocably by the evidence which I have seen. I wanted to share News Group's secrets just as they have shared mine. Unfortunately, that legal recourse is not available to me or to anyone who does not have countless millions of pounds to spend on the pursuit of justice. Such is our world. Until someone comes along who can confront the Murdochs' endless means, all that I have left are these words. And they are the truth.' Miller settled her case in 2021.

Actor Hugh Grant, giving evidence at the Leveson Inquiry, railed against the constant invasion of his privacy by the press and its impact on his life. Grant rejected suggestions that it was in moviegoers' interests to understand the true character of the stars they worship. Indeed, even when his mugshot was splashed across the world's front pages after his arrest for a liaison with a sex worker, it had little impact on his fan base. His next movie broke box office records.

Trading on the public's appetite for other people's misfortunes and misdeeds, the Sunday weekly *News of the World* was the only one sent to the news knackery by its owner Rupert Murdoch. The 168-year-old masthead, enjoying the highest circulation in the English-speaking world, was offered as the sacrificial lamb to atone for the unethical practices that had infected the News International machine at least a decade before they became public knowledge throughout 2011.

The final nail in the *News of the World* coffin came when *The Guardian* (a not-for-profit enterprise) broke the story that journalists had hacked the phone of murdered schoolgirl Milly Dowler during the search for her in 2002. A desperate mother trying to reach her thirteen-year-old couldn't leave a message because the messagebank was full. When she tried again a day later, some messages had been erased. It filled Sally Dowler with false hope that Milly had listened to her messages and was still alive. In fact, *News of the World* had accessed her voicemail and deleted her messages. The truth wasn't revealed for nine years.

The Murdoch family claimed ignorance over the entire hacking enterprise. On 15 July 2011, on the steps of a hotel in central London ahead of a meeting between Rupert Murdoch and the Dowler family, I jostled to the front of the press pack and asked the News boss how it was possible that he signed a cheque for £750,000 to Gordon Taylor without ever asking what the money was for. It had demonstrated either negligence or deceit.

I'm not naive enough to suggest that news is not a business, but it shouldn't be for sale to the highest bidder. For decades, it's been corrupted by the influence of money and might. It shamelessly barracks for parties during their election campaigns and can even determine the outcome, as evidenced by the 1992 UK election when the unexpected victory of the Conservatives was followed by a pointed front-page headline: It's The Sun Wot Won It.

The Leveson Inquiry found the relationship between politicians and journalists was too cosy; Andy Coulson, the former editor of *News of the World*, was hired by then prime minister David Cameron, to run his media strategy in 2007. In 2010, he was appointed the Downing Street communications director.

As *The Guardian* published story after story documenting the criminal behaviour at the heart of the News International operation, the BBC invited me to appear on its Media Show to discuss the topic from an Australian perspective. I talked about tabloid television because, in

Australia, that was the closest equivalent to the tripe served up in the British red tops.

During my time at *A Current Affair*, we would pay tens of thousands of dollars to secure stories. When we didn't want our rivals at the Seven Network to interview someone we had already secured on tape, we'd hide that person in a hotel room for the day to fortify our exclusive. One time we even bought a Nissan WRX, wired it with cameras, put a crew in a van nearby and waited for it to be stolen on camera. One famous interview of a motor mechanic who'd been overcharging and under-servicing clients ended tragically when the target of the 'investigation' committed suicide.

Thankfully, that kind of journalism is fading from view as the money that funded it finds better content to support. A more mature and discerning consumer is seeking out trusted individuals and funding their content directly through newsletters and podcasts.

The industry doesn't need more money. It needs the money to be distributed to where it counts. It needs influence over what constitutes news taken away from business and politics. More than 5000 Australian journalists have lost their jobs over the past decade, yet quality publications overseas like *The New York Times*, *The Guardian*, *The Atlantic* and the BBC have grown revenues and audiences. Arms-length trusts have been created to ensure editors and reporters are truly independent and detached from their paymasters. Purpose and profit have never been a palatable cocktail.

The notion that the press is the fourth estate, and, by extension, an integral feature of any modern democracy, is founded on the idea that the function of news is to act as a guardian of the public interest and as a watchdog on the activities of government. While media houses continue to undermine the trust bestowed on them, younger audiences and readers vote with their feet, taking advertisers and philanthropic money with them.

Emma Alberici spent thirty years as a journalist across print (*The Herald Sun*), commercial television (Nine) and ultimately as *Lateline* presenter, finance editor, economics editor and foreign correspondent at the ABC. She has authored three bestselling books on small business and is now working in executive search at Derwent.

20
CROSSING THE LINE: ONE MAN'S LIFE OR THE STORY

Sophie McNeill
Jerusalem 2015–2018
ABC

With Nazieh and family Heidelberg, Germany.

IT WAS A modern exodus of biblical proportions. In the northern summer and autumn of 2015, over one million refugees and migrants landed on Europe's shores, the majority of them fleeing war and persecution in the Middle East. Half of those seeking safety were Syrians, who, after spending years being bombed and slaughtered by their own government, gave up waiting for the rest of the world to notice their suffering. A determined, resourceful and brave people, more than half a million Syrians took matters into their own hands, walking out of the decrepit camps they had been stuck in for years in Lebanon, Jordan and Turkey, and making their way to the Turkish coast, where they could easily find a seat on one of the hundreds of smugglers' boats leaving each day for the Greek islands.

I had arrived in Jerusalem a few months earlier with my husband and two young sons in tow. Having spent much of the past decade reporting on the Middle East for SBS's *Dateline* and ABC's *Foreign Correspondent*, it was a massive honour to have now landed my dream job: Middle East correspondent for the ABC, covering the whole region for radio, television and online. But looking at the horror unfolding in nearly every corner, it was hard to know where to begin. From Gaza to Yemen, Iraq to Syria, millions of men, women and children were enduring unspeakable fear and suffering. Civilian homes, markets and schools targeted. Food used as a weapon of war. Cluster bombs. Poison-gas attacks. Hospitals bombed. The denial of medical care to civilians, including children, as a deliberate act to achieve a political or military objective. My days were spent trying to weigh up which alleged war crime should be in the headlines. Airstrikes and barrel bombs in Aleppo, children starving in Sanaa, or the latest ISIS car bombing in Baghdad – it was a smorgasbord of horror, and it was very easy to understand why tens of thousands of parents across the region believed it safer to place their children on a boat to Europe than to stay where they were.

The island of Lesvos was one of the closest points of Greek territory to the Turkish coast. Our ABC Middle East bureau producer Fouad Abu Gosh, cameraman Aaron Hollett and I stood on its sandy shores, watching as four cheap, inflatable dinghies sped steadily across the water towards us. More than thirty thousand people had landed on these beaches in just a fortnight; the Greek coastguard were so overwhelmed, smugglers no longer sought the cover of darkness. On a calm day it only took an hour or two to make the crossing, and today the sea looked smooth and glassy. Not everyone was so lucky to get these kinds of conditions. If the wind quickly changed and the swell rose, these inflatable craft would be tossed around like bath toys and many of the refugees couldn't swim. Hundreds of people had drowned in just the past few weeks.

There was a cheer and a clap as the first dinghy ground up onto the sand right next to us. A group of young men were the first to jump off, amused to see a camera greet them as they landed. They gave each other high fives and hugs. 'I'm from Syria,' declared a teenage boy, wiping tears from his eyes. 'Thank you, thank you!' Mums and dads stepped cautiously ashore, holding babies, toddlers and small sports bags stuffed with belongings. Many wept to be safely on European soil; others collapsed in exhaustion.

A Syrian father carefully helped his young son alight. The dad shrugged sadly when I asked about the rest of the family. It had cost him US$1200 for two seats on the boat, and that was all he could afford, he told me. His wife and younger children had to stay behind. 'I told him, I'm doing this for his future,' he said quietly, with his arm around his son, who stood overawed and silent next to his dad. 'He is nine years old and has never been to school. You know what it is like in Syria.'

In these days of tighter budgets and constant around-the-clock deadlines, the pressure to file constantly when covering a big story was immense. I had to do radio, live crosses, online, TV news packages and, often, longer in-depth current affairs pieces for ABC TV's *7.30* program as well. There was barely enough time to eat or sleep, let alone do anything else apart from 'get the story'. My team and I had been asked to find a Syrian family arriving by boat and then follow them on their journey across the island, until they boarded a ferry for Athens to continue their way across Europe. But amid the mayhem on the beach, I noticed one old man standing alone, leaning on a cane and quietly crying. Fouad and I quickly went over to ask him what was wrong. 'I've been separated from my wife and my children. I don't know what to do now!' he said.

A sixty-one-year-old Syrian refugee, Nazieh Husein was lost. He had no money, no phone and no contact numbers for his children or wife, who he'd been separated from on the crossing. He also had a bad leg, and it was clear he couldn't walk unassisted the fifty or so kilometres to Mitilini, the main town where the ferries left for Athens. All he had with him was his cane, his identity documents, and the family Quran which he carried in a plastic bag. He also hadn't had any food or water for two days as he waited in the bushes for the people smuggler to give them the all clear to get in the boat. Nazieh didn't meet the brief we had been given and we had many other filing tasks to complete that day. But I knew we couldn't just leave him. It was a battle for survival here. Every asylum seeker was desperate to try to get across Europe to a country like Germany before the weather turned. It was hard enough finding food and shelter for themselves and their families, let alone taking on an old man who wouldn't be able to keep up. Surely, we could film Nazieh and help him at the same time?

Fouad and Aaron both agreed. We hugged Nazieh and told him not to worry. We promised we would help him get to a safe place and put him in touch with groups who could begin the search for his loved ones.

Our driver on Lesvos told us about a new regulation: it was now illegal to provide transport to asylum seekers. But we all agreed it was worth the risk to assist Nazieh. We picked up some food and water and began the two-hour drive to the main port where the ferries were leaving for the Greek mainland. The town by then resembled a refugee camp as thousands of refugees slept rough in the streets or in small tents while they waited for a ferry. We took Nazieh to look for his wife and children among the crowds, but despite hours of searching, we had no luck. There was every chance they had been put on a boat to a different Greek island altogether, or that they had never even left Turkey. Nazieh couldn't stop crying. He told us that his life wasn't worth living without his wife and kids. They were all he had left. 'I just need to see them again,' he told us, tears running down his cheeks. 'This is my only wish in life.'

The International Committee of the Red Cross (ICRC) had set up a missing-persons tent on the outskirts of the main town. The volunteers wrote down Nazieh's details and took his photo to add to their family tracing register. 'Your picture will be published on the Red Cross website and hopefully they will help you find your family,' a young Greek volunteer explained kindly to Nazieh through an interpreter. 'What was your family's target destination?' 'Almania,' Nazieh said sadly. Germany. We didn't want Nazieh to join the thousands of others sleeping on the streets, so we found him a room at our hotel and Fouad gave him some of his clothes to wear. While still managing to meet all our filing requirements that day, we didn't tell our bosses quite how much time we had also spent helping Nazieh.

The next morning, Nazieh spotted a Syrian family who'd been on his boat from Turkey. They offered to help him cross to the mainland and take him to the main ICRC office in Athens. Nazieh decided this was the best option; he was sure he would have more luck finding them there than on this small island. That afternoon, he hugged us tightly and we said a tearful goodbye before he joined the other family and limped up the long walkway leading onto the ferry, turning back and waving at us several times before disappearing inside. It would be the last shot of our feature report on Nazieh's story for *7.30*.

We left Lesvos that night and flew back to Athens. But Nazieh was still firmly on my mind. I couldn't stop worrying about what might happen to him. I was about to board my flight back to Jerusalem in the early hours of the morning when the Syrian family looking after Nazieh called. They were worried the Macedonian border was going to close and had decided to leave Athens immediately. They wanted to know what they should do with Nazieh. It was 2 am. I was terrified that he might be dumped on the streets of Athens with no ability to communicate, no money and no proper jacket to keep him warm. I went up to the check-in desk and told the hostess I wouldn't be boarding and urgently needed to get my bags offloaded. The family said they would leave Nazieh with some Syrian friends who would deliver him to the Red Cross headquarters in Athens at first light. I promised to meet him there.

This wasn't under the cover of work anymore. There was nothing more to film; the story on Nazieh had ended once we got the shots we needed on Lesvos, and Aaron, the cameraman, had flown back to his base in Beirut on an earlier flight. But I couldn't turn my back on him now. I got a cab into Athens and found a hotel to try and get a few hours' sleep before meeting Nazieh. I arrived at the Red Cross where Nazieh was supposed to meet me at 7 am. But there was no sign of him. After an hour, I started to get really stressed. Had the family given him the right address? Had they really left him with someone who could help him make it here? Finally, at close to 9 am, I saw a figure slowly limping up the street with a cane. Nazieh! He saw me and started crying, and I rushed over to hug him and help him cross the road. He looked absolutely exhausted, and I felt awful. We had told him he would be looked after, but it hadn't gone to plan.

We went inside the Red Cross building to meet the Syrian refugee case workers. There was no news yet on his wife or children. So was there somewhere he could stay in the meantime? I explained Nazieh's inability to walk very far, his lack of money, and that he only spoke Arabic. They looked concerned. The cash-strapped Greek government was overwhelmed, they explained. Tens of thousands of asylum seekers were arriving each week and there were now hundreds of vulnerable cases like Nazieh that needed the extra help and protection provided by the authorities. 'Let us make some calls and get back to you,' they promised.

Back out on the street, we weren't sure where else to turn. So, we went for lunch and did some shopping to get Nazieh new clothes, cigarettes and a phone. Just as I was beginning to worry about just how long I might have to stay in Athens, the Red Cross called. They had found him a bed in a camp on the other side of town, where he could stay for free and receive meals and medical care while he waited for news of his loved ones. We jumped in a taxi and headed straight there. The staff were extremely lovely, welcoming Nazieh and introducing him to his Arabic-language case worker. Nazieh was assigned his own little demountable hut with a small single bed and even air conditioning. Refugees were not locked up here in Greece – they could come and go as they pleased – but most of the families didn't leave. They needed the free services provided. Many like Nazieh were waiting for lost relatives or had run out of money and couldn't continue on their planned journey to Germany.

This time when I left Nazieh, I knew he was in safe hands. Thanks to my producer Fouad's excellent sleuthing skills, a few weeks later we managed to track down Nazieh's daughter in Syria on Facebook and discovered that his wife and children were now in Germany. They had been distraught, desperately searching for him all along the route. Now they could hardly believe he was still alive. In the end, we produced a 'part two' program; I flew to Germany and filmed beautiful scenes of them reuniting.

Despite all that, I was in deep trouble with my boss. I was told I had 'crossed the line' and 'placed too much stress on the team' on Lesvos by prioritising helping Nazieh – and they didn't even know about the Athens side trip! While it upset me greatly that they felt that way, I had absolutely no regrets.

PTSD (post traumatic stress disorder) and moral injury are very real risks when reporting on deeply traumatic and emotional events. I always found that the best way of avoiding the guilt that I saw eat other colleagues up was to help whenever I could. That episode with Nazieh cemented that I would always be a humanitarian first and journalist second. No 'story' was more important than someone's real life.

The belief that reporters must be dispassionate, neutral observers is built on a fallacy. While I'd never pick a military 'side' in a conflict, I was always firmly on one side – that of the civilians, the women and children, the victims of the violence and the war crimes, the ones caught in the middle without the power of the gun or the warplanes. It doesn't impact my commitment to the truth, to verifying the evidence, or getting it right. I just believe that centring ethical decision-making at the heart of what you do makes better journalism. The people you meet along the way also know if they mean more to you than just a story – they give you better access and are more honest if they feel they can trust you to act ethically and make decisions that place their wellbeing first.

I've been told my approach is unique (and mostly not as a compliment) and I wonder if it's because I didn't do any formal journalism training. I didn't really know how you were supposed to do it. I didn't really know what the rules were. I just did what felt right, what I could live with, my heart and gut leading the way. As a result, I now sleep better at night and can deal with all those ghosts from the road. I don't really have any 'what ifs' or thoughts of 'if only I had just helped that one person', because I always did.

Ultimately, though, I have left this great profession. I was just not convinced this was the best way to achieve change and make the world a better place. I could have easily spent another decade or two on the road, showing you more of all the terrible things, but that felt like the easy option. Now, as a researcher for Human Rights Watch, my job is to investigate and expose human rights abuses, but also to advocate and lobby for change. That's the hard part I've learned, not just telling people what's wrong, but coming up with solutions and working to get them implemented. But all the brave, amazing people that I met along the way, like Nazieh, keep me inspired and fighting for change. I hope, too, that young journalists coming into this profession will push back against those editors who might try and tell them not to 'care so much' or 'get too involved'. Because nothing is ever just a story for the people who are in it.

Sophie McNeill is Australia researcher for Human Rights Watch. A multiple–Walkley Award winner, she was an investigative reporter with ABC TV's *Four Corners* and was posted to the Middle East as ABC correspondent. She is the author of *We Can't Say We Didn't Know: Dispatches from an Age of Impunity.*

21
ONCE UPON A TIME IN INDIA

Melissa Roberts
Delhi 1981–1983
Freelance

On the Afghan Pakistan border with the Mujahideen.

'I SAY.' THE softly spoken Reuters correspondent one row in front of us on the Indian Airlines plane caught the attention of the flight attendant. We were still pushed back into our seats by the sharp angle of the take-off from Jaipur. Jeremy gestured out the window; the attendant placed her hand on the back of the seat and bent down to look. 'Should there be flames coming from the engine?' he asked.

'Fasten your seatbelts!' the flight attendant screamed and ran towards the pilots' cabin.

Ever the optimist, I turned to my partner, Trevor Watson, the ABC Delhi correspondent. 'That's normal, right?' I asked. Maybe the engines were old, or just burning off some excess fuel. Maybe we weren't about to crash into the wasteland around the airport and die in a conflagration among the makeshift camps of people coming to town in search of a better life.

A white-knuckle flier in India at the best of times, Trevor clasped my hand. 'No. It's not normal.'

The Fasten Seat Belt and No Smoking signs pinged back on. The flight attendant strapped herself into her seat by the door with shaking hands.

We watched the flames kill the port engine.

In the row behind us another journalist couple, Trevor Fishlock, *The Times*' Man, as he was always known, and the *Daily Mail*'s Penny Simon, were doing a fine line in British stiff upper lip.

The pilot pulled the Boeing 737 back into an even steeper climb through the bird strike zone, the area of sky above the airport where vultures hung high over the illegal new villages, waiting to spot the dead and dying. And waiting, on occasion, to be sucked into a jet engine.

Then there was silence. The other engine had failed.

Captain Gupta, who we would later learn was an ex air force fighter pilot, dumped fuel over the homes below. Then, at the apogee of the climb, he turned the plane sharply to starboard – and rushed headlong back towards the earth. The dive kickstarted the one good engine. At the last moment, he pulled the nose up and we skidded sideways along the runway, back on solid ground. The passengers erupted into applause and, as we headed down the emergency exit, a tour group of Europeans shared a pre-breakfast bottle of Cinzano, swigging desperately from its neck.

It was 1982. Weeks earlier, a messenger had arrived at our door in New Delhi with a gilt edged, printed invitation. The Maharana of Udaipur requested our presence as his guests at his City Palace, on the shores of Lake Pichola. Udaipur had starred in the latest James Bond film, the Lake Palace was already a hotel, and Maharana Bhagwat Singh Mewar wanted us to have a look around his digs and let him know if we thought he should take in paying guests.

The 600-odd royal families of India had kept their crowns through the long British Raj. They had been extraordinarily wealthy – the Nizam of Hyderabad was said to have used enormous diamonds as paperweights while rats ate his cash. In return for their support at Independence in 1947, they received millions of rupees a year, until in 1971 Prime Minister Indira Gandhi turned off the tap, forcing them to earn a living. Most chose to commercialise a palace or two.

When we finally made it to Udaipur in the desert state of Rajasthan, we were welcomed with garlands of yellow marigolds, our foreheads were marked with sandalwood paste, and we were deposited in front of the massive clifftop palace, built of golden stone. The front door was closed, so we knocked. It was opened at once by a prince, the handsome and resolutely royal-looking younger son, Arvind Singh Mewar. He wore a double-breasted navy jacket with brass buttons and an elegant turban; his luxuriant black beard was neatly parted down the middle of his chin and brushed to curve up towards his ears.

We were shown to our old-fashioned yet luxurious rooms (our massive patio had a flower-garlanded swing) and then left to ourselves, the five of us wandering the palace, poking around, finding treasures like the collection of vintage cars that included a Rolls Royce Silver Ghost, and naughtily sitting on the throne.

Finally, at dinner, we were joined by the Maharana, who slipped into his place at the head of the long, heavily decorated table. He was a diminutive, clean shaven, quietly spoken man in a safari suit. We five journalists were uncharacteristically quiet, until Penny gestured to the huge stuffed black bear looming over us. 'Magnificent beast!' she said. When the Maharana retired for the evening, the Indian whisky came out and the party started.

The City Palace was never to take in guests. The Maharana left his fortune and title to his younger son, a decision that has been disputed ever since by elder brother Mahendra, who did not come to dinner. Arvind lives there still, running other hotels as the Indian legal system slowly grinds away. Perhaps sometimes he looks out over the lake at the view we once shared to the glowing hotel on the island, wondering what might have been.

OLD INDIA LIVED on in the princes, the seemingly eternal villages and the echoes of the Raj still found in hill stations, rundown hotels and the memories of old people. There was a sense of the fairytale about it. At the Republic Day parade, along with the tanks, the artillery and the crack troops, the mounts of the Bikaner Camel Corps were festooned with rainbows of pompoms, the riders were equipped either with a spectacular turban or fatigues and an assault rifle. Now ceremonial, the corps once routed the Turks in a World War I camel charge and joined the Relief of Peking that ended the Boxer Rebellion, albeit on foot.

Pride in their national dress lent everyone a glamour, and English usage often remained peppered with 1930s Bertie Wooster–style Britishisms, full of spots of bother and old chaps. A clerk filling in one of India's endless forms needed my address. 'Where are you putting up these days?' he asked. Some correspondents joked that when the colonial masters departed thirty-five years earlier, they left behind the instructions on how to run the country, but in a locked box to which no one could find the key. They called India a functioning anarchy.

I freelanced for *The Australian* and a bunch of radio networks including National Public Radio and NBC in the US. Trevor and I wrote our stories on ancient typewriters and filed our copy by telex, a hulking machine in the corner of the office. I typed in my story to record it as punched holes on a long ribbon of paper. After dialling repeatedly, possibly for hours, until I got a line, I would feed the ribbon back into the machine, and hope that at the other end, foreign editor and mentor Piers Akerman was waiting. During the monsoon, the telex could go down for a month. From his recording booth, Trevor filed radio stories to Sydney via London, down the phone line that, when it worked, was so crackly as to sometimes make the stories unintelligible.

The ABC employed numerous servants – a cook, bearer (housekeeper), driver and chowkidar (night watchman) – who lived with their families in a compact block of flats in the backyard. It would have been impossible to work without their help, but their presence also brought responsibility, like the day Padma, the bearer, came to ask us to do something about the man in the garden whose dancing bear was frightening the children.

The garden was lush with bougainvillea and was a sanctuary or a circus, invaded daily by various wallahs, the men who provided a specific service. There was Hamid the carpet wallah, the monkey wallah, men with baskets of dancing snakes, and Mr Singh, who made safari suits to measure for all the male members of the press corps. Outside, bicycle rickshaw wallahs touted for business.

But India was also a grinding and confronting place to live, and to work. At that Republic Day parade, I had narrowly missed being injured as police managed queues with mounted lathi charges, beating the people around me with long sticks. Classified by the ABC as a Hardship Post, extreme poverty and death were always close: the unclaimed dead child lying in the street outside our house, floating half-burnt bodies in the Ganges, lepers banging on the car windows. The barrage was dark, constant and draining. These were real people, and the suffering of each one seemed more awful than the next. And then there was the parade of Australian travellers at the door asking for help, the young man bitten by a rabid dog (Yes), the man overwhelmed by India who wanted to stay with us because his aunt had been a receptionist in a regional ABC office (No).

ADDING TO THE otherworldly feeling was the absence of imports. We drove a locally made Hindustan Ambassador – or, rather, our driver Joseph drove it. A kindly and intelligent man, he was guide, translator at times, and friend. He could also be an intermediary, calmly negotiating between inquisitive crowds that could suddenly turn tense and a frustrated ABC correspondent, trying to record a piece to camera amid constant chaos. The Ambassador was a brand new, locally built 1953 Morris Oxford. The manufacturing plant had been bought from Britain in its entirety, and as it aged, each new Ambassador was slightly inferior to the one before. The car's great benefit was that it was so simple it could be easily repaired by a village mechanic when it broke down, as it inevitably did.

India's first prime minister, Jawaharlal Nehru, had believed political freedom depended on complete self-sufficiency, that foreign nations could suddenly cut the supply of heavy machinery and weapons, causing Indians to 'thus remain slaves'. He banned imports and India was obliged to produce every single thing it needed, from bicycle rickshaws to pharmaceuticals and the raw materials to make them, to every scrap of cloth and every bite of food. It was a policy continued by Nehru's daughter, the country's second prime minister, Indira Gandhi. But with few savings to draw on for investment, inefficiency and shortages were assured. There was a one-year wait for an Ambassador; some people, it was said, could expect to wait twenty years for the phone to be connected (which didn't work during the monsoon anyway). For those lucky enough to win a manufacturing licence from the government, the upside was huge profits; one downside was Thums Up, a rather unpleasant locally made soft drink.

I WAS DRAWN to stories about women, like Phoolan Devi, the Bandit Queen, who, at twenty-five, had a price of 10,000 rupees on her head for the murder of thirty men. The equivalent of US$1000, it was a fortune to a villager. Devi's territory was the dusty villages and ravines of Uttar Pradesh, where gangs of dacoits, or bandits, terrorised the countryside. They rarely attacked tourists, but no one took the road to the Taj Mahal at night. When anger over the predations of dacoits almost brought down the state government, the chief minister cracked down, claiming his men had killed 1500 outlaws with the loss of only thirty-nine police.

Married to an old man at eleven years of age, Phoolan Devi eventually ran away to join the dacoits. When her gang leader boyfriend was murdered, she led a massacre of the killer and twenty of his fellow villagers. The myths (and a movie) quickly followed. She was beautiful; she killed men with her bare hands; she sang from the rooftops as her men robbed and pillaged; she had a prodigious sexual appetite.

Her reign of terror was short. In a ceremony straight out of Bollywood, she laid her gun at the feet of her adversary, the chief minister, and spent the next eleven years in jail (which was probably not quite what she was expecting). Then, in a plot twist, she was elected to parliament, representing Delhi. But in Bollywood, women who stray get their comeuppance, and in 2001, a gunman appeared at her door and shot her to death. It was retribution for the massacre that had earned her fame almost two decades before.

Other women had a different kind of price on their heads.

At a cocktail party, an Indian man told me he was worth half a million rupees, a sum that, while it could not be converted into hard currency, had a local buying power just as great as it sounded. He had no assets, just a Western education, high social status and a well-paying job with a foreign company. He was referring to the dowry he could demand from a future wife in cash and gifts like refrigerators or motorbikes. About 85 per cent of marriages were arranged, and dowries were both banned and demanded. Many matches began in the pages of the Sunday papers, where prospective brides and grooms listed their attributes, like the paleness of their complexion or their US residency rights. The same newspaper might also carry a paragraph about a young bride whose sari caught fire while she was making tea on the gas stove. Every day, in Delhi alone, another two women died of burns, likely murdered by their mothers-in-law in a dispute over their dowry.

After the marriage, when the dowry agreement had long been settled, the new family demanded more. 'Even when confronted with their bruised and battered daughter, the bride's parents seldom intervene,' I wrote. Nor did husbands: their brides were virtual strangers and second marriages meant second dowries, activist Subhadra Butalia told me. She had sat by Hardeep Kaur's hospital bed in 1978 as the young woman died of burns. Hardeep's in-laws went free. Despite her feminist organisation Kamika's campaign against dowries and violence, Mrs Butalia had compassion for the mothers-in-law. They too had been mistreated in a loveless marriage.

But dowry was firmly linked to greed, penetrating areas of the country where it had no basis in tradition. It also contributed to the desire for baby boys and the mistreatment of women from the uterus to the grave, with girls more likely to suffer malnutrition, more likely to be illiterate and 60 per cent more likely to die in infancy. Gang rapes were frighteningly common. In Amritsar, the wealthy capital of Punjab, doctors were advertising amniocentesis tests and abortions for female foetuses. Women took to the streets. 'It's shocking that in the Punjab, which already has the lowest female ratio of 875 women to 1000 men, these tests are being conducted so blatantly and brazenly,' said feminist member of parliament Susheela Gopalan. But for one father at Amritsar's Bhandari Hospital, a test was cheaper than a dowry. 'Better to pay 500 rupees now than one lakh [100,000] rupees later,' he said.

INDIA IS INDIRA, crowds would chant. Indira is India.

This was also a country where a woman could lead with an iron grip. Gandhi's party was Congress (I) and the I stood for Indira. Her control was such that she personally chose every candidate, and every senior party functionary. Her son Sanjay was expected to continue the dynasty, but he died in a light plane crash just before we arrived, leaving behind a grim legacy of forced sterilisations and compulsory slum clearance. His brother Rajiv, a thirty-nine-year-old Indian Airlines pilot, agreed to step up, as he said, 'to help mummy'.

The most powerful woman in the world, at sixty-five Mrs Gandhi had held power for a decade and a half in the world's most disparate nation. She would often proudly point out that India was the world's largest democracy – but she had also declared The Emergency in 1975, during which she ruled by decree for two years, cancelling elections, suspending civil rights and jailing opponents and journalists. India, I wrote, was the only country to throw out a dictator in a fair election that she had called, and promptly vote her back in at the next opportunity.

There was another woman bearing the famous Gandhi name with her eyes on the prime ministership: Maneka Gandhi, Sanjay's young widow. The traditional tensions between mother- and daughter-in-law were played out in the national papers.

When Maneka forged the National Sanjay Party from her husband's band of hardline enforcers, Indira threw Maneka and her infant son out of the official residence at night. Maneka hit back with full-page ads in the newspapers addressed to 'Dear Mummy', accusing the PM of torturing her in 'every conceivable way', including making her eat in her room and insulting her in front of the servants. The pro-Indira camp accused Maneka of chain smoking; Indira blamed 'foreign forces' for infiltrating Maneka into her family; while, for her part, Maneka noted her mother-in-law's advanced age and erratic memory and offered her best wishes for a speedy recovery.

'We are very alike,' Maneka told me. 'One day she will come to me and ask: Why are you doing all this? And I will say: Because I am you.' Indeed, they were very alike – strong, intelligent and suspicious.

'Wherever I go, the government is absolutely paranoid and does whatever I want them to do. I can't achieve anything directly, but I can focus attention on a problem and then the government rushes in and does the job. It's really quite amusing,' Maneka said. 'I mention it in all my speeches.'

Mrs Gandhi was a towering figure on the world stage. As head of the Non-Aligned Movement, which claimed to be united by their independence from both the Soviet Union and the United States, she hosted the biggest summit in history. It featured every despot of the late twentieth century, and the kings, presidents and prime ministers who ruled two-thirds of the world's people.

There was Cuba's Fidel Castro, Egypt's Hosni Mubarak, Lee Kuan Yew from Singapore, Libya's Colonel Gaddafi and Zimbabwe's Robert Mugabe along with Malaysia's Mahathir and Pakistan's martial law ruler General Zia ul-Haq. Saddam Hussein brought his own bodyguard of

150 commandos. Delhi, or at least the parts on display, was beautified and security was tight.

The Research and Intelligence Wing (RAW), India's foreign intelligence agency tasked with counterterrorism efforts, had already investigated an anti-tank missile fired over the wall of the US Embassy, which they said had been cleverly designed to look like an iron tube when dismantled. All police on Non-Aligned duty were told to be on the lookout for suspicious characters carrying iron tubes and to arrest them immediately. Journalists were briefed: 'Police have been ordered to watch for Ananda Margis, Nigerians, Lebanese, militant Sikhs, Assamese, Burmese, Afghans, Iranians and anyone else who could mean trouble, while plain clothes police will be hiding in treetops, on roofs, behind boulders and in jungles looking out for suspicious characters, in particular, foreign ones.'

The summit threw up some curly diplomatic questions. Who should represent Cambodia, then called Kampuchea? The South-East Asians wanted Prince Sihanouk, but others, unhappy with his links to murderous Pol Pot, wanted Vietnamese-backed Heng Samrin. In the end, the seat was vacant. Chad posed the opposite problem, with representatives of two national governments turning up.

Cheerfully, Mrs Gandhi opened the summit by declaring that the world was on the brink of total economic collapse and nuclear destruction. 'The hood of the Cobra is spread. Humankind watches in frozen fear, hoping that it will not strike. Never before has the earth faced so much death and danger,' she said.

But while the summit struggled with the big issues like the Soviet invasion of Afghanistan and the Iran–Iraq war, little was achieved. Members simply refused to allow interference in their internal affairs.

THERE WAS NO shortage of 'colour stories' to write: the public servants who took to the streets in their undies to protest their homespun uniforms, or the traffic system that saw entire families of four on motor scooters with sari-clad ladies demurely riding side-saddle, fabulously adorned Tata trucks more sparkly than a Rajasthani dancer, and the capital's new traffic lights that were largely regarded as decorative symbols of sophistication. And in the jungle, tigers stalked people and ate them.

'I knew I was going to die.' Shivshankar, a canefield chowkidar, showed me his leg scored with claw marks. He beat the tiger until it released him and bounded into the cane to crouch, watching and waiting. In his fear, the old guard knocked over his kerosene lamp, setting his hut on fire and bringing villagers to his aid. His village was on Man-Eater Road, just a few kilometres from the edge of Dudhwa National Park, 500 square kilometres of jungle on the Nepali border, and the crowded home of sixty Bengal tigers. 'There are tigers everywhere in the jungle, in the cane fields,' a woman yelled. 'Something must be done. We want them killed.' This tiger was not killed, and it would come back for Shivshankar.

Nine people in the Lakhimpur Kheri region had already been killed and eaten that year, at a rate of about one every two weeks. The tigers were no respecters of the park's borders and preferred hunting in the golden stands of cane. Billy Arjun Singh, who ran Tiger Haven, a small private park that abutted the national park he helped establish, wanted to create a people-free buffer zone. The local people preferred to keep their farms. We stayed with Billy, rode elephants through the long grass and crouched, one night, in a hide, listening to the tigers' howls that called up a visceral fear, and watching as a mother taught her cub to kill a buffalo.

THE LATE TWENTIETH century was a dark time. After three wars, the relationship with Pakistan was tense. In the once-cosmopolitan country over the border, martial law ruler President Zia ul-Haq was sponsoring Islamic fundamentalism, and women were being pushed into purdah, the traditional seclusion of women from a male-focused world. Suddenly, few women outside the major cities would venture out without a chador, a large light shawl that wrapped them from head to knees. 'A chador doesn't stop you going out to the market or to work,' one professional woman told me. 'In fact, it makes you feel more free. It's a sign of respectability. It means you can go about your work without being given undue attention. No-one looks.' Pressure was growing on schoolgirls and public servants. Women declining to veil were harassed on the streets and denounced in prayer meetings.

General Zia was replacing the British legacy legal system and winning the support of the mullahs. Islamic theologian and TV personality

Israr Ahmed, a member of Zia's Council of Islamic Ideology – tasked with establishing Koranic law – told the nation that a woman's place was in the home: 'The actual field of movement for a woman remains within four walls,' he said. The council wanted to halve the value of a woman's testimony, halve their compensation payments and remove the right to vote, to drive and even to ride in buses. But when he went on to explain that women must hide their bodies, as they were responsible for sex crimes, women poured onto the streets, demonstrating in violation of martial law regulations. They were dispersed with tear gas and baton charges. But they did win a victory of sorts. The uproar cost Israr Ahmed his TV spot.

One of the most serious incursions into women's rights was the change to laws around rape. A conviction for the crime carried the penalty of death by stoning. But for a guilty verdict, the victim had to produce four men of good character who witnessed the entire act, which would, I reported, seem to indicate that the men were not of particularly good character. One senior male official in the Pakistani foreign service observed: 'If a man commits a rape in front of four potential witnesses, he deserves to be stoned to death for stupidity.' The changes also meant few women were prepared to take their cases to court. Sex outside marriage, consensual or not, was a crime punishable with a hundred lashes.

Pakistan shared a porous border with Afghanistan, where refugee camps were staging posts for anti-Soviet jihadis. The Mujahedin were supported by the US in a proxy war against Soviet forces, who had invaded and staged a coup in the final days of 1979. Afghanistan, sitting at Asia's crossroads, had been invaded with varying degrees of success by the Moghuls and Persians, by Alexander the Great, by Tamerlane, and by the British three times. It was also the third crack by the Soviets.

There was little hard information to be had. The Soviets said very little, while the CIA and Britain's MI6 gave secret weekly briefings that could only be reported as 'sources say ...' It was those sources who told us that almost 3000 Soviet soldiers and Afghan civilians had died in a single disaster in the Salang Tunnel, through the Hindu Kush mountains, north of Kabul. A fuel tanker exploded in a collision with the lead truck in a military convoy. Traffic continued to flow into the tunnel and Soviet military officers, fearing a terrorist attack, sealed the exit. There was silence from the Afghans and the Soviets, and there has never been a real accounting of the death toll.

Following the Russian invasion, one in five Afghans were said to have fled to Pakistan, and with so little information to hand, we decided to go and take a look, at least as far as we could. Trevor and veteran ABC cameraman Willy Phua, Brian 'Digger' Williams, from Reuters' Islamabad bureau, and I, along with a guide who seemed to have little or no idea of where we were, set out in an old car with a single cassette jammed in the player. We edged into dusty, brown Afghanistan across an unmarked border while a country and western singer repeatedly pleaded with us not to go up Wolverton Mountain.

At the Park View No. 6 camp, one of many along the rugged and remote Afghan frontier, refugees and rebels lived in UNHCR tents and ate bread made from Australian wheat. The camp's guerrilla commander, Baran Khan, who claimed to have killed 200 Russians, said he was wintering there but would walk the 160 kilometres back across the mountains to rejoin the fight in spring.

Dressed in a modest Indian churidah kurta (tunic and pants), with a dupatta flicked over my head and shoulders, I was adopted by Mujahedin fighters as their Little Sister of the Revolution. They proudly displayed their old Enfield rifles left over from the British; Kalashnikovs stolen from the Russians (in reality supplied by the US); and their ability to ignore the rules about women when it suited them. The rules were bent for me, but Afghan women were not so fortunate. While the men and boys played sport and attended school, women and girls were nowhere to be seen. We were given a stern warning that if women were filmed, hands would be cut off.

PAKISTAN WAS THE product of Partition, the division of British India at Independence into new religion-based homelands just thirty-five years earlier, which had sparked astonishing slaughter and cruelty. In the greatest mass migration in history, up to 20 million people fled between India, West Pakistan and East Pakistan, which would become Bangladesh. Villages were razed, whole trainloads were slaughtered, women were raped and children dismembered. One older friend told me she had carried cyanide capsules for her and her baby son should their train be stopped as they fled to Delhi. It's said a million people died. The origin story of three nations is one of horror.

Communal violence between Hindus and Muslims continued. In 1982, in the remote north-eastern state of Assam, 3600 people died in riots, bombings, arson and murder in a single month. In one massacre alone, Assamese tribesmen wielding machetes descended on a cluster of Muslim villages. The 600 victims of the eight-hour-long rampage were nearly all women and children. The Assamese claimed immigrants from Bangladesh were taking their jobs. The victims said their families had been in the region for hundreds of years, pre-dating the borders drawn and redrawn during colonialism and its bloody end.

In the Punjab, Sikh activists demanded an independent homeland in the fertile north, a claim Indira Gandhi saw as secessionist and likely backed by Pakistan. The militant Sikh leader, Jarnail Singh Bhindranwale, turned the spiritual heart of Sikhism, the Golden Temple, into a fortress. 'We know how to sacrifice our lives,' he said. 'We know how to cut others to pieces.' Bhindranwale would be killed with hundreds of others when Indira Gandhi ordered police to storm the holy complex in 1984 – and everything changed.

Months later, I was back in Sydney, on *The Australian*'s foreign desk. One night, driving home after work, Trevor's successor in Delhi came on the air. Indira Gandhi was dead, assassinated by her Sikh bodyguards in retribution for the attack on the temple.

We turned the car around and went back to our offices. There was one final India story to write.

Melissa Roberts has reported as a freelance correspondent from India and Papua New Guinea for *The Australian*, from China for *Time* magazine and *The Christian Science Monitor*, covering the chaotic years around the Tiananmen Square uprising, and from Singapore and Australia for *Newsweek* magazine. She has worked on staff for 2UE, *The Australian* and AP DowJones. Melissa has written five children's books, published by Addison Wesley Longman and Macmillan, and is co-editor of *The Beijing Bureau*, Hardie Grant Books, 2021.

22
HITCHING TO THE AFTERMATH OF A GENOCIDE

Candace Sutton
Central Africa 1994
The Sun-Herald

The tools of genocide.

THE CAMP WAS strewn across a vast African valley, between the smoking mouth of Mount Nyiragongo, The Great One, and two bluish peaks which descended into foothills scattered with cypress and eucalypts. As far as the eye could see, lean–tos fashioned from tree trunks and UN–issue plastic stretched over lava–hard ground littered with football–sized lumps of volcanic rock.

Up to half a million people had surged into the big camp north of the city of Goma in the great exodus after the Rwandan genocide, and the queue of those hopeful of setting up home under garbage bags in this massive car park of sorts stretched across Zaire, as the Democratic Republic of Congo was then called, and back over the border. The terrain of hardened lava made it difficult to build latrines, and one of the worst cholera epidemics in modern history was raging through the camp.

It was mid-afternoon as I picked my way gingerly along a culvert by the road bisecting the camp. Bodies rolled up in woven papyrus bound with rope lay toe to toe in the warm sun. A man sitting on a bucket perched on the culvert's edge had his head in his hands, which were thrust into a pair of pink washing-up gloves that appeared to be helping him to block out the present. At his feet, one smallish woven cone seemed to belong to him. Another larger roll alongside also seemed to be his, and when he lifted his face from his gloves, his eyes looked straight through me in a thousand-yard stare. The line of woven bundles along the culvert seemed to stretch ahead for kilometres.

Through the sprawling filth of the camp, which was shrouded in a haze of smoke from thousands of tiny campfires, I could see two trucks slowly ploughing a path through the waves of refugees. Eventually they came to a stop, halted as more people flooded in from all directions. They thronged around the vehicles, threatening to engulf them. The refugees beckoned and shouted and fought over boxes, presumably of food, which were being tossed from the back of the vehicles.

The camp's name was Kibumba and, nearing the end of the long dry season of 1994, in this small city of tired, hungry and ragged people seemingly dying in their droves, the scene was *biblical*. Not for the first time since I'd arrived that morning in the back of a Norwegian People's Aid supply plane, I wondered what in God's name I was doing here.

I'd absolutely busted a gut to make it to the other side of the world, to Zaire, a country I'd barely heard of, where a tragedy of unimaginable proportions had been unfolding on the television for weeks, but in reality for months and, historically, for decades. Back at the newspaper office, I'd lobbied hard to be the one to be sent here – I wasn't exactly a newsroom wallflower who covered the knitting round – but now I had a sudden pang of longing to be there, finishing work after a dull assignment with a nice, quiet beer, and then home to bed.

What had I done?

THE TRAGEDY DOMINATING the nightly news had begun just 150 kilometres away, over the border in Rwanda, a tiny landlocked country in equatorial Africa's Great Rift Valley. Called the 'land of a thousand hills', Rwanda was unknown to most of the world until its mountain apes starred in the 1988 film *Gorillas in the Mist*. The country's long history of violent ethnic division between its two main people, the Hutu and the Tutsi, only came to the notice of your average suburban household six years after the film's release.

On 6 April 1994, Tutsi extremists of the Rwandan Patriotic Front (RPF) shot down the airplane carrying Rwanda's totalitarian, pro-Hutu president Juvénal Habyarimana and President Cyprien Ntaryamira of neighbouring Burundi, killing all on board. What happened next was inspired by government extremists, and by Rwanda's 'free' radio station, RTLM (Radio Télévision Libre des Mille Collines), inciting Hutus, in nearly a month of broadcasts, to wipe out the Tutsi 'inyenzi' (cockroaches). Machete-wielding mobs rounded up Tutsi villagers and herded them off to be killed.

A hundred days of slaughter ensued – with Hutu militia killing nearly a million Tutsi men, women and children, along with sympathetic moderate Hutus.

The scope of the Rwandan genocide is perhaps best exemplified by the church massacre at Ntarama, 30 kilometres south of the Rwandan capital, Kigali. Hoping for protection against the genocidal Hutu militia – the merciless Interahamwe – 5000 Tutsis sheltered inside the church. It did them no good. They were murdered in the pews where they sat. Those that tried to flee were macheted through their Achilles tendon or simply clubbed to death. Soldiers returned repeatedly to ensure nobody remained alive.

The killing continued until July 1994, when the RPF, led by Rwandan reformer Paul Kagame, rounded up government forces, surrounded Kigali and took control of the country. Fearing reprisals, two million Hutus fled Rwanda, over the borders to neighbouring countries like Zaire. The new Tutsi government left Ntarama as the Interahamwe had, a scene of unbelievable horror, as a reminder and a record of the crime. Inside the church, stacked three or four deep, and lying outside where they had fallen, slumped against trees in the churchyard, the bodies turned to skeletons.

Aid workers, doctors, nurses, peacekeepers and preachers converged on Zaire, and, when the refugees began dying from cholera and dysentery, pneumonia, malaria and other diseases, the stage was set.

AS CENTRAL AFRICA was seized by a humanitarian disaster on a colossal scale, the media flooded in to cover what had become the biggest story in the world. I wanted to be there, but there was a problem. *The Sun-Herald* had already assigned a reporter to the story. He was the sort of tall, confident type who got tapped for the big jobs, and I don't know whether he'd asked to go or had just been given the nod.

But I had an idea, and I started ringing around aid agencies who were sending their workers to central Africa to help. The sight of dying African kids had become a nightly horror show on the news and appalled Australians were opening their wallets like they had never done before or since. I found an aid agency willing to fly a journalist over to cover its work with children in the Rwandan camps.

I told the editor, who informed me he was not prepared to send two reporters to cover the one crisis. When I looked a little crestfallen, he laughed and said what editor wouldn't agree with the one proposal that would save him money? The journalist who ordinarily got tapped for the big jobs was not impressed.

Two weeks, seven inoculations and a course of anti-malarial tablets later, I was seated on a stack of rice bags in the back of a Hercules as it dipped between low hills clustered with smoking huts onto the lumpy runway of Goma airport. I stepped down in what I had christened my 'Rwanda boots', thick rubber-soled footwear designed to keep the cholera-infected ground of Zaire's camps as distant as possible.

Cargo flights were arriving at the rate of two a day into Goma. With the influx of nurses, doctors, aid workers, UN officials, administrators, statisticians, logisticians and journalists, along with blankets, vaccines and thousands of bags of rice, Goma's post-genocide economy was booming.

Goma airport was like a film set. Photographers, TV crews and reporters stood around writing scripts, doing their make-up for their on-camera appearances, filing stories on satellite phones the size of suitcases, smoking, chatting and laughing.

I couldn't have been more intimidated.

I found a kind-faced reporter who recommended I go into Goma and then on to the largest camp, where the rising death toll was the subject of daily press conferences. The foreign correspondents, he said, tended to travel with a crew, a photographer and sometimes with a fixer in hot spots. But hiring a driver from Goma at the going day rate would do for me, even if it had recently inflated to US$100.

A picturesque little border town on the north-eastern corner of Lake Kivu, Goma was ordinarily a stop-off for tourists on the way north to see the mountain gorillas, and a holiday destination for the corrupt despot, Zaire's then president, Mobutu Sese Seko. Goma was literally uprooted when hundreds of thousands of refugees burst over the border, ripping up the civic gardens and every decorative tree and shrub by its roots to make thousands of tiny fires as they camped in the streets. The fleeing Hutus were promptly herded off: poor villagers to farflung locations, and soldiers and suspected war criminals to camps closer to town.

Journalists helped fuel the local economy by hiring drivers to take them to camps or into Rwanda to see the genocide's ghastly aftermath. I foolishly exchanged one of my US$100 notes in the town bank for a large envelope stuffed with Zairean dollars bearing Mobutu's image, their value plummeting even as we drove off north to the camps.

Along with the aid workers distributing food and tending to the dispossessed, the media, the UN officials and the peacekeeping soldiers, there were seasoned visitors to trouble spots who had gathered at the Kibumba camp. When humanity screwed up, in from the four corners of the earth came the righteous and the merciful: Mother Teresa's tea towel nuns, Lutheran World Relief, the Mennonite Central Committee, and lone mercy givers like the American 'homemaker and child of God' from Houston distributing pamphlets printed in English promoting Truth, Justice and Peace in the World.

And strolling through Kibumba was a man who looked faintly familiar, or possibly just famous, and his entourage. Dressed in matching desert storm fatigues, the men strode to a position slightly up a rise and formed a circle of four. They closed their eyes and held hands while the fifth held up a video camera to capture the scene. The group's leader began incanting a prayer: 'Bless this troubled land, oh Lord, and keep it free from disease and bloodshed between its people'.

I stopped and listened and when the prayer ended, I asked the cameraman, 'Excuse me. I'm a reporter from Australia, can you tell me who this guy is?'

'You never heard of Al Sharpton from New York City? He's going to be a US Senator.'

The Reverend Al ended his prayer and walked over, holding out his arms to embrace me. 'Al Sharpton. Who do you represent, sister? My congregation raised $50,000 so we could come over here and see what's happening to our black brothers. You're welcome to join us on our tour.' He looked around at the scene. 'This is something, isn't it. Nowhere else like this on God's earth. Are you staying in town? Have dinner with us.'

It was getting towards late afternoon when I got back to Goma and paid an American TV crew to use their satellite phone to file my first story. In 1994, filing copy from a different time zone to a Sunday newspaper was reporting into a vacuum. No feedback, no one to talk to for reassurance that I was even doing a competent job. The sat phone connection cost was US$100 a minute, so I kept it reasonably short.

I was beginning to realise that US$100 seemed to be the going rate for everything, so I kept the colour piece to a description of the largest refugee camp on the planet, the rows of bodies, the stories about the dying. My photos of the man with the pink rubber gloves beside his dead infant daughter and wife would have to wait for another day. They were too expensive to be sent right now, I thought, although I was to learn that other correspondents demanded and got what they wanted in relation to their work, like a budget. As far as writing about the aid agency that had paid my airfare, and its life-saving work, I'd have to get to that. The story of the families dying in the camps was too big to ignore.

The agency had booked me into a basic room in the only place to stay in Goma: the only place with running water. The Hotel Karibu, down the Avenue des Volcans, was set apart from the ravaged centre of town torn apart by the refugees. It was in picture postcard Africa, with hibiscus trees and bougainvillea tumbling over white rendered walls, a red clay tennis court and neatly clipped lawns bordered with flowerbeds above the intense blueness of Lake Kivu.

At the Karibu, which meant 'welcome', seasoned correspondents gathered on my first evening to forget the dark hole of the day's business amid a committed downing of extraordinarily well chilled booze. Gathered around the bar were men and women of different nationalities, British, American, Swiss, German, Dutch, and a few Australians. They all seemed to know each other from previous or current conflicts, Bosnia, Kosovo, the Gulf War, Iran–Iraq, and there was even one man who had covered the Russian invasion of Afghanistan.

Waiters in faded blue uniforms delivered tall sweating bottles of Primus, 'the queen of beers', to rows of long tables in a room overlooking the curve of the lake's edge below. I would later lose the beginner's shoulder chip, but for the first night, enough back slapping and exchange of war stories managed to render this comparative ingenue in crisis coverage mute. So when I spotted Al Sharpton and his retinue at a table and he beckoned me over, I gratefully accepted.

Reverend Sharpton sipped on soda water as he sat silhouetted against the gathering dusk, surrounded by his aides. In a pre-Google era, I had managed to do enough research with one of the friendly Americans to confirm that Al Sharpton was a famous civil rights leader who worked for the Reverend Jesse Jackson helping poor black youth. Defending the rights of African Americans who had been unlawfully attacked or killed, he was a kind of Black Lives Matter campaigner of the late twentieth century.

His publicity man, Theo Timms III, filled me in some more about Sharpton's feats for the black American community while the Reverend's security detail, an enormous former guard for the New York Giants football team, Elwin Reuber, sipped silently on his Coca Cola.

'I never seen anything like that in all my days,' Reverend Al said, shaking his head.

'Lordy, Lordy,' said Winston Deans, a fellow preacher from the New York Baptist Church, his head moving in unison.

'Well, as I've always said, sometimes you've got to holler like hell to get what you want and I'm going to holler like hell to tell people what I just saw,' Sharpton exclaimed. 'People will not believe, will not bee-leeeve!'

A waiter approached the table with a pad and announced the menu. '*Oeufs à la russe*, tilapia with *pomme de terre*, suh,' he said.

'Erf ah la russe,' Elwin repeated, 'tee-lapeea and poms, what's that?'

'Eggs in mayonnaise and lake fish with potatoes,' translated Moncef Bouhafa helpfully. Moncef, an old Africa hand on detachment from Liberia, where he was working with UNICEF (United Nations International Children's Emergency Fund), had just joined the table after recognising Sharpton.

The waiter looked like a smallish teenager, with the cuffs of his faded trousers and shirt turned up several times, and Bouhafa explained the man was a member of the Twa, Rwanda's third ethnic and even more marginalised group, known more commonly in colonial Africa as pygmies.

'Hey' said Elwin, 'does that mean this fish comes from that lake?' He jabbed a thumb towards the now darkened shape below, on whose shores dead refugees had been washing up before the living were banished to the camps to the north.

'I've been eating it for weeks,' said Bouhafa, 'I haven't been sick yet.'

'Okay,' Sharpton nodded, 'we'll take the fish.'

The tilapia arrived whole, black and steaming on trays from the kitchen. Biting through the crunchy coating, it tasted fresh and sweet and I hoped Bouhafa was right. Although I had packed tablets for what seemed like every disease known to humanity, getting food poisoning or diarrhoea in a refugee crisis would be disastrous.

With his aides, Bouhafa and me as his audience, Sharpton was formulating a plan.

'We must go to Rwanda. See the US ambassador. Talk to him. Acti-vate! We will go tomorrow. Sister, would you like to come?'

'I don't know,' I ventured, turning to Bouhafa, 'shouldn't I stick around and report what's happening in the camps?'

The Africa veteran looked at me and asked, 'How many conflicts have you covered?'

I told him this was my first, and that I worked for a weekly tabloid newspaper which was eager for exclusive stories of as extreme a nature as possible.

'Go with the Reverend Sharpton,' he advised. He nodded towards the other side of the room where the tables were now forests of empty long-necked bottles surrounded by journalists, photographers and cameramen who were tired, dirty and more than a little drunk. 'You've filed your first story, you say, of the refugees dying in the camps. They will continue to die. You could stick around for another week, or see something different. You're in Africa. It's an interesting place. The aftershock of the genocide still has a long way to go. People are still getting put in jail.'

Sharpton and his men went off to bed. Moncef Bouhafa took me over to a table where correspondents were complaining about the current exorbitant price to hire a driver in Zaire.

The Primus was ice cold and malty and the night rolled on. Correspondents boasted about their exploits in Chad and Somalia, in Ethiopia and Mozambique, all the trouble in the world.

The next morning, after sleeping on a hard floor, I woke up to catch the Reverend's ride, with all my belongings and a special sort of pain gripping my head.

Outside the Karibu was a white minibus which seemed far too small for another person to join Sharpton's men already crammed inside the vehicle. I crawled in and Gerard, the French-speaking driver, slid the door shut. It was twenty minutes to the border. We stopped outside a squat yellow concrete building from which a man emerged and spoke to Gerard, who turned and asked, 'Passport, mademoiselle?' Outside the Office des Douanes et Accises, the customs office, machetes, fire-arms and ammunition lay in piles on the ground, where they had been stripped from refugees – as much as you can disarm people arriving at the border at a rate of five hundred a minute. Officers with rifles on their shoulders slouched against the yellow walls. Inside, an indignant bodyguard, Elwin Reuber, was trying to argue with an officer from the Rwandan Patriotic Front who would truck no opposition.

'You will take an escort,' he told Reuber, pushing forward a young officer in a neatly pressed brown uniform, 'the road is *dangereuse*'.

IT WAS LATE afternoon and we still hadn't reached the Rwandan capi-tal, Kigali. We had passed through ghost towns and miles of beautiful empty country. Only twice had we seen people, heavy with belongings, making the eight-day trek on foot along roads cutting through lush slopes terraced with coffee plantations, the ripe red plumes of sorghum and endless banana groves heavily laden with the September harvest.

Reverend Sharpton's face was gloomy. 'It's like in the Bible. Pesti-lence and plague! I'm going to tell the American people what's happening to our brothers here. We're gonna stop this suffering. Man, we gonna fight!'

More people began to appear as the mini-van drew closer to the city centre. Children played on the footpaths of streets bereft of traffic. On Avenue Paul VI, the stars and stripes fluttered above a bunker-like building and a harassed-looking man eventually answered Theo Timm's attempts to buzz someone from the gate.

He was unimpressed by Reverend Sharpton's demand to see the US ambassador, but disclosed that US President Bill Clinton's Assistant Secretary of State for Democracy and Human Rights, John Shattuck, was flying in and there would be a press conference. At the sight of a soldier balancing a television camera and a GI holding a long-handled microphone, Al Sharpton's mood brightened.

'You guys are doing a great job here,' he said as the camera started rolling.

I left the aspiring senator and his entourage and caught a lift with a British journalist to spend the night at an abandoned monastery, where, it was said, priests had been murdered by the Interahamwe. The journalist was planning to visit a girls' school the following day where, he claimed, there had been a massacre of Tutsi students. I wanted to go to the jail at Gitarama, where hundreds of Hutu massacre suspects were being held. The British guy, David, was keen to split the driver's day rate, which inside Rwanda had skyrocketed to the princely sum of US$150.

Rulindo secondary school was an hour's drive north of Kigali, on badly maintained, twisting roads full of potholes. The school was eerily quiet, the floors of its empty classrooms cluttered with books, notepads and pens, and dozens of schoolgirls' identity cards. Like every Rwandan's mandatory ID, each one bore the holder's ethnic identity, Tutsi or Hutu, in capital letters just below their name. The rooms appeared to have been ransacked and two wells in the school grounds were stuffed with clothing and belongings. David claimed they smelt of death. He also suggested the uneven grass around the abandoned school covered the corpses of massacred Tutsi school-girls. I thought it unlikely. Even if the girls had been the victims of a massacre early in the conflict (which you'd think would have made the news), grass wouldn't grow that lushly and evenly over a mass grave in the dry season.

A short man in a pastor's collar arrived at the school and rushed over, telling us in heavily accented French to leave. It was 11 am, and we had a long drive ahead of us to Gitarama prison, south-west of Kigali. Conditions at Gitarama were so squalid that it had been labelled the worst prison in the world. David left the school reluctantly, claiming the pastor's demeanour indicated a guilty secret lurked beneath the surface at Rulindo, possibly a world exclusive that I was doing him out of. I made a mental note never to share a day rate with another correspondent bent on his own quest for fame.

Gitarama was built for 500 men on a red dirt rectangle about half the size of a football field. In August 1994, with close to 1500 inmates, it was so crowded that the men slept sitting up. The stench of the latrines hung over the prison quadrangle, where miserable-looking men squatted where they could. Hutu militia, soldiers or just members of mobs who rose to the Rwanda Free Radio call to exterminate the *inyenzi*, they were now in danger of dying themselves.

Within a few years, Gitarama would house between 7000 and 8000 prisoners, meaning they would be forced to stand twenty-four hours a day. The shocking overcrowding resulted in frequent fatal fights. The victors ate the bodies of the dead in an effort to stay alive. The squalor and the standing caused prisoners to suffer from gangrene of their lower limbs, forcing amateur amputations and often death. If they lived long enough to be tried for their alleged crimes in one of the community justice courts known as the *gacaca*, it would be a miracle of survival.

We left as night was falling over the putrid yard and drove the two hours back to the monastery. I felt filthy and a little hopeless, but in the priest's quarters I found an American photographer who graciously allowed me to file some copy overnight for the cut-price sum of US$80 a minute. Early the next morning, I used the satellite phone again and spoke with my news editor, who talked too slowly as I watched the time tick away; he told me the editor was very happy with my stories and that they were running my prison piece under the headline, 'The Butchers of Rwanda'.

'So, the subs were asking this arvo, when do we get your follow-up, The Bakers of Rwanda?' he asked. He told me the radio broadcaster Frank Crook wanted to interview me for an eyewitness account of the horror of the camps for his show on 2UE Sydney. 'Plus, he wants an idea of what the conditions are like for correspondents on the ground. Get 2UE to pay the bill,' he said, before hanging up on a US$400 phone call. Frank Crook would agree to footing a bill of several hundred dollars for an interview with me, and that proved something.

I'd learned lessons about going it alone in a foreign country that I would put into practice on later assignments, and I guess I knew that as a correspondent I'd graduated.

Candace Sutton is a former North America correspondent and foreign affairs reporter who has covered events from the Bougainville civil war to the Bali bombing, the MH370 disappearance and the Christchurch massacre. She has worked at both the former Fairfax newspaper group and at News Corp and now writes about crime and major issues for *Daily Mail Australia*.

23
FORGIVENESS, JUSTICE AND LUCK IN WEST AFRICA

Prue Clarke
Liberia 2004
The Times

With Chuckie, Liberia.

ARRIVING IN A war zone is always a shock. You leave a peaceful, functioning place and land, a short time later, in a hellscape. But the West African nation of Liberia in 2004 was something else again. Ten years of economic freefall under the dictator Samuel Doe had given way in 1989 to an insurgency led by a tyrant whose name became synonymous with the term warlord: Charles Taylor. On Christmas Day that year, Taylor's forces invaded, plunging Liberia into fourteen years of civil war filled with horror that shocked even the hardy crew of humanitarian workers and war reporters who had already seen too much.

Child soldiers, cannibalism, sex slaves, rape and violence against women and children happened on a scale rarely seen before. Taylor also stoked an insurgency in neighbouring Sierra Leone, fuelled by the violent exploitation of diamond mines and inspiring the film *Blood Diamond*.

I arrived on assignment for *The Times* as the carnage abated, travelling on the first UN flight returning some of the three million people who had been displaced by the fighting. The scenes of devastation were almost too much to take in.

The capital, Monrovia, teemed with people – most dressed in worn-out clothes, dragging jerry-rigged carts selling peanuts, palm oil, sugarcane, coconuts – anything they could coax, without tools, seeds or fertiliser, from depleted tropical soils. Outside the convent where I found a bed, boys tried to sell me a baby chimpanzee they had named Chuckie after Taylor's notoriously vicious American-born son. The boys had likely killed and eaten its mother.

The city had once been the proud beacon of a Pan African effort to return Africans stolen by the slave trade. Now its grand buildings were burned and broken by bombs, bullets and neglect. People squatted in the ruins, risking death from their collapse, to escape the drenching equatorial rains. Garbage piles, storeys high, lined the streets. Islands made from garbage rose from rivers. After nearly two decades with no public services, powerlines dangled in sewage-filled streets. Beaches had become public toilets. Craterous potholes severed the city's main arteries. Not that it mattered. The only transport available was a small fleet of rundown 1970s-era cars, packed with as many as ten people, and motorbikes given to ex-combatants as part of a weapons buyback and rehabilitation program.

Those ex-combatants, many of them still children, addicted to drugs and missing limbs, were shunned by survivors, including their own families. Most were too mentally broken to acquiesce to the demands of a tiresome UN bureaucracy that was implementing a multi-million-dollar rehabilitation effort. They lived in ghettos, stealing to survive. Interviewing them was almost impossible. They were too broken or angry to hold a coherent conversation. It was hard to see their way back. Many had been kidnapped as children, given brown-brown – a mix of cocaine and gunpowder – and riled up on Rambo videos before they were sent into battle. Among the many depravities of this war, some had been forced to rape their own mothers or sisters before killing them. Some ex-combatants were so numb that they lived in cemeteries, moving aside the bones to sleep before rising each morning as the real-life zombies they had become.

As a cadet journalist in ABC TV's Sydney newsroom ten years earlier, the long civil war in Sierra Leone had given me my first lesson in international reporting: sometimes the truth is too shocking to report. Taylor's rebels became notorious for asking children if they wanted 'short sleeves' or 'long sleeves' and then hacking off hands or arms with machetes. In the ABC newsroom, we curated the vision to find images the audience could stomach. On the ground in Liberia, I did the same thing. Finding ways to tell stories that editors deemed too dark would become a big part of my job.

The head of the gender-based violence unit of the International Rescue Committee, a US NGO, told me she had never seen anything like the suffering of Liberians. And she would know. A Rwandan Tutsi, she had survived the hundred-day genocide in her own country that left a million people dead.

'In Rwanda women and children were raped,' she said. 'But in Liberia they were raped over and over again for fourteen years.'

THE UN FLIGHT carrying the returning refugees flew in from nearby Ghana. It was two hours by plane, but for the passengers, it was a million miles from what was awaiting them. They knew it. In Ghana, they lived in squalid conditions, and were barred from jobs, schools and public services, but most had not wanted to make this journey home.

Tens of thousands would never return. Liberia's brain drain has few parallels. Anyone with an education left and, eventually, secured asylum in the West. Helene Cooper, the Pulitzer-prize winning *New York Times* correspondent, is one of many successful Liberians lost to their homeland. In Australia, head of the Aminata Maternal Foundation, Aminata Conteh-Biger, was part of the exodus from neighbouring Sierra Leone. In 2022, the two countries flail at the bottom of UN development rankings – a lack of educated teachers and technocrats is a major cause.

As we landed and the returnees stepped onto the crumbling tarmac, Gyude Bryant, Liberia's interim leader, led a ceremony that seemed more of a show for visiting journalists than a genuine welcome. Bryant urged the returnees to 'let bygones be bygones' – an expression I would hear repeatedly – and help rebuild the country. His administration of former warlords would soon be accused of embezzling US$1 million in aid money during their two-year reign. The returnees appeared to wholeheartedly embrace the call for forgiveness. They sang the national anthem and cried, and pledged to work for peace.

I was documenting the return of twenty-four-year-old Edmund Doe and his sister Fatu, eighteen. Fatu was quiet and reserved, but Edmund, a rotund fellow, had a quick smile and joyful demeanour that tricked my brain into believing that maybe the horrors he and Fatu had endured weren't so bad.

Fourteen years earlier, in 1990, their mother had been away visiting their grandmother when Taylor's forces besieged Monrovia. Their father packed the children up and led them out of the city on foot with thousands of others fleeing the rain of bullets and grenades. At a makeshift checkpoint, a leader with Taylor's rebels recognised the children's father as a government official. The pair had been friendly before Taylor's invasion, but that would not save him now. The rebel shot Edmund's father dead. Strangers covered the children's mouths to stop them screaming. Had the rebels known they were his children, they would have shot them too.

Now Edmund took me to the site where his father had died on the side of a busy road leading out of the city. He had not been there since he was ten years old, but he found it immediately. Edmund looked at the spot where he last saw his father, as he and his sister were carried, distraught, through the checkpoint by caring strangers.

'We left my father here on the side of the road, dying in a pool of his own blood,' Edmund said softly, bearing a son's shame; by tradition it was his responsibility to ensure his father had a dignified burial. It was clear he had imagined this moment many times, hoping to see some sign of his father. He found none.

My privileged life and Edmund's could not have been more different and yet I felt a pang of recognition in this moment. My family also carried this particular grief. My grandfather had been a child when his father was gunned down in war.

Christopher Clarke, my great-grandfather, had been a captain in the Royal Irish Constabulary in 1922 when he was executed by the Irish Republican Army (IRA) in Belfast. Christopher was murdered as he was leaving the funeral of a colleague slain during the conflict that would lead to the division of Ireland. He knew death was coming. As a Catholic in a British uniform, he had earned the ire of the IRA. He sent his beloved fourteen-year-old son, my grandfather Patrick, home from the funeral by a different route to save him. Patrick's mother, her husband dead, and fearing her young son would be next, put him on a boat to Australia. They never saw each other again.

Patrick's experience, along with that of my maternal grandfather, who had fought the Japanese invasion of Papua New Guinea, formed a heavy backdrop to my childhood. They both died before I was able to ask them real questions. I'm sure their stories drove my desire to be a journalist, to try to understand the cruelty and resilience of which humans are capable. My grandfathers were with me as I told Edmund's story.

I'D HAD MY own close-up with human cruelty three years earlier, on 11 September 2001. I was reporting for the *Financial Times* (*FT*) in New York City when terrorists attacked the World Trade Center. All the sensible people were running away from the burning towers after the first plane went in that morning in downtown New York. But that's not an option for a reporter. I did what I'd been trained to do as an ABC cadet. I pushed past the fleeing river of people and ran towards the towers.

In Australia, the most dramatic event I had ever covered was an election. In the next hour, I would report, a block away from the towers, as America went into crisis – facing an unimaginable attack by terrorists on the central pillars of the nation. I watched in disbelief as dozens of people flung themselves to their deaths from a hundred storeys above. When the first tower crumbled, and 110 storeys of cement and steel collapsed in the streets in front of me, I thought I was going to die, too.

September 11 would have profound and devastating consequences for millions of people around the world. For a young country girl just starting out in journalism, it was a catalyst to better understand the forces that brought us to that moment.

Every journalist has her own reasons for putting herself in difficult or dangerous situations. I am there to learn – about humanity, development, myself. My university friends still chuckle at my capacity to sleep through lectures. I have to learn from experience – to touch, smell, question. Liberia opened a door into a new world for me, blowing away the last vestiges of my comfortable worldview that had shaken loose on 9/11. I threw out everything I thought I knew and started again.

For nearly two decades since, I have worked with Liberian journalists as the head of New Narratives, a not-for-profit newsroom and NGO. Through postwar reconstruction, the 2014 Ebola crisis, and their quest for justice for war crimes, Liberians continue to teach me more about humanity than any book.

AFTER THEIR FATHER died, Edmund and Fatu eventually made their way to Ghana, 1500 kilometres away. They had heard rumours their mother had made it to the United States, and now, coming back to Liberia, they hoped to learn more. They planned to stay with their Aunt Natalie, whom they had just learned was alive. They took me to see what had been their childhood home. Once a solid four-room cement-block building, bullets, thieves and the tropical climate had left nothing but a few crumbling walls.

Edmund was still reeling from his return to the devastated city when he happened upon his biggest mental demon: the rebel who killed his father. The man now lived a few blocks from Edmund's house. Just as he had mentally prepared to return to the place where his father died, Edmund had prepared for this moment, too.

'I have forgiven him, I have forgiven everybody,' he declared with enthusiasm. The shock on my face must have prompted more explanation. 'Killing him would not bring my father back. I want to move forward and see what I can do to build a future for my family tomorrow.'

The same scene was playing out across the country. There was no capacity to try hundreds of thousands who had committed war crimes. Charles Taylor had been granted exile in Nigeria. And the deal between warring factions that brought peace had meant the former leaders were all given a place in the government. (Taylor would later be convicted by the UN-backed Special Court for Sierra Leone for war crimes committed in that country. He is serving a fifty-year sentence in a UK prison. His son Chuckie is serving a ninety-seven-year sentence for war crimes in a Miami prison. Neither has been tried for crimes committed in Liberia.)

Complicating everything was the fact that so many people had been pressed into service against their will. Fifteen years later, New Narratives journalists would play a crucial role in Liberians' quest for justice for war crimes, but for now, survivors had only one choice: to move on. It was almost impossible for me to comprehend, and I told Edmund so. Perhaps that was why he took me to a broken-down building where his family and friends had gathered that afternoon for a makeshift Christian prayer service led by Aunt Natalie. They sang and praised God for bringing them back together.

After a childhood with parents split between warring Anglican and Catholic families, I had no use for religion until then. During the previous nine months I'd lived in Ghana, I had been annoyed by Africans' fervent devotion to a religion brought to them by colonisers. But in this ramshackle church, it was clear that religion was one of the few things that kept Liberians going through so much darkness. Belief in a better life in heaven had given their suffering purpose. On my first day in what was the closest thing I had seen to hell, religion suddenly made sense.

IN THE FOLLOWING years, I would return to Liberia over and over again from my base in New York City and London. As the country emerged from a war that had destabilised all of West Africa, there was a lot of interest from the news organisations in the UK, US and Canada for my freelance reporting. That received a boost in 2005 when this broken, conservative country surprised everyone by becoming the first nation in Africa to elect a woman leader.

Ellen Johnson Sirleaf was the best person for the job by any measure. A darling of the West, she was hard working, driven and fearless. Ma Ellen, as Liberians know her, had given birth to four sons by the age of twenty-two, before she left her abusive husband, studied at Harvard, worked for Citibank and became her country's first woman finance minister. She was imprisoned and nearly killed after the 1980 coup. With her international experience, connections and smarts, she was the best hope for Liberia. It was a testament to Liberians, and a hopeful sign for progress, as they overcame deeply patriarchal beliefs to elect her. Her Nobel Peace Prize in 2011 was an international seal of approval for their decision.

The ructions that would up-end the global news business had already begun. But for a few magical years, I, and other young freelancers – some of them in this book – had opportunities that had previously been reserved for staff reporters. And because so often it had been men who had climbed the ladder to staff positions, it was women who benefited most now.

The iPhone would not arrive until 2007, but the digital world had already begun to chip away at traditional news revenue; craigslist, started in 1995, took away the classifieds business that had funded the papers and the first major cuts came to international news. In a few short years, US news organisations cut 80 per cent of their international correspondents. Big papers like *The Philadelphia Inquirer* and *The Boston Globe* cut international news gathering altogether. Others pulled back to major global cities – Hong Kong, Beijing, London, Moscow, Jerusalem.

But US interest in international news stayed strong, helped in part by US interventions in Afghanistan and Iraq. In the absence of staff reporters, freelancers filled the void. With contacts in the US, where I attended Columbia University Journalism School, and from the *FT*, I built a stable of clients. A US radio program took two stories a month at US$1500 per story plus expenses. I'd sell the same reporting in different formats to *Foreign Policy*, *The Globe and Mail*, *The Times*, *Newsweek* and CBC radio and, later, *The Washington Post*. It was nothing like the $4 a word big-name journalists still get, but with a husband on a good income, no kids and a lean budget, it kept me going. I reported from Liberia and across West Africa. I went to Rwanda, Congo, Uganda, and further afield to post-tsunami Indonesia and to Australia to cover Afghan asylum seekers caught up in the offshore detention scheme.

That glorious freelance window began to close in 2009 with the Global Financial Crisis. The shows I relied on in the US and Canada ended. *Newsweek* all but collapsed. The 2014 videotaped beheading by ISIS of American freelance journalist James Foley, two years after he'd been kidnapped in Syria, was the final blow. The costs of the search crippled *The Global Mail*, a startup media organisation that Foley had worked for. Media houses faced overdue pressure to provide better safety and insurance for freelancers. As advertising revenue bled to Google and Facebook, many media outlets simply cut back on freelancers.

From 2014, as the best media houses began to rebuild businesses based on reader revenue, quality international coverage regained its appeal. The most successful news businesses, *The New York Times*, the *Washington Post, The Guardian, Financial Times* and *The Wall Street Journal,* rebuilt serious international news operations.

IN LIBERIA, ELLEN Johnson Sirleaf's election had made little difference for women. In 2005, I visited the village of Sanniquellie, a transit point between Liberia and Guinea that had seen a lot of fighting. The International Committee of the Red Cross was here educating women and men about rape; not, as one might expect, how to prevent it or seek justice after it. The ICRC trainers were teaching people what rape was, and that it was bad.

A kind woman instructor in colourful Liberian dress stood at the front of the room pointing to hand-drawn pictures of people in sexual positions on posters. Few people here could read. 'You know when a man forces himself on you and has sex with you?' she said to twenty women riveted by every word. 'That is called rape.'

The catalyst for these sessions was Johnson Sirleaf's commitment to legislate to make rape illegal. For these women, acquiescing to a man's demand for sex was just her lot in life. During the war that had had a cataclysmic impact on Liberian society, men deserted wives who were raped; women were left destitute with children they could not afford to care for. For years, I did not meet a married couple.

One thing that had puzzled me in Liberia (and later in the war zones of Congo) was that no one ever cried. I had spoken with former child soldiers, too many victims of rape, and survivors of horrors that still haunt me. Everyone narrated their stories in cold, clinical detail, without emotion. This, and the almost robotic repetition of the phrase 'let bygones be bygones', made it appear that there was something different about Liberians – something in their unique and difficult history that I needed to understand.

In Sanniquellie, the reason for their cold demeanour became clear.

Edith was in her thirties, slightly older than I was at the time. Like most women in Liberia (at least 70 per cent, according to the UN), she had endured gang rapes. Her husband had been killed. Three children had died of hunger or illness. Another became a 'war wife', a euphemism for slave. Like so many people before her, Edith shared these stories with me without emotion, until I asked about her brother.

As Edith thought of her big brother Jeremiah, tears began to flow.

Jeremiah, Edith and her two small children had been crossing a checkpoint. At different times during Liberia's civil war there were as many as half a dozen different militia groups operating. They would set up random checkpoints to steal and terrorise civilians, who could be singled out and tortured, raped or murdered for looking at the fighters the wrong way. People avoided checkpoints if they had any choice. But there were few ways through one of the world's densest forests. To escape fighting, people often had no choice but to risk their lives passing through the checkpoints.

Jeremiah, Edith and the children waited anxiously in the line. When their turn came, the leader of the young rebels began menacing Edith. He tried to pull her away to the bush, where, it was clear, he would rape her. Brothers, sons and fathers had told me how they had endured these moments in silence, knowing they would be killed if they intervened. But Jeremiah couldn't stay silent. As the rebel dragged his baby sister away, he challenged him. The next moments were a blur but Edith remembered the end with clarity. The rebels tied Jeremiah to a pole and, strip by strip, skinned him alive.

'They let him walk away,' she recalled through her tears and gesturing with her hands, 'with all his strips of skin hanging.'

As Edith sobbed, I tried to comfort her. But I was overwhelmed with shame. Who was I to be asking this woman to relive such horror? This was far out of my league. I felt the ICRC staff's disdain. I still cringe at my next words – a reflection of the cosy world from which I came.

'I don't know how you go on,' I said.

Edith looked at me, incredulous.

'What choice do I have?'

Suicide and depression were unheard of here. There were no psychiatrists in the country. Only a handful of counsellors. In the years to come, through deprivation, injustice and the world's worst Ebola outbreak, that didn't change. Survival, devotion to God, resilience was all they knew.

After that, I mentally committed to Edith and all the survivors to learn everything I could about trauma, to minimise the harm I caused them and better explain their experience to audiences. I came to understand that Liberians' lack of emotion reflected a deep trauma that, after so many years just trying to stay alive, had rewired their brains. As time went on, it was remarkable to see their sense of humour and joy return.

I admired the different approach African cultures take to trauma and healing. At an Ebola survivors' camp in 2014, when I was heading emergency Ebola programming for the BBC charity arm, BBC Media Action, I had tagged along with the indomitable Liberian journalist Mae Azango, now head of New Narratives in Liberia, when she interviewed a midwife who had brought Ebola home from her job and infected her entire family. The midwife was the sole survivor. I was trying to process the guilt and grief the midwife must have lived with, when, minutes later, Mae pointed me to a group of dozens of people singing, dancing and praising God. The midwife was leading the celebration.

In Rwanda, counsellors had told me they could not understand the approach psychologists from the West had brought after the genocide. Taking people to small rooms and asking them to relive their trauma made no sense. They believed in community – dancing, drumming and singing to 'get the blood flowing' – everyone joining together to lift you up and cast out the grief.

Smart journalists like Peter Cave at the ABC and Bruce Shapiro at the Dart Center at Columbia University would spearhead an industry-wide rethink of how trauma impacts journalists and our sources. Trauma in journalism would be a central theme in the International Reporting Program that I headed at the City University of New York's Graduate School of Journalism.

OVER TIME I began to lose faith in journalism's ability to do anything for the people I was reporting on. My audiences overseas knew more about why bad things were happening here than the people who were affected. Journalists in Africa rarely had the funds or the freedom that I had to report.

This led to me joining with my New York–based friend, Susan Marcinek and Liberian journalist Rodney Sieh to form New Narratives. The idea was to leverage our privileged positions to bring funding, editorial and business support to help Rodney support journalists in low-income countries. Because of the longstanding discrimination against them, women journalists were a key focus.

New Narratives has gone on to become a force in West Africa. Reporting in four countries, our work has led to a ban on female genital cutting, a UN investigation into sex abuse by peacekeepers, exposés of international sex trafficking rings and misconduct by police and the Catholic Church. New Narratives journalists have travelled to Europe and the US to cover the trials of accused West African war criminals for media across the region. That reporting has led to an upswell, finally, in support for a war crimes trial in Liberia. For nearly two decades, Liberians have had to watch the warlords who tore their country apart and killed their families take leadership positions in government and stuff their own pockets. Fear of retribution forced people to 'let bygones be bygones'.

The trials and convictions of warlords that have followed New Narratives journalism have led Liberians to believe that they too might see justice for their dead. A bill to establish a war crimes court has passed the parliament. The only obstacle now is President George Weah, the former FIFA Player of the Year–turned politician, indebted to the warlords who keep him in power but facing growing pressure from his people and the international community to bring justice.

Nearly twenty years after I first arrived, Liberia has come a long way. As a journalist and human, I have too.

Prue Clarke's reporting and commentary have appeared in *The Washington Post*, *The New York Times*, *Foreign Policy*, *The Guardian*, *Financial Times*, *The Times* and on the BBC, CBC and CNN. She has won numerous reporting awards, including the Edward R. Murrow award for radio reporting and a United Nations World Gold Medal for investigative reporting. In 2010, she co-founded New Narratives, a women-led non-profit organisation that builds independent news organisations in the global south.

24
THE ARC BENDS SLOWLY

Kylie Morris
The Middle East, Asia, US 1999–2019
BBC, Channel Four News

Another mass shooting, Orlando 2016.

SOMETIMES THE STORIES you're assigned to cover can take over. Not only your waking hours, but your sleeping ones too.

I talked with a therapist in the city about one of my dreams. We talked once a week. Or I talked. He nodded and summarised and prompted. I never shut up. Sometimes he'd nod off. Who could blame him? The afternoons were hot. And, even to me, this was repetitive, getting nowhere kind of stuff. But we were enjoined by a pact to get somewhere, and so I talked about nothing and everything. Relationships. Work. Family. And I cried. He put out a new box of tissues before our sessions, for mopping up. Afterwards, I'd stop at a roadside stall for chicken and rice, drink iced tea so sweet it set your teeth on edge, then go home and sleep.

It was nearly a year since the tsunami, and my dreams had descended underwater. In them, I moved around as though I was on land. I only noticed I was underwater when a cow or a child, even a car, floated by.

It was still. Quiet. In the dream, I suspected that I was dead, but didn't want to rush to any conclusions. There was no secondary independent source I could draw on for confirmation. So it was just me, floating about with my suspicions.

The ceremony to mark the first anniversary of the disaster took place on a beach where many had died. We journalists stood among the grieving. That had been our job, after all, for those intervening twelve months. To stand among the grieving and tell their stories of searching and of loss. By extension, their grief had rubbed off on us. We didn't talk about it in those terms among ourselves, but it was there. On weekends. On aeroplanes. Lacing microphones up shirts. It was so real it could have drawn a seat up to the editing table.

I recognised a friend on that beach – a correspondent from another network. We stood quietly together, waiting for the ceremony to begin. People were already holding onto one another and crying. My friend turned to confess a kind of envy. The mourners on the beach were moored in place by a love for the people they'd lost. She'd been so busy telling their stories, she'd had no time for for her own friends and family. There was no one special in her life she would need to mourn. She is an empathetic, respectful person. But for lots of journalists I know, there is a very real tension between telling other people's stories and living their own. It can shut you down.

Another journalist I worked alongside in the Middle East would say at the end of a fraught day, I don't care what we do this evening, but please don't make me talk to any more strangers.

I used to think the job of a foreign correspondent assigns you permanent observer status. You don't belong where you live. In fact, you can't belong there, because your currency depends in part on being a stranger and telling stories that describe and capture it for other foreigners. Yours needs to be a neutral presence. You can't feel involved.

But that's actually not true:

a) Not all correspondents are foreign to the crises they cover – it's no longer some exclusive club for white folk, flown in from Western capitals, or it shouldn't be.

b) Whoever you are, you bring a point of view to the job. That's inevitable. And the more diverse the points of view of those telling these stories, the better. Of course, that doesn't relieve you of the core responsibility to seek out the truth, regardless of your own biases.

c) You need to get involved, at least to some extent, to understand what's going on around you. So that when the editor of a program in Europe asks you, in happier times, to prepare another report about Afghan women learning to drive, or joining the police force, flying planes, or otherwise throwing off the shackles of patriarchy, you can argue your case. You can tell them, yes, that's happening in small pockets, but no, it's not representative of a broader reality. It's happening nowhere near as much as anyone involved in the international intervention would like it to be. And then, instead, you can pitch a report on the prison where young women are locked up for falling in love against their family's wishes.

I REMEMBER ONCE worrying out loud to a fellow journo working in international news that I wouldn't get a posting I wanted because I'd had a family and might not always be able to travel at the drop of a hat. I'd not invented that fear – I'd heard the muttering from mostly male bosses, but not exclusively, about women in the field for years, about how they wouldn't continue to turn up once they had children. They weren't talking directly to me, but I was listening all the same.

In truth, the fear was one I'd internalised. And as a result, I never said no.

When I moved to South-East Asia, after covering Afghanistan, the Iraq war, and a posting in Gaza, a colleague gently suggested that I might want to consider doing a yoga class. But how would that be possible, I asked, if you couldn't take your phone in with you? To go offline and be unavailable for an hour? I couldn't imagine it.

I invited a friend to my new apartment. It was still largely empty – I'd arrived with a backpack stuffed with clothes and mementoes. A flak jacket. A gas mask. Furniture was something I'd not yet considered. I made a salad for him, chopping the tomatoes with my pocketknife, which I'd depended on and travelled with as an essential, for years. He was clearly horrified and chided me. Maybe shop for some kitchen basics, now I was staying put for a while?

AFTER MORE THAN twenty years in foreign news, there's not one singular story that all at once neatly illustrates the joy, drama and slog of being a foreign correspondent. But when you've stopped travelling and come up for air, there are scenes that stay with you: memories so intense that they unexpectedly interrupt your thoughts years later as you walk the dog or wait at the window of the fast-food drive thru.

I've a clip reel in my mind. Of a city under aerial bombardment and without power, where men sit in the streets, on chairs brought out of their apartments, drinking tea and playing cards while kids play in their pyjamas. Of Bruce Springsteen singing to Philadelphia. Of swimming on the Great Barrier Reef, in the Dead Sea, or at the beach in Gaza. Of the migrant caravan camping out in Chiapas. Of mulberry season in Wardak. Of a wedding in Vegas. A market in Damascus. Of Mark Zuckerberg facing the Senate. Of a very old lady in Arizona who sings to her flag every morning and drinks a beer every night.

I should say that if you watch too much TV (and who doesn't?), you could mistakenly assume the foreign correspondent works alone. For there she or he is, on the news. Gesturing down the road, in her flak jacket, as the tanks shell the city; walking through a demonstration, shouting into her microphone; or sitting alone in an intimately lit living room, asking careful questions of a tearful interviewee.

But, of course, that's not so. To start with, the picture you're seeing is filmed by a camera operator. That's who she's talking to. The story is most likely cut together by a video editor, as the correspondent writes and voices a script to match the footage. And then it's beamed back to the program. And that interview? That woman who spoke through her tears? She was probably first approached by the team's producer, who may have found her through a cascade of phone calls and conversations over weeks or maybe months. Any member of the team might have originally pitched the story. A local fixer may have been involved along the way, to arrange a location, or a translator, or come up with a plan b, or c, for when everything that was set up fell apart.

The reality is, it's a team sport.

The broadcast news team I worked with in Washington between 2014 and 2019 in the intersection of the Obama and Trump eras held itself to high standards in everything, even fast food. Given there were so many options on any American freeway, we agreed we could never eat from McDonald's, except in times of absolute desperation. It was a pact which ensured a real variety of culinary delights over five years, from pancakes and shakes across the Midwest, to delicious Vietnamese in the suburbs of New Hampshire, spicy fried pickles in diners everywhere, tacos in Albuquerque and minced meat burgers in Iowa. I recall just a few moments in five years when our McDonald's desperation clause was invoked.

Once was after Aretha Franklin died in 2018, and we were among the foreign broadcast hordes who descended on Detroit for her memorial service. It was a raw, hot day, I remember. The grief at Aretha's passing and the joy at the life she'd led mixed together in the streets outside the Greater Grace temple. She was in the atmosphere. There were pink Cadillacs, and a sea of exuberant hats worn by ladies who'd lost a sister in the Queen of Soul. There was nowhere near enough room inside the church for all the mourners, let alone the foreign media. A cavalcade of stars and civil rights icons eulogised her on stage. Jennifer Hudson roared and whispered through 'Amazing Grace'; Stevie Wonder leaned into his harmonica, flanked by a gospel choir; Bill Clinton and Al Sharpton stood alongside historian Michael Eric Dyson, all swaying in time to the music, in appreciation of a life so richly lived.

The American networks carried the proceedings live, but we watched and listened from a gas station just along the road from the temple. Folk from the neighbourhood gathered there, playing her music, singing along, providing a lively commentary on the service. An impromptu wake among the bowsers.

The funeral rolled on for an extraordinary nine hours. It was gloriously messy, and overblown, and moving. We couldn't leave until it was done. We didn't want to. But starvation set in midafternoon. We retreated to the car, and got a McDonald's delivery to our address, namely where the hire car was parked a few blocks from the gas station. Never had a fillet of fish tasted so delicious, a bun so artificial, a tartare sauce so tart.

When Aretha Franklin performed at the inauguration of Barack Obama in 2014, she said she was delighted to be there, to see 'the promise of tomorrow coming to pass'. But by the time of her passing, a different tomorrow was dawning. The anti-Obama himself, Donald Trump, would soon be president. Giants of the civil rights era were fading and white supremacism was bursting into broad daylight. Aretha's friend Muhammad Ali had died only a few months before her. The day after she was buried, we flew back to DC to cover the state funeral of Republican senator and Vietnam veteran John McCain.

President Obama liked to quote Martin Luther King's pronouncement, that 'the arc of the moral universe is long, but it bends toward justice'. I think we foreign correspondents often come into the story when the arc is bending, but most often not towards justice. Usually, it's bending in the opposite direction. My own arc isn't long enough to know how it turns out, in the end.

A FEW MONTHS after I'd moved with my husband and our two small children to Washington, there was a paroxysm of protest in cities across the United States. They were sparked by the killings of black men by white police officers. In Ferguson, Missouri; on Staten Island; in Baltimore. Those nights were vivid, full of emotion, anger and hope. The police turned out tooled up in the kind of military gear I'd most recently seen in Iraq, or at Gaza's border with Israel. The protesters were a cross-section of each place. Young people, some of them parents with toddlers sitting on their shoulders. Older couples. Pastors. Sisters. All sorts of people. United in exhaustion at the persecution they faced, and the violent end of another one of their community's sons.

I remember we'd been out one night for hours, dodging tear gas, conducting interviews, filming buildings and cars set on fire, trying to read what might happen next, when we just sat down on the footpath to catch our breath. A couple of young protesters did the same. They were swiftly moved on by a police officer wearing a combat helmet and carrying a gun, who reminded them that if they stopped, they could be arrested. He then came to us to explain that it wasn't true for us. This was just an advisory for 'these people' (by that I think he meant the black protesters) because if they stay in one place, then arguments break out and violence follows, he said. He was white. I'm white. He assumed I'd get it. I did, but probably not in the way he'd meant it. In reality, he'd casually confirmed the kind of systemic racism that the protests were against.

When the protests were closer to home, we'd drive back to DC from Baltimore. One night, as soon as I walked inside our home, I went upstairs to check on the kids. I sat on the bed by my daughter for a few moments. She woke up spluttering, asking about a weird smell.

It was only then that I realised I'd brought the tear gas home with me, on my clothes, and in my hair.

PEOPLE OFTEN ASK whether being a woman meant I did my job differently to male correspondents. It's hard to know. Watch my reporting and on average you hear from more women than men. I was more interested in the intimate truths of life in a community in conflict than in talking to powerbrokers, although I did both. I wasn't immediately seen as a threat. I could disappear more easily. Militia leaders have made me tea. And passed me slices of apple.

Marie Colvin, Lyse Doucet, Carlotta Gall, Lindsey Hilsum, Alex Crawford, Christina Lamb, Janine di Giovanni, Maria Ressa, Christiane Amanpour, Orla Guerin. There is a pantheon of women correspondents on whose shoulders we stand. And we're blessed by an elite band of women producers and editors and camera ops; online storytellers and program editors; lawyers and studio directors. At every layer of the industry now, there's a critical mass of women.

In Afghanistan, in the early 2000s, it was hard work to access women and tell their stories. I was always struck by their absence as I passed through small remote towns. You'd see none on the street at all. It was as though they'd vanished. I remember one trip to the provinces when we finally gained access to a family compound after dinner with the men of the family. I asked if I could meet their wives and daughters. It was agreed. My (male) translator would have to sit outside the curtain to the room, but I could go inside.

We walked to the back of the building, I drew back the curtain and there were a dozen or so women and girls, crowded together. None were wearing burqas. They were modestly dressed in shalwar kameez. They were shy. My Pashto was non-existent. I started talking loudly in English, and my translator shouted from behind the curtain the Pashto version of what I was saying. Before I left, I asked if any of them had any questions for me. One young woman smiled and asked how had I gained the permission of my husband to be a reporter and travel far from home?

I explained I wasn't married. At their reaction, my translator shouted, 'They say that is very pitiful and they are sorry for you.'

The young woman had a follow up ... How, then, had I gained the permission of my father?

I AM STANDING by the side of a busy road, in the middle of the day, in small-town Florida. It is 2018. It is hot. My shirt is sticking to me, and I'm coated in sweat. We're about to cross live into the program and the police have stopped in the middle of the road to find out why we might be impeding traffic. We're not really impeding traffic, but our broadcast signal is poor, and it just so happens that the only place it seems to function is here on the fringe of a four-lane highway.

We can't stand on the pavement, where it's quieter, and calmer, because it feels wrong. There are scores of people walking along it, dressed in black. A student killed in the Parkland school shooting, Meadow Pollack, has just been remembered at a service at a nearby synagogue.

The reason why we're waiting there at all is because we've asked to talk to the student's teacher, and the only way we can speak to her while the program is on is by interviewing her immediately after the funeral finishes.

While the police wait to one side, the teacher, Melissa Falkowski, appears. I say hello, and we quickly clip a microphone onto her shirt, and then, through an earpiece, I can hear the London presenter introducing us. I've not had a chance to talk to Melissa directly beforehand, so I don't know how prepared she is for this. It's been a traumatic twenty-four hours. We have come to speak to her because her students have told us about her bravery and calm, as the shooter stalked the corridor outside their classroom in Marjory Stoneman Douglas High School.

I ask her first about Meadow Pollack, the eighteen-year-old whose funeral she's just attended. She answers calmly, remembering and describing her for television viewers in the UK. Melissa taught her last year. She remembers her student's loopy handwriting on the work she handed in. She was a joy, Melissa says, always optimistic.

Melissa explains that, at first, she had thought the shooting was a drill. There'd been some talk of staging a drill, perhaps that week, and there was a new protocol at the school for managing them. But she thought the timing was off. It was only a few minutes before the end of the school day. When she and her students sought shelter in the closet, they were able to use their phones, and found out soon enough.

This was no drill. A gunman was active in the school. And students had died. In total, seventeen students and teachers were killed.

She tells me she rejects President Trump's immediate reaction to news of the shooting, which is to suggest arming teachers to defend themselves and their students. Melissa says she doesn't want to carry a weapon. In fact, she wants gun laws tightened so fewer people can carry weapons, and certainly so that young people can't get access to military style assault rifles.

She confesses she's worried about going back into the classroom. She'd found it confronting enough just stopping by the school to collect her car that morning. I try to end the interview by telling her that when she does return, she should know there are those in her classes who say her swift action saved their lives, and they are very thankful. She starts to cry, and so do I.

I turn around, so I'm not on camera. She walks out of shot. It's an exhausting day.

Only a week before, when I was at home in Washington DC, our seven-year-old wandered in from a day at her elementary school. She told me that afternoon, that the whole class had sat in the closet with their teacher in the dark. It was a boring lesson, she says, and they couldn't talk. When I ask her why they did it, she tells me it was a 'bad guy' drill.

It's part of American school life. Regardless of whether you're visiting, or a citizen; a journalist or a bus driver. We would talk as a family sometimes about staying on in the US, maybe permanently. The kids have lived there longer than they have anywhere else, we'd say. They have American accents. They don't remember London, and Australia they only know from summer holidays. We have good friends and kind neighbours. It is in large part the place we have felt most welcome. But the politics around gun ownership revealed extremes that were hard to reconcile. We have friends who, before their kids' play dates, call the hosts to check whether the weapons in the house are secure.

Another election is looming, and that means weeks and months on the road again. There will be feverish interest, because of Trump, but, in all honesty, it's a story I've run out of energy to tell. The last campaign turned into a relay race of hate-fuelled rallies, with jeering crowds threatening the 'mainstream media', whipped up by the ringmaster candidate himself.

We decide not to stay, to leave the story to the next correspondent, to go back to the place I've not lived in for twenty-one years – Australia – to be with ageing parents and extended family, and to give the kids a home away from the hustle. It's not a surrender. We intend to keep travelling and reporting, although for now the COVID pandemic has different ideas.

We're sitting in our new living room in a very different city, Newcastle, New South Wales, when insurgents storm the Capitol building on 6 January. I watch television most of the night, as my friends and former colleagues file their reports.

I don't exactly have riot envy, but I feel the push and pull acutely: the excitement of what it is to have a front row seat to historic events, versus the need for ballast to keep you steady. And that for me, comes from the messy reality of family life and relationships and belonging. My younger self would laugh at me. But she hasn't seen what I have.

Kylie Morris has reported for the ABC, BBC and Channel Four News UK over the past three decades, with postings in the Middle East, Kabul and Bangkok. In 2014, she was appointed Washington correspondent by Channel Four News, and returned to Australia in 2019. She lives with her husband, Bharat Nalluri, two children and their dog in Newcastle, New South Wales. She travels with a lucky compass.

25
MARGARET JONES:
THIS AMAZING INTRUSION

China 1973–1976
The Sydney Morning Herald
by Trevor Watson

'GENTLEMEN OF THE National Press Club,' Australia's Prime Minister Harold Holt said, as he opened his groundbreaking 1966 address to an audience of Washington's leading journalists and its most powerful editors. Unexpectedly, Holt then ad-libbed another greeting to 'other types not otherwise included'.

There is little doubt that this unscripted addition to his official speech, which was met with titters from the otherwise all male audience, was delivered in recognition of the unauthorised presence in the audience of *The Sydney Morning Herald* Washington correspondent, Margaret Jones.

Washington's National Press Club, which provided a news-generating platform for the capital's most senior politicians and businessmen as well as foreign dignitaries, was a male-only domain. But Jones could hardly ignore an appearance there by the Prime Minister during his historic 'all the way with LBJ' visit choreographed to reinforce Canberra's commitment to the defence of South Vietnam. Having walked into the club and selected a seat, Jones later wrote that 'nobody quite had the nerve to ask me to leave, realising, I suppose, that it would cause more trouble than it was worth, but a photographer came and took a picture to commemorate this amazing intrusion'.

Jones was deeply disturbed by the exclusion of women from the National Press Club. 'What I found really devastating was that most of the gossip and working procedures were discussed by men in the National Press Club, and I couldn't take part in that, so at the end of a working day I went home to my solitary apartment while all my colleagues, unless they were kind enough to ask me, which they seldom were, went off to the bar and discussed the news of the day, and exchanged notes and comments and bits of information and so on. And I was totally cut off from that,' she told an interviewer.

The *SMH* sent Jones to New York in 1965, and on to Washington in early 1966. It was a turbulent year of black versus white and East versus West. It was the year that Martin Luther King inspired the civil rights movement and the Black Panthers inspired violence. In that year, President Lyndon Baines Johnson declared that the US would remain in Vietnam until 'communist aggression ends', and Leonid Ilyich Brezhnev ruled over an inefficient and economically stagnant Soviet Union. At forty-three years old, and after twenty years in journalism, Jones saw the North America posting as her 'first big break'.

In 1969, Jones moved to London: the Beatles, the IRA, Carnaby Street and the Labour Government of Harold Wilson ('a week is a long time in politics'). It was also a time when China, on the other side of the world, was warming to the West as a counterbalance to an antagonistic Soviet Union. President Richard Nixon went to Peking (now Beijing) in early 1972; Australia's Prime Minister Gough Whitlam was there a year later to normalise relations with the People's Republic.

The new relationship between Canberra and Peking included a deal that would see three journalists from each country posted to the other's capital and the *Herald*'s foreign editor, Stephen Claypole, appointed Margaret Jones as Australia's first resident China correspondent since the 1949 founding of the People's Republic. Jones was later told that she had been chosen for the post in the hope that it would do the paper's image some good to send a woman into something of a risky situation. 'I thought that was a bit of a cheek in view of the paper's long record of discrimination against women, but I wasn't about to turn it down,' she said.

Jones' understanding was not shared by Claypole, who had himself reported for the *SMH* from China, and shared his recollections in an interview for *Through Her Eyes*. 'I recommended her to the *SMH* management because she was an accomplished and seasoned foreign correspondent,' he said. 'There were few others like her on the staff.'

Claypole was very much aware of the importance of Jones' appointment. 'The Chinese saw the first correspondents posted towards the end of the Cultural Revolution as representatives of their countries as well as journalists. Margaret was a proconsular figure who would make a real impression on the Chinese. That was important first time around and Margaret was certainly a fine Australian. I don't think there was ever any risk of correspondents being put under house arrest as they were at the height of the Cultural Revolution, but mature judgement and intuition were necessary in those posted there as China opened up,' he said.

Peking was a tough assignment. Foreign journalists were required to live in guarded compounds; they were not permitted to speak to ordinary Chinese or travel outside the capital without permission. They had no access to newsmakers and relied for information on the government's tightly controlled media. Journalists became keen observers: has the mood in the street shifted; has the order of officials lined up for a *People's Daily* photograph changed; has there been a leadership reshuffle; is a popular cadre missing and has there been a party purge?

In June 1974, Jones herself became the story when Chinese officials refused to attend a dinner hosted by the Australian Ambassador, Stephen FitzGerald, in a protest over the ABC's decision to broadcast the less than flattering Michelangelo Antonioni documentary on China, *Chung Kuo, Cina.*

'The director of the press section of the Information Department, Mr Ma Yu-chen [Ma Yuzhen], said: "At this time we cannot sit down with Australian journalists,"' Jones wrote for the *SMH.*

> The Ambassador and his wife waited for more than an hour before being able to contact Mr Ma who said he and the other two men had not come because of the presence of the Australian correspondents. Officials have assured the Ambassador that the Chinese feeling was not directed against the Australian Embassy or the Australian Government but against the Australian correspondents because of the attitude of the Australian press towards China.

During her two years in Beijing, Jones lived in a new diplomatic compound of large, semi-modern and liveable apartments for diplomats, foreign correspondents and trade emissaries. It also housed the first US Mission and the first Australian Embassy to be established under the Communist regime.

'She would have socialised with other Western correspondents and diplomats (the French and Canadian embassies were the best informed in those days) and the then small staff of the Australian Embassy led by the first ambassador from Canberra, Dr Stephen FitzGerald,' recalled Claypole. 'Margaret could be a forbidding figure but her conversation was always laced with acerbic comments, witty observations of other people's character and love of journalists and journalism.'

She formed a strong bond with Clare Hollingworth, Beijing correspondent for London's *The Telegraph,* who in 1939, as a young journalist, extraordinarily broke the story of World War II when she reported the German army massing tanks on the Polish border. Claypole said that Jones and Hollingworth were both immensely strong willed: 'Margaret statuesque and waspish, Clare diminutive and questing. The air crackled around them when they were together.'

While on later postings to London they were to fall out irredeemably, Claypole said that in Beijing, Jones and Hollingworth were very close. 'They used to mount bicycles and disappear into the vast columns of cyclists at the side of the main routes to see what they could find out,' he recalled. 'It was the only way of shaking off the minders who constantly shadowed them, drivers, translators, office assistants, cooks and maids. Amid the columns they used to encounter George H. W. Bush, the first head of the US Mission in Beijing. They were always greeted with: "Good morning, Miss Jones, good morning, Miss Hollingworth," by the ever-polite future president. Side by side at the pedals he would impart a few observations about life in Beijing.'

During her China posting, Margaret Jones visited North Korea on an assignment that Claypole said would probably now get him, as her foreign editor, blackballed by INSI, the International News Safety Institute. 'She was taken almost immediately to a hospital, shown into a large conference room and told to take off all her clothes. Well, it takes only limited imagination to visualise the scene. She mobilised the Australian language and sent it into battle (I never knew her to utter an expletive). Her minders then asked her whether she would mind meeting some medical students. She agreed, believing this to be the best means of tactical retreat to her hotel. At this point, sliding doors to the conference room were eased back to reveal that it was actually the stage of a large lecture hall containing about one hundred or so medical students who had never before seen a white Western woman,' Claypole said.

Jones later returned to North Korea to report on the small Australian diplomatic mission in Pyongyang (members of which were eventually expelled 'in short order' for the heinous diplomatic offence of eating ice cream in the street). She also went south to the armistice line at Panmunjom on the 38th parallel. 'The idea was that she would meet me, the *SMH* Foreign Editor, on the other side of the line,' Claypole revealed.

> It would probably have amounted to no more than a bit of journalistic braggadocio. We missed one another by 24 hours, she was delayed by her minders. It's possible they knew what was afoot. At this distance I shudder at the recklessness of this. Panmunjom was a dangerous place, all sides watching through binoculars and all military carrying weapons with live rounds. Margaret dismissed it as being marginally less threatening than the Sydney Press Club.

Claypole said that 'perhaps the unkindest thing I ever did to Margaret Jones was to ask her to return to Sydney for Christmas leave in 1974 on the Trans-Siberian Railway, from Beijing, via Ulan Bator to Moscow. This was a tourist-free route during the Cultural Revolution and I thought Margaret would produce a fine full page spread for the Christmas editions of the *SMH*. Indeed, she did. But what I hadn't taken account of was that once the train reached the blasted Steppes, all the windows would be covered in frost. Conscientious as ever, Margaret breathed on the windows to open small, round views of the passing world only to see the frost return in about sixty seconds.

'Before entering the Soviet Union, the cars of the express had to be lifted by crane on to new bogies that matched the different railway gauge north of the border. While this was going on, passengers were entertained with grim revolutionary movies in a small cinema near the track. Margaret was followed in by a Soviet colonel who sat down beside her and promptly put his hand on her knee. It was likely the only time an Australian slapped a Russian officer in the entire Cold War,' Claypole said. 'The train had three restaurant cars, Chinese, Mongolian and Russian but no other passengers apart from a well turned out, personable Russian couple who spoke fluent English. Inevitably, they turned out to be KGB and it was not until she reached Moscow that she got shot of them.

'Margaret dismissed all this high adventure as being just in a day's work and the full-page feature she wrote was one of her best. It brought the Sydney Christmas temperature that year down by a degree or two.'

Jones returned to Australia before the deaths, in 1976, of Communist Party Chairman Mao Zedong and Premier Zhou Enlai, two of the towering figures of twentieth century history, regretfully leaving her successor Yvonne Preston (see *The Beijing Bureau*, Hardie Grant Books) to report on these world-shaping events.

After a stint as the *Herald*'s Sydney-based literary editor, during which she wrote *The Confucius Enigma*, Jones returned to London in 1980 as the paper's Europe correspondent. Her book *Thatcher's Kingdom: A View of Britain in the Eighties* was published in 1984. It was followed in 1985 by another novel, *Smiling Buddha*.

Jones' career began at Mackay's *Daily Mercury* in 1948. In a 1954 application for a job at *The Sydney Morning Herald*, she wrote, 'As you may see by my signature, I am a woman and I know that, even yet, a certain amount of prejudice still exists against women in journalism.' She was offered a position which included a Dog of the Week column. By the end of her career in 1987, she had earned a reputation as one of Australia's leading correspondents and a trailblazer for women in journalism. Jones died in 2006 at the age of eighty-three.

26
'RACE TRAITOR'

Sue-Lin Wong
China, Hong Kong 2014 – present
Reuters, *Financial Times*, *The Economist*

On the China North Korea border.

G ROWING UP, I dreaded Saturday afternoons. While my friends played in the park or lazed about at home, I sat in a classroom at my local Chinese school, near Sydney's Central train station, and tantalisingly close to a swimming pool. I longed to swap my exercise books filled with rows of Chinese characters for my swimmers. For most of my childhood, I just wanted to fit in.

It wasn't until the end of high school that I became curious about my heritage. Many of my classmates at Sydney Girls High School were Asian-Australians who spoke their heritage language well. China was increasingly in the headlines. And I wanted to have adventures, to see the world up close.

When I finished school, I decided to spend a year teaching English in China before I started university. I read on online forums that schools in China were desperate for English teachers. But there was a problem, I found, as I unsuccessfully applied for tens of jobs. Interviewers bluntly told me that parents didn't want their children learning English from someone with a Chinese face. Even Russians who spoke English as a second language were preferred.

Eventually, I found a job at a summer camp–style school in rural Hunan, a province in the middle of China known for its spicy food and as the birthplace of Mao Zedong. While my ancestors are from southern China, my parents were born and raised in Malaysia; I had never been to China. It was here, in the countryside, surrounded by factories that produced much of the world's fireworks, that I became captivated by China.

I made friends with the local mainland Chinese teaching assistants who were English majors at nearby universities. We travelled together after the semester finished, to visit the Terracotta Warriors in Xi'an. There, one of my fellow travellers tried McDonald's for the first time. One colleague invited me to her hometown in a remote part of Ningxia, in north-western China. Her parents had built a court-yard home with a vegetable garden in the middle, near the tree that her father lived in as a child after he was orphaned. In the final three months of my gap year, I studied Chinese with other foreign students in Beijing. It was thrilling to meet overseas Chinese from Argentina, Denmark, France, Myanmar, Panama and South Africa who had had such different, yet similar, upbringings to me.

I returned home for university and promised myself I would find a way back to China. In my fourth year, I went on exchange to Beijing, with a generous scholarship from the Australian Government that required I study Chinese and do an internship. I found one with *The New York Times* Beijing bureau. It was an exciting time. They had just launched their Chinese-language website, poaching top Chinese journalists from the best mainland Chinese publications. The Shanghai bureau broke stories about the wealth of the then-premier, Wen Jiabao's family, prompting the Chinese government to block the newspaper's website. I traversed the country on pre-reporting trips in search of interesting stories for a series of features about the largest migration in human history: the urbanisation of China.

In my final year of university, I applied for several jobs. In the middle of one interview for a job in management consulting, the interviewer paused. 'I don't think this is the job for you. Go and be a journalist,' she said. I was lucky to receive an offer to join Reuters' graduate trainee program. At the time, Reuters was especially keen to recruit native English speakers who also spoke Chinese, Arabic or Russian. I trained in Sydney, Singapore and Shanghai, covering everything from climate change to football and the world's largest auto show.

After my training year, I was given a permanent job on the economics team in Beijing. For two weeks each month, I would write up monthly economic data for the wire. I worried this would be the rest of my life. But for the other two weeks of each month, I jumped on trains to travel north and south, east and west. I visited factories, farms, villages and towns, finding stories to illuminate under-covered aspects of the Chinese economy. I roamed across China, from the tropical island of Hainan in southern China to the frigid north-east to meet striking coalminers. On one such trip, the wind blew so fiercely that I couldn't stay upright. I paused in the middle of a street to clutch hold of a freezing telephone pole.

Reuters had a target to automate more of its monthly economic data. The bosses reassured us this would allow us more time to go out and find stories. I figured it was safer to find a new beat.

I covered China's relationship with North Korea, frequently travelling to Chinese towns and cities along the border. I wrote about how North Korea evaded UN sanctions on its seafood, coal and textiles; I interviewed Korean-Chinese traders who told me they worked with factories that stitched 'Made in China' labels into clothes made in North Korea. Eventually, I visited North Korea on a press junket. But I preferred the relative freedom of reporting on the Chinese side, where the locals frequently travelled in and out of North Korea, and spoke more freely. One of my favourite stories was a feature on life along the border; to research it, my colleague and I spent a week driving along the 1400 kilometre frontier.

In 2019, I joined the London-based *Financial Times* as its South China correspondent. The week I received the official paperwork to open the *FT*'s bureau in Shenzhen, a major city bordering Hong Kong, street protests broke out in the former British Crown colony. Millions of Hong Kongers marched through the city to protest a government bill that could send people to mainland China to stand trial. The movement morphed into the largest uprising on Chinese soil since the protests in

Tiananmen Square in 1989. At Reuters, veteran correspondents spoke about 'the holy trinity' – being in the right place, at the right time, with the right beat. 'If you get that once in your career as a foreign correspondent, you are lucky,' they would say. I felt like I was covering the story of a lifetime. The protesters began demanding genuine universal suffrage. The government cracked down, enabling its police force to act with impunity. By early 2020, as reports of a mysterious virus were emerging across the border, the protest movement started to fizzle.

Our attention shifted to covering the pandemic. In January 2020, I visited a hospital in Shenzhen that I had heard was looking after patients with a new SARS-like virus. The outbreak of severe acute respiratory syndrome in 2003 that emerged in China had killed hundreds in Hong Kong and the mainland. As with most reporting in China, it was difficult to learn anything by going through the front door. Instead, my colleague and I loitered outside, asking any doctor, nurse or hospital staff we saw if there were patients from Wuhan that had been sent to their hospital. We confirmed there were tens of such patients in a ward at a far end of the hospital.

In March, as the world turned upside down, China expelled American journalists working for *The New York Times*, *The Wall Street Journal* and *The Washington Post*. The announcement came less than a month after the Trump administration capped the number of Chinese citizens working in the US for five state- and Communist Party-owned media organisations. The foreign press corps watched in horror as our friends (many of them who were covering the early days of COVID and the Chinese government's attempt to cover it up) scrambled to pack up their lives and those of their families. We wondered who would be next. Most foreign correspondents in China know that at any moment, we may be expelled, often for reasons beyond our control.

A year and a half later, it was my turn. By then I was working as a Hong Kong-based China correspondent for *The Economist*. I was supposed to be in Beijing but the Chinese government had not approved my visa application, submitted more than a year and a half earlier. Now, I wasn't even able to report from Hong Kong. The local government declined to renew my work visa, and I was effectively expelled.

The authorities gave no reason for the refusal. I still don't know what happened. A few days after the news broke, the Chief Executive of Hong Kong, Carrie Lam, was asked at a press conference about my case. She responded that America had denied her a visa and governments had the right to decide who they issued visas to. Then she mentioned Hong Kong's new national security law. The legislation crafted in Beijing made crimes of secession, subversion, terrorism and collusion with foreign forces punishable by life in prison, further curtailing the Territory's remaining freedoms.

I received an outpouring of support and sympathy from fellow journalists and organisations that promote press freedom around the world. Zanny Minton Beddoes, our editor-in-chief at *The Economist*, released a statement: 'We are proud of Sue-Lin's journalism. We urge the government of Hong Kong to maintain access for the foreign press, which is vital to the Territory's standing as an international city.'

But inside China, the reaction was vitriolic. One of China's most popular and influential news organisations accused me of smearing the Hong Kong government's crackdown on protesters and accused Western media more generally of distorting facts. This article was then shared on the official news app of the *People's Daily*, the mouthpiece of the Chinese Communist Party. I was accused of being biased in favour of democracy. My current and former employers at *The Economist* and the *Financial Times* all believe in democracy (as do I). Comments on Chinese social media were hateful and personal, attacking me and others of Chinese heritage who do not unconditionally support the Party. Many labelled me an *erguizi*, or race traitor, a derogatory term for Chinese who had helped Japan during World War II.

Never mind that my family left China generations ago, before the Party took power. Even if I had been born and raised in China, it does not make sense that I should love the Party. But this is now the orthodoxy promoted by the Party across China – in schools, in newspapers, at the movies and online: the Party and the people of China are the same; if you are a person of Chinese heritage, regardless of when your ancestors left, or your nationality, you should love the Party. In my view, to be defined by my race is both racist and unacceptable anywhere in the world. It would be racist if a right-wing Australian politician were to say that a Chinese immigrant was not a 'real' Australian. Similarly, it is racist for the Party to view an Australian of Chinese ancestry as less Australian than a white foreign correspondent from Australia.

Racism isn't the only worrying aspect of surging nationalism in China. Across the board, foreign correspondents in China are under attack from online nationalist trolls who are enabled by the Party machine. But the sexism and chauvinism experienced by younger ethnic Chinese female correspondents is particularly acute. Many of my friends at other publications who are also younger women of Chinese heritage have faced much worse and more frequent abuse. I worry that the online abuse will soon move offline and someone will be physically hurt.

It is even worse for mainland-born Chinese journalists. When I started working as a journalist in China, our newsrooms were filled with brilliant and brave locally engaged journalists who broke important investigative stories and illuminated our understanding of Chinese society, politics and business. As native Chinese speakers who were born and raised in China and deeply immersed in Chinese society, they knew more about China than I ever will.

But China has changed since I first visited in 2007. Now, it is much more authoritarian and closed. During a visit to the Chinese state broadcaster, CCTV, in 2016, China's leader, Xi Jinping, said that Chinese media must serve the Party. Most Chinese journalism is now about promoting and amplifying the Party's perspective. Local Chinese journalists who work for foreign media are constantly harassed by the police and state security. Many Chinese journalists I know have left the industry, often to work in public relations for China's tech giants.

I write this from my parents' house in Sydney, a few train stops away from where I learned Chinese as a child. Being a China correspondent in 2022 can take you to some unexpected places. Since I was forced to leave Hong Kong in a hurry, I have felt a sense of loss, a grief even. I ache for a China that doesn't exist anymore. I miss my friends there. There are so many stories I never got to write. Sometimes I wonder if the Party plans to eventually ban every foreign journalist, or only allow a few wire reporters and business journalists to stay.

Yet the world's press corps will continue to cover China, whether we receive visas or not. The story is too important and too fascinating. Perhaps the Party thinks it will receive more flattering coverage if we are all stuck outside. But North Korea has almost no resident foreign correspondents and its coverage is hardly flattering. Our job as foreign correspondents, whether in China or America or anywhere else, isn't to mindlessly promote a government's perspective. Our job is to report and write the truth.

Soon I will start a new role as South-East Asia correspondent for *The Economist*. Like my high school self, I am looking forward to the adventures that lie ahead and to seeing a different part of the world, up close. And I hope that, one day, I will be able to return to China for another posting.

Sue-Lin Wong is a China correspondent for *The Economist*. She was previously a correspondent at the *Financial Times* and Reuters. Sue-Lin was born and raised in Sydney and graduated from the Australian National University.

27
A FIGHT FOR FREEDOM IN PARADISE

Sue Williams
New Caledonia 1985–1987
Freelance

With Mark Baker (*The Age*), Trevor Watson (ABC) and
John Dunn (*Time*), Noumea.

T HE FRENCH PRIME MINISTER Jacques Chirac strolled into the
welcome reception at Nouméa's elegant High Commission
flanked only by a few aides. It was August 1986, and the atmosphere
was relaxed and friendly. Apart from a couple of French photographers,
the journalists who had accompanied Chirac from Paris or flown up
from Sydney were nowhere in sight.

For a young, green correspondent, the opportunity was too good to
be true. I had a glass of champagne in my hand, no notebook or tape
recorder – both were buried deep in my bag. But I knew what the
visiting PM had said to the Australian Consul-General on his arrival in
New Caledonia earlier that day. I had to seize the moment. I grabbed
the arm of my friend Meredith Schroder, the Australian Consul to
New Caledonia, and we introduced ourselves.

266

'Good evening, Mr Prime Minister, my name is Sue Williams. I'm a journalist for Radio Australia. Why are you so angry with [Australian Prime Minister] Bob Hawke?' Seven whole minutes later, I bid good evening to the PM and, adrenaline pumping, bolted out to file.

It was a front-page story and bound to exacerbate existing tensions between Canberra and Paris. It was also my story. But as a junior female stringer who basically turned into a tea lady when my bosses sent in their big guns to cover major events, there was little chance of it carrying my by-line. And yet, I was determined, ambitious, excited and, I believed, good at my job. I would find a way.

I'D ORIGINALLY BEEN sent to the French overseas territory for a week in January the year before by Sydney commercial radio station 2WS to cover a snap twelve-hour visit by French President François Mitterrand. I spoke only a smattering of schoolgirl French and knew next to nothing about New Caledonia, its history or its people. I vaguely understood it to be an exotic tropical holiday destination with a French accent, not far from Australian shores. I spent the hours before my departure reading everything I could get my hands on.

The indigenous people, the Kanaks, were demanding independence from France, white settlers were strongly opposed, and violence was escalating. Ten pro-independence Kanaks had been ambushed and murdered by white anti-independence militants in the northern town of Tiendanite not long before I arrived. A state of emergency had been declared throughout the archipelago, just 3000 kilometres from Australia's eastern coastline.

I watched as Le Caillou, the pebble, as the main island is known, filled with several thousand heavily armed soldiers and the intimidating black-uniformed Republican Security Corps, the CRS riot police from Paris.

It was nigh on impossible to leave the capital, Nouméa, so the days were spent attending press conferences at the High Commission, meeting with the leadership of the Kanak and Socialist National Liberation Front, the FLNKS, or interviewing leaders of the conservative, anti-independence party Rally for Caledonia in the Republic, the RPCR, and other like-minded groups. In between times, the French journalists, photographers and TV crews who had also remained hung out on the terrace of the Hotel Le Paris, overlooking the Place des Cocotiers in the city centre, drinking endless espressos, smoking Gitanes, swapping tales of their professional and other exploits, working out the angle for the day's news story and waiting for something to happen. Despite the palpable tension in the city and the real danger of deadly confrontation, these moments had their comical side, heavily reminiscent of Evelyn Waugh's *Scoop*, the 1930s satire of sensationalist foreign correspondents.

For me, fresh out of the commercial radio scene in Sydney, it was a pure adrenaline rush. New Caledonia is only a dot on the world map, but at that time it was the centre stage of a conflict that had the potential to reshape politics and power in the South Pacific: 'a microcosm, as you might say, of world drama,' in the words of Waugh's venal newspaper proprietor, Lord Copper.

The story pulled me like a magnet. I knew it would capture media attention beyond Mitterrand's visit. It had all the ingredients: an oppressed indigenous population of a colonial outpost on Australia's doorstep was demanding independence and was ready to fight for it, taking on not only a privileged, affluent white minority, but also the might of one of the world's major powers.

I was excited about rubbing shoulders with reporters from leading international media outfits and meeting the actors in a story that had serious geopolitical implications. France was already a thorn in the side of South Pacific regional governments because of its nuclear testing program in French Polynesia. Heady stuff for a young journalist looking to move onwards and upwards.

There were no Australian or anglophone media based in Nouméa. There was one very brave young Australian woman living in New Caledonia, Helen Fraser, who reported occasionally on the story, but she had taken a clear stand for the pro-independence Kanaks and was deeply mistrusted, shunned and, ahead of her departure, regularly roughed up and threatened by the fiercely pro-French population. Imbued with a sense of destiny, I decided to fill the gap. It never occurred to me that my gender could be an issue, and by and large it was not. Although foreign correspondents' jobs, and indeed the whole profession of journalism, were still largely a male preserve, I had cut my journalistic teeth in Sydney's rough and tumble, hyper-macho news environment and come through relatively unscathed. So, I decided to set up as a freelance reporter for English language media in a place where there was a hot story and no one else to cover it.

It seems quite extraordinary when I think back and realise that I was able to up anchor, throw physical and financial security to the wind and dive headlong into a violent conflict in a country whose cultures, languages and history I knew little about. I made a brief return to Sydney to pack up my life and was back in Nouméa. I had enough cash to tide me over for a few weeks, and a return ticket to Sydney if it all went belly up. I had negotiated agreements with Radio Australia, the regional magazine *Pacific Island Monthly* and 2WS. I would provide regular coverage of the story and that would guarantee me at least a trickle of income. Over the next few months, I couch-surfed and house-sat for Australian ex-pat friends working at the regional multi-government development body, the South Pacific Commission, and finally moved into share accommodation with a French doctor newly arrived in the Territory and not yet tuned in to the political and social realities of the place. The story continued to draw international media interest, and I was soon retained as stringer for *The Age* newspaper in Melbourne, the BBC and *The Economist*, along with the ABC. I also reported regularly for the American Broadcasting Company, Radio France International (RFI) and occasionally for *The Bulletin with Newsweek* magazine in Australia.

The locals in Nouméa were initially warm and friendly. Australia was not only a leading source of tourists for New Caledonia, but a holiday destination and business partner for the *Metros*, the temporary residents from France, and the Caldoches, the locals of European origin. But as the independence movement grew, the tourists stopped coming and production at the Goro mine, which exploited one of the world's largest nickel deposits, slowed. The economy was suffering, and that threatened the easy tropical lifestyle of the self-styled loyalists who were opposed to any change in the status quo. Tensions over the Territory's status also hit the handful of wealthy families who controlled its resources and politics. They were furious at the Australian Labor government's support for the Kanaks and believed public opinion was being influenced by misinformation and biased reports. At first, they saw me as a way to get the 'true' story out.

But within months, I was under regular attack from the local daily *Les Nouvelles Calédoniennes*, which distorted and misquoted my reports, broadcast into New Caledonia in both French and English by the ABC's international shortwave service Radio Australia. I was accused of pro-Kanak bias, tagged as a rabid left-wing sympathiser come to foment unrest, and called a spy for Canberra. The newspaper's sister publication in Tahiti joined the fray, in one editorial labelling me as a harpy that Nouméa would best be rid of. An operative for the French military intelligence service, the DGSE, took me for coffee to have 'a friendly chat' about who I was, who I worked for, who I was in contact with, and how long I would be staying. Through a friend, the governing RPCR party even offered me work in the local library. This would be a much more elegant and suitable way for me to stay in Nouméa, they said, protecting the friendships I had made, the reputation of my French partner and my own security. The Australian Consulate staff warned me to be careful – they were sure their own phones were tapped and their every move outside of Nouméa was followed. In a memoir about her tumultuous, life-changing first diplomatic posting, *Red Passport, Red Beret*, Meredith Schroder recalls the panic buttons and safe rooms in the homes of all Australian staff in Nouméa.

The danger was real and I couldn't ignore it. I found myself looking over my shoulder, limiting telephone conversations and rarely venturing out alone at night. I had evidence that the anti-independence militia were smuggling arms into New Caledonia by private yacht. Rumoured to be funded by the loyalists, these guys were hard core. They included descendants of the original white colonialists, refugees or their descendants from the old French empire – Algeria, Indochina, Congo – and ex-army types who had invested their pensions in New Caledonia and enjoyed their simple life in the tropics recalling France's glory days. I was woken up one night by a huge bomb blast not far from my home. It destroyed the Territory's taxation office and came just one day after Jacques Lafleur, head of the RPCR, criticised a proposed tax on business to fund development outside of Nouméa to benefit Kanaks. No one was arrested for the attack.

Getting caught in military or police operations was also an ever-present danger. During a fierce clash in Nouméa between Caldoches and Kanaks, riot police used tear gas to disperse the crowds. One officer fired from directly behind me. The canister zipped over my head so closely that it literally parted my hair. 'Sorry,' he yelled, grinning, as I dropped to the ground. On a trip north with the ABC's John Lombard, we pulled over to the side of the road, I opened the car door and almost stepped on a grenade that had fallen off a soldier's belt. The soldier saw what happened and, red faced, raced up to recover the device, which our car tyre had missed by centimetres and my foot by even less.

WHEN I ARRIVED in New Caledonia, my reporting focused on the threat of a looming bloodbath as fear and anger rippled through the Territory. But soon, another story began to unfold.

From the first, I had reported the Kanaks' grievances and why they were seeking independence from France: 150 years of colonial oppression, denial of their culture and civil rights, exclusion from political and economic life and entrenched racism – the list of injustices was long, and incontestable. The words flowed easily enough for rapid-fire news reports. But my understanding of the real issues only came when I was able to experience New Caledonia firsthand, without the pressure that came with visiting VIPs and hourly news deadlines, and when I had the time to explore and spend time with people from all communities. I developed a deep admiration for FLNKS leader Jean-Marie Tjibaou, whose intelligence, dignity and eloquence shone like a beacon. He was a man of peace who had given up the priesthood to devote himself to fighting for the rights of his people. He knew it would be long and hard, and he knew he would probably pay for it with his life. Tjibaou would indeed be assassinated, along with his deputy, Yeiwéné Yeiwéné, on 4 May 1989, by a rival Kanak leader during a commemoration ceremony to remember the nineteen militants killed a year earlier in a military assault on a cave that ended a hostage drama on the island of Ouvéa.

The experience of plunging into another cultural and linguistic sphere, to delve into its history with all its complexities and contradictions, and to witness the impacts on people's lives, to share their fears, their hopes or their hopelessness, and their aspirations, is one of the greatest rewards of being a correspondent. My time in New Caledonia was a period of intense personal growth that reshaped my future and changed the vision I had of my own country and its history. I found myself questioning what it meant to be Australian. I am embarrassed to admit that it took the Kanaks' fight for freedom to open my eyes to the struggles and sufferings of Australia's First Nations peoples, and to the complex and bloody legacy of British and European colonisation in the Pacific.

BY THE TIME of Prime Minister Jacques Chirac's visit, eighteen months after I arrived, my French had vastly improved, as had my understanding of the complex situation facing the Territory's different populations. His recently elected conservative government had wasted no time dismantling a plan developed by Edgard Pisani, Mitterrand's High Commissioner for New Caledonia, to guide the Territory towards 'independence in association with France'. For Chirac, New Caledonia was a French possession and would remain so. No opposition would be tolerated. His minister responsible for the Territory, Bernard Pons, had warned, 'If (the Kanaks) move, we'll wring their necks.'

The new Prime Minister's stand comforted the loyalists, enraged the FLNKS and reignited tensions, which quickly spiralled into a new round of violence. It also inflamed relations between France and the Pacific region stunned by the DGSE bombing of the Greenpeace boat *Rainbow Warrior* in Auckland Harbour a year before, which killed photographer Fernando Pereira.

Concerned by the explosive situation on Australia's doorstep, Bob Hawke labelled Chirac's position 'a backwards step'. Chirac read the comments, reported in *The New York Times* and *Le Monde*, on his flight to Nouméa. By the time he descended onto the tarmac at Magenta Airport, his aides later told me, he was bristling with rage over what he saw as more Australian interference in French affairs.

I was at the airport for his arrival and the meet and greet handshake with local dignitaries and diplomats, including Australia's consul-general, John Dauth, and his team. When Chirac reached the consul-general, he grasped his hand tightly, leaned in close and whispered in his ear. John's relaxed and open smile suddenly became a thin, pinched grimace and he visibly stiffened. Chirac hopped into his waiting car and sped off to the French high commissioner's residence. As soon as I could, I called John Dauth to ask him what Chirac had said. He hesitated only a fraction of a second before responding: '"Your prime minister is a drunken bastard." Chirac spoke in perfect English. There was no mistaking what he said.'

John had given me the quote off the record, knowing I would not be able to use it. There was an important story here, but how could I tell it? Then came the evening reception at the High Commission, and my serendipitous encounter with Jacques Chirac.

'*Monsieur le premier ministre d'Australie dit des betises sur la Calédonie et la politique de La France dans cette région,*' he replied sharply, when I asked him why he was angry with Hawke. 'The Australian prime minister has been saying stupid things about New Caledonia and French policies in this region.' It was much milder than his remark to the consul-general, but *betises* can be interpreted several ways, from silly to mischievous to nonsensical, inept, ignorant or stupid. Jacques Chirac's meaning was made very clear when he added that it wasn't Australians who were the problem, it was their prime minister, and he would heartily welcome a change of government.

I couldn't believe my luck. I went over everything that was said with Meredith to make sure we had heard right. I had a story. But who would I write it for? *The Age* had sent senior reporter Mark Baker to town for Chirac's visit, which meant that I would have to give the information to him so he could write it up. It would be his by-line on the article. I admired Mark and was very proud to be working for *The Age*, even as a stringer. While I thought it grossly unfair that I would be totally side-lined on my own front-page exclusive, I did my duty and gave Mark the story. In detail, we discussed the Chirac quote and exactly how we should translate *betises*. I also sent a report to Radio Australia. Then, figuring that as a stringer I was free to work for whomever I wished, and quietly annoyed with *The Age*, I also offered the story to the rival Melbourne *Herald Sun*. It was not a well-considered decision, a naive reaction born of frustration, wounded pride and a sense of injustice, and it almost cost me my much-valued retainer with *The Age*. I should have tried harder to negotiate, but I didn't know how.

The *Sun* didn't put my piece on the front page the following morning, but *The Age* and its sister publications around the country certainly did, with the headline blaring that Jacques Chirac had called Bob Hawke stupid. I was delighted and mortified. Even if that's what he meant, he could truthfully deny saying Bob Hawke was stupid.

Sure enough, as soon as I joined the press team heading up into the bush with Chirac that day, I was pounced on by his angry aides, demanding to see my notes and accusing me of not telling the PM

I was a journalist. 'Not true,' I countered, 'and I have a witness. The Australian consul was with me when I spoke to the prime minister.' They told me he would deny the story at a press conference that evening. Later in the morning, Chirac sought me out. Oh no, I thought, here we go. But, beaming, and with Gallic flourish, he took my hand and kissed it, wishing me a good day and congratulating me for such a splendid article. In a flash I understood the headline was exactly what he had wanted, and he'd given me the story in a way that ensured he had deniability. He wanted to send a clear message to Hawke without causing a major diplomatic rift, and he had succeeded. Feeling flattered, outraged and very worried all at once, I called John Dauth and shared my concerns. He did not want to let Chirac off the hook, and he reassured me he would have my back.

That evening, back in Nouméa, we all gathered for the press conference. The word among my peers was still that the prime minister would deny the story. Just before the start, John Dauth coolly strolled in. We took seats side by side in the front row, directly in front of Mr Chirac. The French leader smiled at us and nodded. The first question came from a French colleague, who asked whether he had really called Bob Hawke stupid. I held my breath. Looking directly at John and me, he said he had made some comments during an off-the-record conversation at the reception and would say nothing further on the matter. But he went on to say that the Australian Government's stand on the situation in the Territory was 'unacceptable' and 'false' and that 'it was not in Australia's interest to see France excluded from the region'. I breathed a huge sigh of relief.

I HAD DEVELOPED a strong attachment to Le Caillou – it is a beautiful place and I had lived through some extraordinary moments, and had even married a French anthropology student there. I'd met wonderful people on all sides of the political spectrum. But it was exhausting, and constantly being on alert for my own safety was wearing me down. I was no war junkie.

A decisive moment came several months later during an angry protest march organised by French public servants posted to Nouméa, many of them teachers. Riot police had set up a cordon along their route. A group of them – all men – spotted me on the sidelines and began to chase me, shouting furious insults and threats. I ran towards the wall of riot police and asked them to let me through their cordon. To my stupefaction, they refused and closed ranks to block my escape. Then someone grabbed me, pulled me behind his back and turned to face the rioters. He commanded them to stand back. My unexpected saviour was none other than the extreme–right wing crime author Alain Dreux-Gallou, or ADG, as he was known, a virulent anti-independence royalist who had moved to New Caledonia in 1982 to rally support for the National Front. His newsletter *Combat Caledonien* constantly urged the anti-independence forces to rise up and defend their flag. He pushed me hard through the line of riot police yelling, 'Cours, vite!' Run. Fast.

I don't know why he helped me, perhaps because he was an ardent defender of press freedom. Whatever the reason, he saved me from a beating. A good friend and fellow journalist, Olivier Couhé, corre-spondent for *Le Matin*, was left fighting for his life when he was beaten senseless at his home late one evening just before the first referendum on independence in September 1987.

The strain was taking its toll, aggravated by the knowledge that as a freelancer, I was on my own. With attention now focused on the French government's hardline position, it seemed a logical step for me to cover the story from France.

I was settled in Paris and focused on the upcoming second round of a French presidential election when, on 22 April 1988, the world's attention suddenly switched back to New Caledonia. Kanak militants had stormed a gendarmerie on the island of Ouvéa, killing four and taking the others hostage. The crisis came to an end on 5 May with a brutal military assault, approved by Chirac (who was one of the presidential candidates) and Bernard Pons. The battle left nineteen Kanaks and two elite paratroopers dead. I was angry with myself for not having stayed.

I continued to file on the outcome of the presidential election, won by François Mitterrand, and the subsequent peace negotiations, but I was moving on, working for Radio France International and Agence France Presse. While I loved living in Paris, professionally it was unsatisfying. New Caledonia had given me a taste for geopolitics, but I wanted to write about the things that encouraged peace and dialogue, rather than cover the savagery of war. So when a door opened for me at UNESCO (United Nations Educational, Scientific and Cultural Organization) to write for a new publication about its work in education, science, culture and communication, I jumped through it.

Nouméa is a long time ago now, but my friendship with Meredith Schroder (Atilemile) remains strong. Her memoir helped refresh my memory of certain events, critical dates and the rich mosaic of personalities we encountered in the Territory. The French flag still flies there, but the Kanak cause has advanced considerably and support for independence continues to grow.

As a journalist, I left New Caledonia behind, but I continued to follow its evolution and build on the lessons I learned there. Le Caillou had been my first and last assignment as a foreign correspondent, but like a first love, it remains unforgettable.

Sue Williams began her journalistic career in Sydney radio in 1978. She moved to New Caledonia in 1985 to cover the Kanak struggle for independence, writing and reporting for Radio Australia, *The Age*, *Pacific Island Monthly*, *The Economist* and *The Bulletin with Newsweek*. In late 1987, she was based in Paris, where she worked for Radio France International, AFP and UNESCO, until 2015.

28
A PRIME MINISTER, A MURDER AND A MISSING DIAMOND

Mary Ann Jolley
Malaysia 2015 – present
Al Jazeera

A departure for North Korea 2007.

'WHAT DO YOU mean, I'm being deported! I'm a journalist, not a drug trafficker, and this is Malaysia, a supposedly democratic country, not some despot hermit state,' I blurted to the bemused official on the other side of the desk, my tone probably embarrassingly shrill.

It was July 2015. I was already familiar with the immigration office in the basement of Kuala Lumpur International Airport. I'd been unceremoniously escorted from passport control down there days earlier, and as soon as I was taken there yet again, I knew I was in strife. Behind the rows of officials in brass-laden uniforms, stamping and shuffling document after document, was a whiteboard plastered with A4 mugshots. One of them was of me.

'Why can't I enter the country? What law have I broken?' I asked, my voice wavering, more from anger than fear. The silence was deafening. 'I know why. It's your repressive prime minister, Najib Razak, isn't it?'

As I glared at the official, he pressed his lips together, drew in his breath, lifted his eyes to the ceiling and then looked at me. 'I'm sorry,' he said quietly, his face deflating with empathy and shame. 'Please don't judge me or my country by him.'

FOR THE PAST six months I'd been working for Al Jazeera's Asia–Pacific program, 101 East, which was based in Kuala Lumpur. I'd regularly flown up from Sydney to edit stories I'd filmed in the region, and more recently to produce stories in Malaysia.

As a foreign correspondent, Malaysia had never been on my bucket list. The closed, the repressive and the remote had captured my attention, and I'd been incredibly lucky to be sent on assignments to some of the most extreme of each: North Korea, Saudi Arabia, Zimbabwe, Libya and Sudan, to name a few.

The dictators and pariahs that led them: Kim Jong Il, Robert Mugabe and the erratic and ridiculously vain 'Mad Dog of the Middle East' Muammar Gaddafi were perversely fascinating. So, too, were their privileged and vile family members: Mugabe's grossly extravagant and maniacal wife, 'Gucci' Grace, Gaddafi's Western-educated, deceivingly Zen, bloodthirsty son Saif and his murderous younger brother Al-Saadi, who pathetically bought his way to a reserve position on an Italian professional soccer team. I wanted to understand how they managed to cling to power and the international forces that enabled them. But, more than anything else, it was the extraordinary bravery of their citizens who stood up against their barbarity, often risking their lives and those of their families to speak out, that gave real purpose to being a foreign correspondent. With no independent media inside these fiefdoms, and until recently no social media, we could help ensure dissenting voices were heard as they applied pressure for change.

In comparison, Malaysia seemed benign and, dare I say, dull.

Sure, I'd read the headlines about the former deputy prime minister turned opposition leader, Anwar Ibrahim, and the shocking way he was sacked from office, brutally beaten and thrown in jail on trumped-up charges of corruption and sodomy in the late 1990s. But I had little idea Malaysia was essentially a one-party state, ruled since independence in 1957 by UMNO, the United Malays National Organisation. Nor did I understand the depth of corruption that came with that.

On the surface, the country was a functioning democracy. There were regular elections, a smattering of independent news outlets, and a rapidly growing economy. The sparkling crystal-encased Petronas twin towers, still the tallest twin towers in the world, were a spectacular symbol of Malaysia's development and modernity.

And then there was the country's seemingly stellar performance on the international stage and the starring role played by its British-educated prime minister, Najib Razak. Najib came from Malaysian political royalty. His father and uncle were the country's second and third prime ministers. In 2009, he became the sixth. Unlike his two predecessors – the notoriously 'recalcitrant' Mahathir Mohamad (to quote Australia's former prime minister, Paul Keating) and the underwhelming Abdullah Badawi – Najib was often described by those who met him in diplomatic circles as erudite, eloquent and charming. But as the leader of a predominately Muslim country in a post 9/11 world, it was his moderate Islamic views and his support for 'the war on terror' that had Western leaders fawning over him.

And there was perhaps no greater example of that fawning than Christmas Eve 2014, when US President Barack Obama took time out from his holiday in Hawaii to play golf with Najib. Photographs flashed across the globe of the two men laughing together as they hopped on and off a cart and strode across perfect greens. The money shot came on the 18th hole when Obama consoled Najib for missing a putt, warmly patting him on the shoulder in front of the media throng. It was the second time they had met that year; in April, Obama had been the first sitting US president to visit Malaysia in almost half a century.

The illusion shattered when I started travelling to Malaysia for Al Jazeera in 2015. Najib's international bromances were a smokescreen concealing what was really going on inside the South-East Asian nation.

While he was teeing off with Obama, his wife, Rosmah Mansor, was hitting the shops, racking up credit card charges of more than US$130,000 at Chanel in Honolulu. It was quite a bill for a woman with no known source of income apart from her husband's annual salary of half that amount. No one knew about the shopping spree at the time, but corruption alarm bells were already ringing.

In May 2015, our cameras rolled as a sea of protesters took to the streets of Kuala Lumpur in response to a swathe of arrests of opposition figures and government critics in a heavy-handed crackdown on freedom of speech. 'Say no to the devil and its puppets, Najib and Rosmah,' read one placard.

Najib and his government had narrowly won power at the general election in 2013, losing the popular vote to Anwar Ibrahim's opposition coalition. In the aftermath, they'd faced allegations of widespread electoral fraud and gerrymandering. Their way of dealing with dissent was to silence it. They deployed archaic sedition laws under the guise of maintaining unity in the racially diverse country, and used the threat of terrorism to introduce a new law allowing people to be detained without trial or judicial review for two years. Leading global human rights organisations expressed outrage. Phil Robertson from Human Rights Watch told us the actions were 'draconian' and a return to the human rights 'stone age'. But the denunciations were water off a duck's back for Najib and his cronies.

One of those targeted was Anwar Ibrahim's daughter and member of parliament, Nurul Izzah Anwar. She had been crucial to the establishment of the People's Justice Party, PKR, while Anwar was imprisoned from 1999 to 2004. In 2008, he made a triumphant return to politics, but as he and the PKR grew in popularity, he was again charged, convicted and jailed for sodomy. In March 2015, Izzah rose in parliament to deliver a scathing condemnation of the judiciary, who she accused of 'displaying subservience by taking directions from their political masters' and selling 'themselves to the devil'. Parliamentary privilege could not protect her. The mother of two young children was arrested and held overnight in police custody before being released on bail.

When we interviewed her at her family's home in Kuala Lumpur, as party members and constituents waited for an audience, she was still under investigation and had to report regularly to the police station. She wasn't cowering.

'If you don't speak out, there will never be an end to this corrupt regime,' she said. 'One thing that's kept my family alive: we shall never surrender to Najib and his authoritarian government.' Her words would come back to me often in the years to come.

Ultimately, sedition charges were not laid against Izzah, unlike Malaysia's internationally celebrated political cartoonist Zulkiflee Anwar Haque. Zunar, as he is known, is a warm, insightful and delightfully mischievous character. When we met in his tiny studio above a suburban strip of shops and cafes in April 2015, he'd just spent three days in a police lock-up, charged with nine counts of sedition for tweeting that Anwar's conviction was politically motivated. His fans helped pay the US$6000 bail, but he faced a potential forty-three-year jail sentence.

When our camera rolled, he was armed with a defiant catchcry: 'I will keep drawing until the last drop of my ink, it doesn't matter what you do to me. If the government wants to stop me, they need to stop the ink coming to Malaysia!'

Zunar had been charged with sedition before, his office raided numerous times, his books seized, destroyed and banned, his printers and booksellers threatened. He'd been a constant thorn in the prime minister's side, his drawings exposing the corrupt underbelly of Najib's government, from the US$11 billion black hole in the country's sovereign wealth fund, One Malaysia Development Bank, or 1MDB – more about that later – to the excesses of Najib's wife, Rosmah.

'She is the Prime Money-ster,' Zunar chortled as he lifted his pen to draw her, complete with a ridiculously large sparkling diamond. He sketched Najib as an elf-like creature, stealthily pouring cash from bags labelled 1MDB into Rosmah's handbag.

'Marie Antoinette, she loved diamonds,' he explained, his voice melodic, as if telling a fairytale. 'Imelda Marcos loved shoes. Grace Mugabe loved handbags. But Rosmah loves all – shoes, diamonds and handbags! I need to thank her. She lets me open up people's eyes about corruption.'

But lurking in Zunar's collection of drawings was a darker subject, and the real reason he found himself at the top of Najib's hit list. 'This is Altantuya, this is the bomb, and this is the submarine,' he said as he drew. 'It's a very sensitive issue in Malaysia.'

He was talking about the sensational murder in October 2006 of a twenty-eight-year-old Mongolian woman, Altantuya Shaariibuu, and its suspected links to an allegedly corrupt billion-dollar submarine deal with France. At the time of the murder, Najib was deputy prime minister. But the tale begins in 2001, when as defence minister, he signed off on the submarine deal, brokered by his key advisor and close friend, Abdul Razak Baginda.

Altantuya, a translator, was Baginda's lover and had accompanied him to France. Later, after the romance soured, she was abducted at night outside Baginda's house in an exclusive gated suburb of Kuala Lumpur, driven out of the city and shot with a high-powered semi-automatic gun. Military grade explosives were strapped to her body and detonated, blowing it to smithereens.

Two elite policemen from Najib's ministerial security detail, Azilah Hadri and Sirul Azhar Umar, were convicted of her murder, but no motive was ever established. Neither had met their victim before bundling her into a car, but they definitely knew about her. Baginda had asked Azilah to 'deal' with Altantuya, claiming she had been harassing him and his family. Baginda later divulged that during their conversation, Azilah had 'boasted' he'd killed six to ten people in the past. Baginda was initially charged with abetting the murder, and jailed, but the charge was dropped when a preliminary hearing found he had no case to answer.

Phone text messages leaked to the press a couple of weeks before he was freed suggested interference in the case by the then deputy prime minister, Najib. And a year earlier, a private investigator, known as Bala, whom Baginda had hired to protect his family from Altantuya, issued a statutory declaration asserting the Mongolian woman had told him she'd had an affair with Najib, was pregnant with his child and had been promised US$500,000 for her help in the submarine negotiations. The next day Bala retracted his claims and disappeared. Years later, when he finally resurfaced, he told a chilling story of how Najib's younger brother, Nazim, had threatened his life.

At his sentencing in March 2009 for the murder, Sirul added more fuel to the bushfire of speculation that Najib was involved in a massive cover-up, when he begged the judge not to sentence him to death, insisting he was a 'scapegoat for those more powerful'.

Just two weeks after Sirul and Azilah went to death row, Najib was sworn in as the new prime minister of Malaysia.

In January 2015, as I was joining Al Jazeera, came another bizarre twist. Sirul and Azilah had been acquitted and released on bail, pending an appeal by the prosecution. Sirul fled to Sydney, where he knew he'd be safe from extradition should the Malaysian appeals court decide to send him back to jail and the gallows – Australia refuses to return anyone to a country where they face execution.

But he wasn't free for long. The Malaysian court overturned his acquittal and an Interpol notice was issued against him. Within days, he was detained by Australian Federal Police and shipped to Villawood Immigration Detention Centre in Sydney, where he remains.

The more I read about the case, the more intrigued I became – what was the real truth behind Altantuya's gruesome and tragic murder and why had there seemingly been no justice for the mother of two young children?

So, in May 2015, I emailed Paul Stadlen, Najib's British international media advisor, asking for an interview on the story with his boss. There was no reply. Stadlen had developed an intense dislike of international media when his exorbitant, several million–dollar salary and his ageing party boy antics were exposed.

In Malaysia, I tried to talk to people from all sides of politics, the judiciary and police, as well as those with personal ties to the case. But as soon as I mentioned Altantuya's name, the fear was palpable. Phone lines went dead. 'How did you get my number?' some asked, terrified they'd been betrayed or that someone might find out they'd spoken to me. For those willing to talk, cars were the preferred location, but the conversations were always preceded with: 'This must go no further.' When I asked why they weren't prepared to speak publicly, one person succinctly summed up the sentiments of many: 'I live and work here and I want to continue to do both.'

Remarkably, the man at the heart of the case, Razak Baginda, agreed to meet me, with his lawyer, in a slick cafe in the luxurious shopping mall at the base of the Petronas twin towers.

A small, impish man, he was frenetic from the moment he arrived. 'You know, the relationship wasn't sexual,' he said before he even sat down. It seemed such an odd thing to say straight up. If he thought it would convince me of his innocence, all I could think of was the famous line of former US president, Bill Clinton: 'I did not have sexual relations with that woman.'

As Baginda bobbed up and down in his chair, leaping from one unfinished thought to another, it was clear that he had little empathy for Altantuya and the shocking way she was murdered, or for her children. He and Najib were the real victims, their careers and lives unjustly blemished by the Mongolian woman and the two 'rogue' policemen who 'took it upon themselves' to murder her. 'And no, I'm not going to do an interview,' he said, adding he and Najib were unimpressed with our recent 'biased' program on sedition laws. The two were obviously still close; Baginda had a desk in the PM's office and was heading there after our meeting.

'Perhaps you could suggest to the Prime Minister he do an interview with us,' I said sharply as we parted. Later that afternoon, in an extraordinary coincidence, Paul Stadlen emailed, agreeing to meet.

We met at a trendy hotel in the centre of the city. He was everything I imagined someone who worked for a prime minister and posted hedonistic and debauched images of himself on social media would be – arrogant, narcissistic and malicious. His eyes piercing and menacing, never looking away, he launched into a tirade in defence of his boss.

'Of *all* the politically motivated allegations against the Prime Minister over the years, the most *ludicrous* is that he had something to do with that woman's murder,' he said. 'There's not a shred of evidence linking him to it.'

He then set about disparaging Razak Baginda, calling him a 'fool' for getting involved with a 'prostitute' (as if that unfounded charge made her life less important) and for having 'hired a killer' to deal with her. Trying not to show my shock, I nodded and frowned, feigning sympathy for his boss. It's the grubby side of the television game, but sometimes you've just got to do what you've got to do to get some people, namely crooks, to agree to go on camera. But, hey, it was nothing a good long shower couldn't wash away, and it was definitely in the public interest!

The next morning, I headed to Kuala Lumpur's international airport, to fly to Hong Kong to film an interview with Altantuya's father, Setev Shaariibuu.

At the passport control counter, as the officer scanned my passport, her eyes locked on her computer. She called a colleague over. 'This is not a good sign,' I muttered to myself. She marched me to the immigration office in the basement, pointed to a chair and told me to wait.

'What's the problem?' I asked.

'No problem,' she replied and headed to a whiteboard at the back of the room, where half a dozen others joined her, talking vigorously and pointing at a document attached to the board, which I suddenly realised was a photograph of me.

'My plane's about to leave,' I yelled out to them. 'Can you please tell me what the problem is?'

There was no reply.

Finally, the officer came back with my passport. 'You should hurry to your flight, it's leaving soon,' she said cheerily.

'But what's the problem with my passport?'

'No problem, all fine,' she repeated, her smile deadly.

But when I flew back into Kuala Lumpur, I was barred from entering the country and, within hours, deported – escorted to the plane by five customs and military officials.

That didn't stop us finishing the story. My Al Jazeera colleagues in Kuala Lumpur continued filming interviews while I turned my attention to Sirul, locked away in Villawood. He refused to engage, but his relatives in Australia were happy to tell us what they knew and, more importantly, hand over the possessions he'd left behind when the federal police took him away.

His diaries had pages and pages of contacts, a 'who's who' of top security chiefs and advisors to senior ministers, including to the deputy prime minister and prime minister himself. But it was Sirul's Australian mobile phones that provided the dynamite. A trail of SMS messages revealed he was desperately trying to negotiate a deal with someone in Malaysia who clearly had a lot at stake. His point of contact was Abdul Salam bin Ahmad.

On 17 January 2015, Sirul sent this text to Salam: 'Greetings, boss. I am in difficulties here. I want 2 million Australian dollars before boss [you] come to meet me, I need to guarantee the future of my children here, after that I want 15 million and I will not return to Malaysia ever boss. I won't bring down the PM.' Four and a half hours later, Salam responded, 'They want to discuss.'

When the story was broadcast in September 2015, there were fervent calls for the Altantuya case to be reopened, but instead, the inspector general of police, Khalid Abu Bakar, launched a criminal investigation into the program for 'publishing material that could cause public harm'. In parliament, Deputy Prime Minister Ahmad Zahid Hamidi labelled me a threat to national security.

Najib issued a statement saying he 'did not know, has never met, has never had any communication with and has no link whatsoever with the deceased'.

But Najib had a much bigger firestorm to smother. *The Wall Street Journal* broke the news that a whopping US$700 million from Malaysia's sovereign wealth fund, 1MDB, had landed in Najib's personal bank account. Then there were leaks to the press that the attorney general, recently sacked by Najib, had been planning to charge the prime minister with misappropriating 1MDB funds. And that was just the start of it.

A year later, the United States Department of Justice (DOJ) released the findings of its investigation into a massive international money laundering scam involving 1MDB. Najib was referred to as 'Malaysian Official 1' and Rosmah as 'wife of Malaysian Official 1'.

Najib had created 1MDB just months after he became prime minister in 2009, ostensibly to drive large-scale strategic developments that would attract foreign capital and grow the economy. But, instead, he and a handful of co-conspirators got together on a luxury superyacht in the Mediterranean and dreamed up a way to defraud it. To quote the US DOJ, they used 'the public trust like a personal bank account', plundering more than US$4.5 billion. All up, the DOJ found that more than US$1 billion of the stolen loot ended up in Najib's accounts. The department dubbed it the 'largest kleptocracy' case it had ever uncovered.

The young Malaysian financier Jho Low, dubbed the 'Billion Dollar Whale' by *Wall Street Journal* duo Tom Wright and Bradley Hope, was the 'mastermind' behind the 1MDB heist. With business associates from Switzerland, the United Kingdom and the Middle East, including a low-level Saudi prince, Jho Low set up a myriad of companies across the globe, their names mirroring legitimate businesses, into which 1MDB funds were diverted and then laundered.

Famous for throwing lavish parties for his celebrity pals, including Paris Hilton and Leonardo DiCaprio, Jho Low also splurged 1MDB money on hundreds of millions of dollars worth of real estate from Beverly Hills and Manhattan to London, on van Gogh and Monet masterpieces, a US$250 million superyacht, a private jet and astronomically expensive gifts. He bought jewellery, not only for supermodels like Australia's Miranda Kerr, but for Malaysia's 'Prime Money-ster', Rosmah, most notably a US$27 million 22 carat pink diamond pendant.

Rosmah's son from a previous marriage, Riza Aziz, had introduced his close friend Jho Low to Najib, and benefited handsomely from their association. Riza received US$240 million from the 1MDB purse, which he used to buy tens of millions of dollars worth of real estate in the United States and to launch a film career, brazenly producing the US$100 million Hollywood blockbuster *The Wolf of Wall Street*.

Despite the tornado of 1MDB headlines circulating around the world, Najib's star on the international stage faded little. In September 2017, US president Donald Trump welcomed him to the White House and thanked him, apparently without irony, 'for all the investment you have made in the United States'.

In March 2018, Australian prime minister Malcolm Turnbull met Najib on the sidelines of an Association of Southeast Asian Nations meeting, the ASEAN–Australia Summit in Sydney. Photographs of the two men shaking hands and beaming at one another sparked 'budding bromance' headlines back in Malaysia, riling the man who had become Najib's nemesis, the country's former prime minister, Mahathir Mohamad. So appalled at the skyrocketing corruption under Najib's reign, the nonagenarian had come out of retirement and formed a new party with his political enemy Anwar Ibrahim. In the lead-up to the summit, Mahathir had told Australian press, 'If you know a man is a thief, he [Turnbull] should not meet with him.'

Not long after, the angry Malaysian public heeded Mahathir's call to shun the 'thief'. Najib and UMNO, the party that had ruled for sixty-one years, suffered a historic and humiliating defeat at the country's May 2018 election, and Mahathir became prime minister for a second time.

Najib and Rosmah were immediately banned from leaving the country. Police raids on their family homes seized hundreds of thousands of dollars worth of luxury goods and almost US$30 million in cash. Their grotesque greed was laid out across a field of trestle tables at a press conference: 234 pairs of sunglasses; 550 handbags, including more than US$12 million worth of the Hermès Birkin variety; more than 400 luxury watches valued at US$20 million; and 12,000 pieces of jewellery estimated to have cost almost US$300 million. But to the outrage of Malaysians, the pink diamond was nowhere to be found.

Najib was arrested and charged. Eventually he'd face more than forty counts of money laundering, corruption and abuse of power. Rosmah would face seventeen charges for money laundering and bribery. But, bizarrely, their lives continued almost as if nothing had happened. Najib still attended parliament along with his corrupt UMNO cronies who also faced charges. He was a welcome campaigner for UMNO in by-elections and posted critiques of the new government's policies on his social media sites for his millions of subscribers.

But now he was no longer in power, I was free to travel to Malaysia, and I had the former first couple in my sights. 'What a reality television blockbuster they'd be!' I thought to myself, remembering Rosmah's music clips on YouTube, serenading Najib with warbling love songs. But unfortunately, UMNO was unlikely to let her talk. I needed to get Najib on his own.

I fired off a WhatsApp message to his right-hand man and UMNO stalwart Tengku Sariffuddin, requesting an interview with his boss. 'We understand Mr Najib is going through a challenging time, but we want to give him a chance to tell his side of the story,' I texted, using the age-old journalists' line.

Less than an hour after I pressed send, I heard a ping. It was Tengku!

Weeks of pandering to the former prime minister's ego ensued. 'Yes, we'll definitely give Mr Najib an opportunity to talk about his legacy and his thoughts on the Mahathir government's economic policy,' I assured Tengku repeatedly. 'But you must understand it's critical he also answers the allegations regarding 1MDB and the murder of Altantuya Shaariibuu.'

Finally, he agreed. Four days later, we were in the sumptuous reception room at UMNO headquarters, with our equipment set up, waiting for our interview guest to arrive.

Suddenly there were muffled voices and movement from behind a closed door at the back of the room. The door was flung open. The former prime minister emerged, surrounded by a legion of minders. Our crew rushed over, cameras rolling as Najib made his way silently towards me.

As the cameras reset for the interview, Najib twisted the large square emerald ring on his right hand and regaled me with a story about the time he was a guest on the Emir of Qatar's 'small' yacht. As the Emir is the patron of Al Jazeera and my ultimate boss, Najib's message was clear: he had friends of influence. But this was Najib's first major interview since his plummet from grace. I dived in.

'Mr Najib, what was your reaction the night of the election and why do you think the Malaysian people, after six decades, decided they wanted a change?'

A tsunami of deluded and ignominious self-pity came crashing back at my feet. 'We lost a propaganda war, you know, the vilification of me and the party,' he began. Like a spoilt child, nothing was his fault; others were to blame or were maliciously trying to tear him down.

He explained away the billion dollars of 1MDB money which landed in his bank account. Gifts, gifts and more gifts was his constant refrain. His venality was palpable. According to Najib, the money had come from Saudi Arabia's former king, Abdullah bin Abdul Aziz Al Saud, who, he said, had pledged to support him. Now dead and unable to verify his patronage, the royal was a convenient scapegoat.

'I assumed everything was going to be done in a proper way and I would not have any knowledge who owns the funds,' Najib insisted, extraordinarily pleased with his answer, casting another sly glance to his cheer squad of minders.

'But you were the prime minister, the minister for Finance, the chairman of the 1MDB advisory board, shouldn't you have made it your mission to know where the funds came …' Najib cut me off, exasperated. 'When I received that money, I assumed it was a genuine gift!'

Rosmah's pink diamond was 'assumed' to be a gift from yet another royal, this time from the United Arab Emirates.

'There's a culture in the Middle East that expensive gifts are given,' he declared condescendingly, then tried to suggest he and Rosmah had no idea of the value of the jewel.

'But Mr Najib,' I said, knowing the US Department of Justice found damning evidence to the contrary, 'your wife had a special viewing of the diamond on a mega-yacht on the Mediterranean. And she had fittings for the pendant at the jeweller in New York, what do you have to say to that?'

The value was of no consequence, he said. There was no regulation requiring politicians to declare gifts from foreign dignitaries. And anyway, he claimed, Rosmah had never received it.

There are no prizes for guessing where Najib 'assumed' the US$240 million of 1MDB money transferred into Rosmah's son Riza Aziz's account had come from: a Middle Eastern royal, of course, their great family friend, the crown prince of Abu Dhabi, Mohamed bin Zayed Al Nahyan. MBZ, as Najib called him, had been keen to invest in Riza's film-producing career, despite him never having made a film previously.

When I turned to the subject of the police raids on his family homes, he became very agitated. 'No, you're talking too much about this. We're supposed to talk about the economy!' he demanded. So, I let him talk. His diatribe on the economy never made it into the final edit of the interview, but his response to my next question certainly did.

'Why did you deport me while I was filming a story about Altantuya Shaariibuu's murder?'

'Good thing we deported you, you were a nuisance,' he snapped back, 'because as far as I am concerned, you were making lies.' And apparently that was also why he unleashed his younger brother to threaten the private investigator who had signed a statutory declaration implicating him in the murder. 'Bala was making lies, he was making baseless allegations,' he cried. 'Oh my God! I have no knowledge of her. I have not met her. As far as I am concerned, I am totally, totally, innocent of the Altantuya case, absolutely!'

When I returned to the 1MDB scandal, he stood up and threatened to leave. 'You're talking too much about this!' he pouted, then literally squealed. 'Come on, you're not being fair to me!'

'Okay,' I said. 'Let's talk about your legacy as prime minister.'

'Okay, let's talk about legacy, I'm fine about that.' He quickly sat back down, puffed out his chest, patted the lapels of his suit coat. 'We'll talk about legacy,' he muttered again, as if he was reassuring himself he actually had one.

I asked him whether he felt 1MDB and Altantuya's murder had tainted his legacy. With that the interview was over. Najib stood up, ripped off his microphone and left.

Surrounded by UMNO officials, we scrambled to get our memory cards out of the cameras and out of the building before they could be taken from us. We squashed into a taxi and headed back to the office, gobsmacked by what we had just witnessed.

When the interview was broadcast later that night, it went viral in Malaysia. Najib was the centre of nationwide ridicule.

I packed my bag and left the country; this time of my own free will.

Since then, Najib has been convicted twice on seven charges and sentenced to twelve years in prison subject to a final appeal. He still sits in parliament and may yet make a leadership comeback.

Former deputy prime minister Ahmad Zahid Hamidi faces forty-five charges of corruption, bribery and money laundering, but is the current president of UMNO and is also eyeing the country's top position.

Najib's former international media advisor, Paul Stadlen, fled Malaysia just before the 2018 election result was announced. In 2019, he was charged with two counts of laundering more than US$3 million, but, in 2021, the charge was dropped without acquittal when he agreed to pay US$1.7 million.

As I sign off, I'm about to head to Cambodia, where Hun Sen has ruled for almost forty years and intends to hand over power to his son; where the only opposition party has been dissolved, many of its members locked up or forced to live in exile or slammed with politically driven charges; where the military is deployed to violently snatch land from the poor for the benefit of business empires run by Hun Sen's family and his cronies; and where critics are shot dead in broad daylight.

It's yet another state getting away with murder, while the international community does little until it suits it. With China's growing investment and military engagement with Cambodia, Western countries are trying to make up lost ground. Australia's recent pledge to support the establishment of a state-endorsed national human rights institute reeks of expedient tolerance of a brutal and nefarious regime.

Journalists sometimes have an impact, but all too often it feels like the wheel of corruption continues turning – even after it's exposed.

Mary Ann Jolley has worked for Al Jazeera since 2015, covering Asia and the Pacific. In 2019, she won the British Television Awards Interview of the Year for her interview with Malaysia's former prime minister, Najib Razak. She previously worked at ABC TV's *Foreign Correspondent* and *Four Corners*. She has won several Walkley Awards, a United Nations Correspondents Association Award, a Grand Jury Prize at the New York Festivals Awards and has been awarded a Nieman Fellowship for Journalism at Harvard University.

29
A DICTATOR, A HOUSEWIFE
AND A COUP GONE WRONG

Gwen Robinson
Manila 1985–1988
The National Times

Reflecting on the end of a dictator's reign.

WITH ITS TECHNICOLOUR characters and chronic addiction to Western media attention, the Philippines in the 1980s was fertile ground for an ambitious young journalist, and a favoured destination for seasoned hacks who wanted a vivid, accessible story and a fun yet comfortable life. Some had probably watched too many replays of Mel Gibson as an intrepid Australian journalist in *The Year of Living Dangerously*.

'I'll let you in on a secret, darling, this is the world's greatest story, and it's a breeze to cover,' an American correspondent once bragged to me over beers in a seedy Manila bar. 'It just writes itself, everyone wants to talk, and you don't need to make stuff up – you just couldn't, anyway.'

He was right about the last point, and more prescient than he could have known about the first. From a steadily imploding country fast losing relevance in its own region, the Philippines became one of the top stories of 1986, thanks to the People Power Revolution which brought more than 1.5 million people onto the streets of the capital, Manila, and catapulted a widowed housewife, Corazon Aquino, to the presidency. Only later did it emerge that the popular uprising was triggered by the failure of a coup plot led by disgruntled officers, aimed at installing Marcos's defence minister, Juan Ponce Enrile, at the helm of a civil-military junta.

In many respects, the Philippines was a bundle of corny clichés. Its macho yet sentimental culture shaped reporting priorities among the press corps of the day and lent itself to over-simplistic renditions of 'good-versus-evil' stories abounding with guns and goons, liberation fighters, obscenely rich business cronies, heart-rending poverty and other human-interest angles – all useful for selling stories to faraway editors.

But these larger-than-life themes often created absurd or misleading illusions, portrayed in stories that rarely looked beyond the noisiest and most visible characters and the easiest, most obvious angles.

It began with the 'singing first lady', Imelda Marcos, later notorious for her mind-boggling shoe collection and outrageous extravagance, who would flirt shamelessly with male Western foreign correspondents at her vaudevillian 'Kapihan sa Manila' coffee mornings at the deluxe Manila Hotel. It continued with perennial stories about the slum-dwelling scavengers who lived around Manila's Smokey Mountain garbage dump. There were press conferences at mountain hideouts with telegenic communist New People's Army guerrillas; invitations from business tycoons to vast sugar plantations, timber-logging operations and luxury countryside residences; and covert interviews with labour organisers and underground activists. The list went on.

In international relations, the Philippines didn't figure prominently on any country's political radar other than America's. Washington's strategic interests were reflected in its vital US military facilities there and its decades-long patronage of their favourite strongman dictator, Ferdinand Marcos. Even so, there was an intriguing expat commu-nity: Manila and other main cities such as Cebu and Davao abounded with spies, dodgy investors, diplomats, ubiquitous journalists and any number of activist NGO types. Heavily reliant on US backing, and with a high degree of English literacy, the country was heaven for hustlers of every description.

Manila remained a semi-regular stop for 'firemen' and regional correspondents who would fly in to regurgitate stories from a well-worn playlist: the communist insurgency, poverty, prostitution, the Catholic church, and the US bases, between hanging out in the Ermita red light district and lounging at one of the favoured five star hotels.

The early stages of my foreign correspondent life were a social disaster but wonderful for character development. A young, green Australian woman reporter was the last thing the hard-drinking, male-dominated 'hack pack' wanted to see – particularly in favourite hangouts such as the go-go bars of Ermita. The jewel of this tawdry district was the Firehouse bar, which was often portrayed as just a convivial meeting place. But customers could pay a 'bar fine' of about 500 pesos, US$25, to take a girl out.

Occasionally one hack or another would invite me to join for drinks, possibly for amusement at my discomfort. One night, one of them, a swashbuckling American sporting a handle-bar moustache and a war correspondent khaki vest, took me aside and said, 'You know, darling, you're swell, but this really isn't a place for *you* …' Of course, there were others who were rarely or never seen in the hack-pack drinking holes, but for a young and hungry journalist, social and professional lives were inseparable. Almost everything I did over those three years was work related, in its broadest definition.

But he was right, and I realised quickly I was on my own in a foreign country with few friends. That changed rapidly as I developed contacts, and drifted towards local reporters, particularly an extraordinary network of brave and talented women journalists, including Marites Dañguilan Vitug and Sheila Coronel, as well as intellectuals such as Francisco 'Dodong' Nemenzo and the sharp yet enigmatic columnist and editor Amando Doronila.

It was true that nearly everyone wanted to talk in the Philippines – often, too much. Even as a fledgling correspondent, I was able to gain access to newsmakers and key officials – from cabinet ministers to underground activists, guerrilla commandos, bishops, billionaire cronies and politicians. Thanks partly to my friendships with local journalists, I came to know military rebels, underground leaders, insurgents, Filipino intellectuals and many others, connections that eventually gave me an edge over my older, mostly male counterparts.

Having made a reconnaissance visit in 1984, I settled in Manila in early 1985. I had been lucky enough to gain a position as a junior writer on *The National Times*, a groundbreaking Australian weekly newspaper known for fine journalism and investigative reporting. The editors had offered me a retainer for a couple of stories per month, with freedom to file for other outlets as well. I had convinced the paper's editors that the Philippines would be a compelling story. My pitch had virtually written itself: a lush, tropical country of 7000-plus islands, ruled by an ageing, ailing dictator and his profligate wife; a Ramboesque and often abusive military; communist insurgents (including several Catholic priests and a military officer who had taken up arms to join the rebels); Muslim secessionists; feudal-style plantation owners; semi-enslaved workers; crony timber and mining tycoons with private armies; and a powerful Catholic Church.

Once there, I travelled constantly, plunging into different worlds with every provincial trip, but often dealing with themes related to the growing insurgency, rural exploitation, abuse of official and military power, and the power of crony tycoons and politicians. I was particularly struck by the central and southern regions, returning often to the central island of Negros and further south to Mindanao, for stories ranging from guerrilla hit squads in Davao to Islamic extremists in the island's north-west.

Negros, with its feudal-style plantation culture, was a striking symbol of all that was wrong with the country: colonial-style plantation owners and downtrodden workers, a powerful but divided church, an intensifying guerrilla movement and an abusive military. I met activist priests, including the memorably named Father 'Baby' Gordoncillo, and immersed myself in the arcane world of what was then called Negros Occidental.

Corazon Aquino, or Cory, as she was known, hailed from a dynastic sugar-growing family. I later visited the Aquino family's Hacienda Luisita, near Manila. The sugar story was an early and valuable lesson on the grievances fuelling the communist insurgency in the Philippines, the entrenched yet anachronistic nature of the landed elite and the growing sway of 'liberation theology' that had rocked South America. Most of all, the stories of plantation culture, as well as logging, mining and big agribusiness, were windows into deeper issues such as thwarted land reform efforts, labour exploitation, vast corruption and the inexorable spread of the insurgency.

Yet, at every level, there was an earnest yet often wacky sense of theatrics and a complete lack of irony. I remember, in a mountain hide-out, several rebels, most of them former sugarcane workers, held forth on a mix of Marxist theories and military tactics, when suddenly one of the women guerrillas piped up: 'Can I ask you a question; is it true that Prince Charles and Princess Diana are having marital problems?' Later, they all had a singalong and shared a meal. It was a typically surreal but poignant session which reinforced my addiction to the country.

There were plenty of dark sides too. Alongside daily reports of human rights violations by security forces were constant reminders of the seamy side of life in the Philippines. On one occasion, I worked with Wendy Bacon of the *National Times* on a report into the sex industry around Olongapo and Angeles, the seedy towns that serviced the US bases. The grotesque sex shows and open sale of young girls at the hardcore bars there made the Firehouse in Ermita look tame. It was a sinister industry, which included thriving paedophile tourism. Such issues were taken up by some militant women's groups, includ-ing the fledgling GABRIELA, which later spawned a political party. But the mainstream (and largely male-dominated) activist movements back then tended to ignore the sex trade. Some time after I left the country, it became such an issue that police were forced to act and many of the red light districts were closed down.

Independent media were often the targets of court actions and harassment. But a striking irony was the obsession with media coverage and the respect – even deference – that Filipinos accorded the Western media. From communist guerrillas to establishment politicians and business tycoons, it was astonishing how the thirst for media coverage drove the news. Coup plotters were caught because they gave inter-views in hideouts. Politicians and bureaucrats would divulge 'top secret' plans. And, in late 1985, President Marcos announced the fateful snap election in a live interview with ABC anchor David Brinkley.

Even Cory Aquino had a weakness for big-name US media. Shortly after coming to power, she gave an interview to a few cor-respondents, including me and a visiting American journalist: NBC's celebrity reporter Maria Shriver, who had recently married

Arnold Schwarzenegger. After the new president spoke of the tense days leading to her inauguration, she turned to Maria, asking, 'Now, I'd like to ask *you* a question: what's it like being married to Arnold?' She then asked Maria for her autograph, saying it was for her daughter, Kris.

There was also a proliferation of what is now called fake news; rumours were reported as fact and stories were typically unsourced. Back then, it was just part of media life. Invariably, the foreign press took precedence over local reporters, and at the top of the pile was the US media. The sense of privileged access and inside information reinforced a kind of arrogance among the correspondents. Yet, it was often an illusion. Local reporters, a vast majority of them women, were often the ones who really knew what was going on and, more importantly, understood the context.

I found myself spending more and more time with local reporters, teaming up with some outstanding women journalists. I benefited greatly from their willingness to share knowledge and contacts, but I realised later the benefit was mutual, when one woman reporter said to me, 'It works both ways, Gwen; you're useful to us, too. Half the time the big people are not interested in just locals, they want foreign correspondents.'

We discussed stories and shared interviews, with military conspirators as well as underground leaders. My little studio flat was a useful safe house for meetings with all kinds of rebel figures, including 'Satur' Ocampo and Bobbie Malay, of the political wing of the insurgency, who would turn up heavily disguised in wigs and sunglasses.

The small community of feisty women journalists among the male-dominated hack pack of foreign correspondents tended to be loners and included Abby Tan, a consummate freelancer who worked for various newspapers, Tan Lian Choo of *The Straits Times*, Catherine Manegold of *The Philadelphia Inquirer*, Louise Williams of *The Sydney Morning Herald* and Daniella Dean of UPI. Among the highest profile women correspondents were Melinda Liu of *Newsweek* and the late Sandra Burton of *Time*. Always friendly, though distant, they would fly in for long stints and disappear on mysterious assignments, suddenly turning out a startling interview or scoop.

One of the most memorable 'fire women' was Kate Webb, who had recently returned to journalism to work for AFP after an earlier stint in

Manila with UPI. On the Philippine campaign trail in the lead-up to the 1986 election, when hotel rooms were in short supply on Cory's provincial barnstorming tours, she offered to share her room with me. I would wake up in the pre-dawn hours to see Kate, sitting on her bed in her signature white shirt and ill-fitting blue jeans, swigging from a bottle of beer and staring into the distance. 'You know,' she'd mutter without looking at me, 'this place is about to completely blow up ... wanna beer?'

Some resident correspondents were sympathetic to young wannabes, others less so. After the People Power Revolution, hordes of reporters swarmed to Manila, making me feel almost like a veteran. By mid-1987, I had established strong networks and, as a hyperactive stringer, had more work than I needed with regular outlets. But I never forgot earlier kindnesses, small and large, including from visiting correspondents like Bill Mellor, then a reporter with Fairfax, who lent me money and gave advice.

THE MILITARY WAS rarely on a correspondent's close contact list, until a small group of mainly freelancers and local journalists began speaking with a number of young officers in early 1985. The leaders of the Reform the Armed Forces Movement, or RAM, would prove themselves adept at propaganda, spin and manipulation.

A point here on spin: Marcos's downfall and Aquino's installation as president has been called the People Power Revolution by some and sneered at as a failed coup by others. But neither really captures the essence of the events of February 1986. It was many things: an ageing despot's desperate attempt to cling to power, a failed military takeover, a people's uprising, and a stunning democratic outcome. The Filipinos call it EDSA, the acronym for Epifanio de los Santos Avenue, the Manila boulevard to which more than 1.5 million people flocked during a three-day siege by rebel military officers.

One day in mid-1985, Marites Vitug, one of my closest friends in the local media, called me, excited about her contact with some young military officers who had staged a public protest at a recent graduation ceremony at the Philippine Military Academy. The issues they raised – crumbling professionalism in the armed forces, the spread of corruption, the expansion of insurgency – were falling on fertile ground, drawing some of the brightest young officers to their circle. They were articulate and ready to speak. 'Let's meet some of them,' she suggested.

That led to my early connection with the ringleaders of RAM, a close circle around Defence Minister Enrile and Armed Forces Vice-Chief of Staff Lieutenant-General Fidel Ramos. Led by Colonel Gregorio 'Gringo' Honasan, Enrile's security chief, they would talk eloquently about the need for military reform and, after Marcos called the snap election, to be held in early 1986, began muttering about possible action against the government. The coup plot became the most important story in late 1985 as the political pace quickened in the lead-up to the poll. Alongside some mainly local correspondents, I alluded to a possible coup and featured quotes from disgruntled officers, but with its shroud of secrecy and uncertain life span, it was impossible to write as fact. We wondered if the RAM officers would dare to launch their planned attack, if they could pull it off and, more importantly, if Enrile would go through with it.

The grievances cited by the RAM leaders were real, although their goals were self-serving and their allegiance was to Enrile. Through remarkably skilful spin, they promoted a dashing, clean and courageous image, pushing forward the more photogenic and personable among them. Yet, the real brains behind the elaborate coup plot and persuasive propaganda were the quiet, faceless officers in the background, including the oversized Vic Batac from the Philippine Constabulary, who ran a crucial think tank that helped organise the RAM network. He was often described as a mastermind of the coup plans, though you would never know it from his understated manner.

There were other officers I got to know, including Ricardo 'Dick' Morales, who was part of Imelda Marcos's security detail. More straightlaced than the others, with a sincere and serious air, Morales had many talks with me, and I was shocked to see him paraded on television the night Marcos discovered the coup plot, reading a confession. Long after, he talked of his growing horror while accompanying Imelda on her wildly extravagant overseas shopping trips in the early 1980s. 'There was no end, no limit to it. My loyalty, I realised, was to my country, not the Marcoses, who were deceiving the people and spending all their money,' he told me.

It is easy with hindsight to say journalists back then fell for the RAM reform line. But it is clear there were genuinely reformist elements within the organisation and, more broadly, within the military and police – particularly among the younger, more impressionable ranks. The tragedy was how it was hijacked by cynical, power-hungry leaders.

The media was also hungry, but for a story. And the RAM officers had an innate flair for the media. They favoured foreign reporters but kept lines open with locals. In the lead-up to the snap February election, Honasan and others would talk about their 'reform' plans in conversations at their headquarters behind the Defence Ministry. Foreign correspondents were welcomed by appointment, but a core of reporters, foreign and local, were free to drop by for a coffee and a chat.

They often alluded to their desire to oust Marcos. At times, they would talk openly of role models where military reformers else-where had come to power. Latin America was a favourite example. Thailand, a coup capital of the world, didn't figure so prominently. With their reform narrative, it seemed RAM had right on its side. They were persuasive, a striking contrast to old, corrupt and repres-sive generals and the pro-Marcos clique under armed forces chief General Fabian Ver. Enrile was a wily old fox but managed to portray himself as articulate and open to the press. His Saturday mornings at the Jeepney coffee shop at the Intercontinental Hotel rivalled Imelda's Kapihan sessions.

When I arrived in Manila in 1985, the world was paying rela-tively little attention to the antics of Ferdinand and Imelda Marcos. According to US diplomats, Marcos apparently took his fateful decision to hold a snap election in response to criticism from Washington over the worsening economy, intensifying communist insurgency and deteriorating human rights situation. He saw it as a way to legitimise his regime. It never occurred to him he could lose – let alone to a woman who described herself as a 'simple housewife'.

Precisely one month later, after receiving a petition of more than a million signatures urging her to run, Cory Aquino, widow of slain opposition leader Benigno Aquino, declared her candidacy on 3 December. Overnight, the country went from a media backwater to an international headline story. By early February, amid a flood of reports about a stolen election, it exploded into one of the world's biggest stories.

On election night on 7 February, the media were rushing from one part of Manila to another, between the headquarters of the opposing parties and the government's COMELEC vote tabulation centre at the International Convention Center. There was an electrifying moment two nights later when, amid allegations of fraud and violence in the election, thirty-five COMELEC computer operators walked out of the counting centre, claiming tampering with the election results.

On 15 February, Marcos and his vice-presidential candidate, Arturo Tolentino, were formally declared the winners. Protests erupted around the country, drawing more than a million people to Manila's Luneta Park the next day. There, Cory Aquino claimed her victory had been stolen and called for nationwide civil disobedience and a boycott of Marcos-owned companies. The RAM leaders knew it was time to move and set 23 February to launch their coup.

I remember discussing with a couple of Australian diplomats that the military reformers were laying plans to take over; it drew thin, sceptical smiles and a feeble 'thanks'. On the night of the uprising, as the nation was seething with rage at the stolen election, the Australian ambassador, Roy Fernandez, had gone away on a sailing trip and couldn't be contacted. Later, a rather officious Australian diplomat, clearly in intelligence, and who had earlier dismissed my coup theories, told me over lunch that the embassy wished to warn me that I was in a precarious position, that my contacts with both the left and the military were 'causing concern' in Canberra, and suggested that maybe I should lay low or 'take a long holiday'. I smiled and said 'thanks'.

Long after the dust had settled on the EDSA revolution, the details of the coup plot emerged. The initial plan by Enrile's team led by Honasan was to launch an assault on Malacañang Palace and arrest Marcos, while other military units would seize strategic facilities including airports, broadcasters and military headquarters. The goal was to install Enrile, not Cory Aquino, as head of an interim ruling council. Cory had not been advised of the plot. But on a pre-dawn reconnaissance mission around the palace the day before the coup, Honasan and his team saw troops guarding key access points. Their plot had been discovered. Marcos ordered the arrest of coup leaders and presented some of the captured plotters on live television.

My pager beeped furiously late that afternoon, alerting me there would be an emergency press conference at Camp Aguinaldo, the

General Headquarters of the Philippines Armed Forces, on EDSA. At 6.45 pm, Enrile and Fidel Ramos appeared together in the social hall of the GHQ building and announced they were withdrawing their support for the Marcos government.

Enrile, always one for theatrics, said, 'We are going to die here fighting.' The more understated Ramos, dressed in civilian clothes, said, 'The president of 1986 is not the president to whom we dedicated our service. It is clear that ... he has put his personal family interest above the interest of the people. We do not consider President Marcos as now being a duly constituted authority.'

Over the next three nights and days, hundreds of journalists who were holed up with Enrile and Ramos barely slept. Half my coverage, including radio and print commentary and reporting, was done in a semi-delirious, sleep-deprived state. Later, many other reporter colleagues inside the siege confirmed they were in the same condition.

We knew that at any minute, pro-Marcos forces could unleash aerial bombardments or artillery fire. There was a massive scramble for any available landline, as correspondents frantically wrote stories and tried to file them by reverse charge calls. I remember managing to get a call through to my family to tell them I was okay. All my other precious phone time was to editors and copytakers – or radio stations who were desperate to find journalists inside the siege.

When an alarm was raised that attack helicopters were heading for the GHQ building, the word quietly went out that Enrile and his crew were transferring across the road to Camp Crame. Seth Mydans of *The New York Times* had sat down on a sofa for a few minutes of sleep. He recently reminded me that I had run by and shaken him awake: 'Seth, quick, we're transferring across the road, move it!'

By the end, when Marcos had fled the country, I was nearly hallucinating. My leg had swelled up after three sleepless days, but adrenaline and bountiful supplies of snack food passed into the camp from the crowds on EDSA had kept me going.

On the final day of the attempted coup, 25 February, after Cory Aquino had been sworn in at the elite Club Filipino down the road in San Juan, and Marcos had staged his own swearing in at Malacañang Palace, we finally left the camp. News later spread of the pre-dawn conversation between Marcos and US senator Paul Laxalt, his longtime friend and a confidant of US president Ronald Reagan. Laxalt told the beleaguered leader, 'I think you should cut, and cut cleanly. The time has come.'

That night, even before receiving the news that Marcos and his entourage had left the Philippines courtesy of US military transport, we knew it was over. I was in a daze of fatigue and pain, trying to put a story together, when I learned that crowds were breaking through the gates of Malacañang Palace. Without thinking, and beyond exhaustion, I made my way there. I remember getting a taxi to the palace, and wandering around palatial halls with grotesquely lavish trappings, gold everywhere, and sombre paintings. I followed the crowds upstairs and along a corridor to the private quarters. I still have no idea how I managed to get back to my little apartment, but I slept for many hours. In the first two months of 1986, I had written more stories than I had in my previous four years as a journalist.

THE EVENTS OF 1986 left a mixed legacy for the Philippines. Despite the ulterior motives of the coup plotters, their claims of a genuine desire for reform within the armed forces were true. This was clear from lengthy conversations with literally scores of military members across the ranks. What wasn't clear until later was the cynicism of the coup leaders, and their skilful messaging after Cory Aquino's ascent that the armed forces had a right to a role in governing the country. Many came to believe it, thanks to their spin.

The People Power Revolution was a turning point. It was a unique and exhilarating moment of national unity. A few years later, disillusionment set in as reformist fervour ran out of steam. Some of Cory's advisors and ministers were exposed as greedy opportunists, not least the 'hero of EDSA', Enrile and his close associates. Aquino ended up dismissing him and, later, some genuinely progressive members of her administration, due to impossible pressure from military-backed elements.

It wasn't long before parts of the RAM group were plotting new coup attempts against the Aquino government – at least six in all, some causing civilian deaths and injuries. In August 1987, I was dining in Malate with Humphrey Hawksley of the BBC and the ABC's John Mills, when the pager beeped, with a message to get to the palace. That led to the narrowest escape in my time in the Philippines.

As I scrambled along a crowded street, a rifle grenade sailed past and hit a group of bystanders just behind me, exploding in a mass of severed limbs and mangled bodies.

It was the fourth and most serious coup attempt, instigated by Honasan. At least fifty-three people died and 200 were injured, most of them bystanders, when rebel soldiers attacked the palace.

So, EDSA was both a revolution and a coup. But I never contradict people who choose to call it the People Power Revolution. It was, after all, the people who transformed a naked power grab by the ambitious defence minister and his team into a massive display of, well, people's power. It also changed the fundamental attitudes and approach taken by many foreign media outlets to their coverage of the Philippines – that it was a fun colour story that briefly flared up. The EDSA events also changed me – journalistically as well as personally.

Gwen Robinson's first tour abroad was in the Philippines, 1985–1988, where she covered the downfall of Ferdinand Marcos for Australian newspaper the *National Times*. She joined the *Financial Times* in 1995 in Tokyo, becoming a correspondent and senior editor until 2013. She is now based in Bangkok as editor-at-large of Nikkei Asia.